INDEX
OPTIONS
&FUTURES

INDEX
OPTIONS
& FUTURES

THE COMPLETE GUIDE

BY **DONALD L. LUSKIN**
COMPUTER RESEARCH BY PATRICK C. CARLYLE

JOHN WILEY & SONS
NEW YORK CHICHESTER BRISBANE TORONTO SINGAPORE

This publication is designed to provide accurate and
authoritative information in regard to the subject
matter covered. It is sold with the understanding that
the publisher is not engaged in rendering legal, accounting,
or other professional service. If legal advice or other
expert assistance is required, the services of a competent
professional person should be sought. *From a Declaration
of Principles jointly adopted by a Committee of the
American Bar Association and a Committee of Publishers.*

Library of Congress Cataloging-in-Publication Data:
Luskin, Donald L.
    Index options and futures.

    Bibliography: p.
    1. Stock index futures. I. Carlyle, Patrick C.
II. Title.

HG6043.L87   1987   332.63′222   86-28189
ISBN 0-471-85464-6

Printed in the United States of America
10 9 8 7 6 5 4 3 2

PREFACE

On February 24, 1982, *the world's first futures contract on a stock price index* was traded—not, as one might have expected, on the floor of the New York Stock Exchange, but rather on the Kansas City Board of Trade (KCBOT). Kansas City may seem like a strange place for the beginning of a revolution in the structure of the international capital markets, but a revolution is precisely what occurred when the seemingly sleepy little KCBOT began trading futures on the Value Line Composite Index.

Today, just a few short years later, options, futures, and options-on-futures on various stock price indexes are actively traded on exchanges around the world almost 24 hours a day. As a means of trading the entire stock market in a single transaction, they have become indispensable strategic tools for almost every type of investor, from individuals to blue-chip institutions. They have acted as the catalyst for a new perception of portfolios, not as collections of individual assets, but as composite commodities.

The most popular index instruments are futures contracts on the S&P 500 Index, traded on the Index & Option Market division of the Chicago Mercantile Exchange. Since their introduction in April 1982, their trading activity has grown to the point of eclipsing that of the stock market itself. As Figure 1 illustrates, the monthly dollar value of S&P 500 Index futures trading surpassed that of the entire New York Stock Exchange in February 1984, and has never surrendered the lead. Altogether, trading in index options and futures is now almost three times the value of NYSE trading every day.

To the hidebound traditionalists of the financial community, index options and futures seem like an uninvited guest at a formal affair—a little too loud, but nonetheless charming and rapidly becoming the life of the party. The critics do not deny the popularity of these instruments, nor ignore their many legitimate uses. In fact, they claim that they may be *too* popular for the stability of the capital markets. They claim that by diverting capital and distracting attention from the stock market itself, the tail may be wagging the dog.

The critics' most often-cited argument against index options and futures is the unpredictable jolt they allegedly give to stock prices once a month when the options and futures expire. The "witching hour," as it has come to be called, is apparently caused by the establishment and liquidation of complex intermarket arbitrages in which index options and futures are hedged against portfolios of stocks. But knowing its cause is little comfort to those who feel the practitioners of such exotic new strategies have no right to crash the private party on the New York Stock Exchange.

---

v

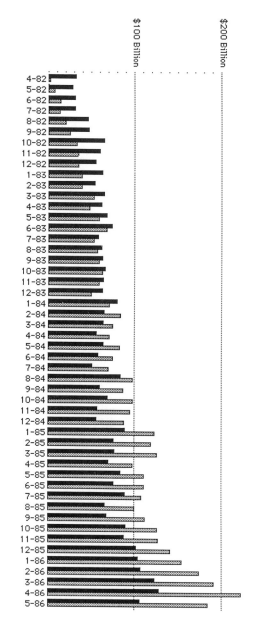

FIGURE 1

This book is intended to serve as an all-purpose atlas of the world of index options and futures, and to answer the many questions investors have about them.

What exactly are index options and futures?

Why have they become so popular in so short a time?

How can conservative and aggressive investment managers best use them to

    Improve performance and lower transaction costs?

    Take the most powerfully levered risk positions?

    Earn riskless arbitrage profits?

    Isolate and eliminate the market component of portfolio risk?

    Create a ''portfolio insurance'' policy?

    Simultaneously lower risk and enhance yield?

    Profit from displacements between sectors of the broad market?

    Make short-sales without the NYSE ''plus-tick'' rule?

    Invest in market indexes without supporting ''immoral'' companies?

    Predict short-term market moves?

How do the options and futures exchanges operate?

What are the differences between options, futures, and options-on-futures?

How should they be priced in a fair marketplace?

What are the differences between the various indexes?

Are index options and futures undermining the stability of the capital markets?

Should more be done to regulate them?

For those with no previous experience with index options and futures, the early sections of this book will make an excellent introduction. For investors who already utilize them, this book will present the broadest possible spectrum of their potential application, with the fine points explored in sufficient detail to benefit even the most experienced professionals. And for those who are merely curious, or concerned about the effects index options and futures may be having on the structure of the capital markets, this book will serve as a forum for diverse opinions.

For traders or students who are interested in the theory of options and futures valuation, this book offers detailed discussions of the most accurate models, including state-of-the-art software that can be run on most personal computers.

The reader should note that the masculine pronoun has been used throughout for ease in reading.

This book would not have been possible without the generous assistance of many friends and associates. For their encouragement and suggestions, I wish to thank Robert Bassi, Nettie Bleich, Kirk Bomont, Edward B. Chez, Sheck Cho, Barbara Cofsky, John and Barbara Cutler, Patrick Faust, Thomas Gilmartin, Jerry Gluck, Tracy Herrick, Chris Hynes, Raymond Killian, Stephen Kippur, Hayne Leland, Joseph Levin, Jean Morley, John O'Brien, Melonie Parnes, Barbara Richards, Mark Rubinstein, Stephen Selig, Bing Sung, Christine VanDeVelde, Karl Weber, Eric Wolff, Leslie Wurman, and Robin Yonis. For help with research I thank Scott Banke, Joseph Eberle, Raymond Murray, Dean Phelps, and John Roesner, Jr.

DONALD L. LUSKIN

Chicago, Illinois
March 1987

CONTENTS

NUTS AND BOLTS

PRICES AND VALUES

STRATEGIES AND TACTICS

NUTS & BOLTS

Index options and futures are exchange-traded contracts for making economic commitments—bets, one might say—based on the shifting values of stock price indexes.

Let's look at the most popular index instruments—*futures contracts* on the Standard & Poor's 500 Index. Like any futures contracts, S&P 500 futures are contractual commitments to make or take delivery of an underlying commodity (in this case, the S&P 500 Index) at a specified date in the future, but with the price locked in today. Today's futures price, determined in a free auction market on the floor of the Index & Options Market division of the Chicago Mercantile Exchange, is quoted in points and hundredths of points, just like the index itself.

Each contract is a commitment of $500.00 times the value of the index; hence, $500.00 is said to be the *contract multiplier*. In the customary language of the stock market, each contract could be thought of as representing 500 "shares" of the index. The dollar value of the underlying index covered by a contract is called its *underlying value*—the price of the underlying index multiplied by the contract multiplier. For instance, if the index were at 240.00, the underlying value would be $120,000.00.

Underlying value		Index price		Contract multiplier
$120,000.00	=	240.00	×	$500.00

The dollar value of the contract itself, the *contract value*, is the futures price multiplied by the contract multiplier. For instance, a futures contract priced at 241.80 has a contract value of $120,900.00.

Contract value		Futures price		Contract multiplier
$120,900.00	=	241.80	×	$500.00

When a futures contract is traded, buyer and seller do not transfer the full contract value when the position is established, as they would had they traded shares of stock. Rather, each posts a small *initial margin* through their brokers with the exchange's *clearing house*, not a downpayment, but a performance bond to indicate their creditworthiness. Then every day that the contract remains outstanding, buyer and seller exchange *variation margin*—the losing party must deposit cash with the clearing house equivalent to the amount of each day's unrealized losses, determined on a mark-to-the-market basis, and the winning party is free to withdraw his unrealized gains. The clearing house interposes itself in all transactions as the buyer to every seller and the seller to every buyer, so either party is free to liquidate his position at any time by making an offsetting closing transaction.

On the day the contract expires, final profits and losses between the buyer and seller are settled in cash based on the *closing price of the S&P 500 Index itself*. In other words, at expiration, the contract value and the underlying value are equal, no matter how they may have fluctuated during the life of the contract.

Unlike traditional agricultural futures contracts that result in the physical delivery of commodities, index futures are *cash-settled*—at no time are any actual shares of stock transferred. And at no time do buyer or seller ever transfer the full contract value. All along, they settle their daily profits and losses through transfer of variation margin—at expiration, they settle their final profits and losses, and the contracts virtually vanish. For instance, if the index were 250.00 on expiration day, each contract would have a value of $125,000.00.

Contract value		Index price		Contract multiplier
$125,000.00	=	250.00	×	$500.00

The buyer's final profit (and, consequently, the seller's final loss) would be $4100.00, the difference between the contract's initial value of $120,900.00 and its expiration value of $125,000.00.

Buyer's final profit		Contract value at expiration		Contract value when purchased
$4100.00	=	$125,000.00	−	$120,900.00

Index *options* are somewhat more complicated than index futures. They come in two distinct varieties: *calls* and *puts*. An index *call* gives its buyer the *right, but not the obligation* to exercise, and thereby receive in cash any amount by which the underlying index is *above* the call's *strike-price*. An index *put*, on the other hand, gives its buyer the *right, but not the obligation* to receive any amount by which the underlying index is *below* the put's *strike-price*. In the case of so-called *American* index options, buyers have the right to exercise at any time during the option's life. In the case of so-called *European* options, the buyer can only exercise when the option expires.

The cash value that an option buyer could receive by exercising is called the option's *exercise value* or *intrinsic value*. Borrowing terminology from world of horse-racing, options with exercise value are said to be *in-the-money*, while options with no exercise value are said to be *out-of-the-money*; when the price of the underlying index is precisely equal to the option's strike-price, the option is said to be *at-the-money*.

The contractual obligations of index options are not equivalent be-tween buyers and sellers (as they are in futures contracts). For the buyer of an option, exercise is a *right, not an obligation.* Sellers of index op-tions, however, have an *unconditional obligation* to respond whenever the buyer chooses to exercise. It may seem that the buyer has all the advantages, and that the seller assumes nothing but liabilities. But that is why the buyer has to pay the seller for the option at the outset, and not the other way around.

Let's examine the most popular index options—calls and puts on the Standard & Poor's 100 Index traded on the Chicago Board Options Ex-change. Just as the contract multiplier of S&P 500 futures is $500.00 times the value of the index, the contract multiplier of S&P 100 options is $100.00. If the index is priced at 230.00, the *underlying value* of a contract is $23,000.00

Underlying value		Index price		Contract multiplier
$23,000.00	=	230.00	×	$100.00

As an example, let's consider a three-month call option with a strike-price of 240.00. With the price of the index itself at 220.00, this out-of-the-money option might be priced at about 2.50. The actual dollar price paid by the call buyer—the option's *contract value*—is $250.00.

Contract value		Call price		Contract multiplier
$250.00	=	2.50	×	$100.00

The buyer must pay cash to the seller for an option's full price. Since this is the most the buyer can possibly lose in the transaction, he is not required to post any additional security as margin. The seller, on the other hand, must post margin with the clearing house as a performance bond, calculated by a formula based on the relationship of the index price to the option's strike-price. Additionally, the seller may be required to deposit additional margin if his position moves against him.

Whenever the buyer chooses to exercise the call, he receives in cash $100.00 times any amount by which the index price is *above the strike-price.* As with index futures, index options transactions are cash-settled against the closing price of the underlying index itself as of the day of exercise, without the requirement of ever transferring actual shares of stock. For instance, if the S&P 100 Index were to rise to 250.00, its exercise value would be $1000.00—$100.00 times 10.00 (the difference between the index price of 240.00 and the strike-price of 230.00).

Exercise value		Index price		Strike-price		Contract multiplier
$1000.00	=	(250.00	−	240.00)	×	$100.00

An investor who bought this option for $250.00 and exercised it for $1000.00 would have earned a profit of $750.00

Buyer's profit		Exercise value		Original contract value
$750.00	=	$1000.00	−	$250.00

But if the index price had not risen above the call's strike-price, the call would have expired out-of-the-money and the buyer would have lost his entire initial investment.

In addition to the cash-settled options just described, a second type of index option exists: *options-on-futures*. At first these may seem like impossibly complex hybrid instruments, but they are really quite simple. At any time prior to expiration the exercise of options-on-futures results in the *purchase at the strike-price* (in the case of a call) or *sale at the strike-price* (in the case of a put) of an index futures contract. Options-on-futures expire on the same day as their underlying futures contracts. For example, three-month options-on-futures apply to three-month futures contracts. Therefore, at expiration options-on-futures are the functional equivalent of cash-settled options because the futures contracts are themselves cash-settled.

As an example let's consider three-month S&P 500 Index call options-on-futures with a strike-price of 250.00; priced at 3.00. Like the underlying futures contracts, the contract multiplier for options-on-futures is $500.00, so the total contract value would be $1500.00.

Contract value		Option-on-futures price		Contract multiplier
$1500.00	=	3.00	×	$500.00

As with cash-settled options, the buyer must pay cash to the seller for the option-on-futures' full price, and is not required to post any additional margin. Again the seller must post margin with the clearing house as a performance bond, and will be required to increase his margin if the position moves against him.

Let's say that the underlying futures contract rises to 260.00, ten points above the call's 250.00 strike-price. If the buyer were to exercise the call, he would become the owner of a futures contract with a cost-basis of 250.00—the option's strike-price. If he were to immediately sell the futures contract, it would show a $5000.00 profit.

Futures profit		Futures price		Strike-price		Contract multiplier
$5000.00	=	(260.00	−	250.00)	×	$500.00

However, we must consider that he paid $1500.00 for the call initially—so his total profit on the entire transaction is $3500.00.

Total profit		Futures profit		Option-on-futures cost
$3500.00	=	$5000.00	−	$1500.00

These three types of index instruments—futures, options, and options-on-futures—can be used alone, in combination with each other, or in combination with portfolios of stocks, to create an almost limitless variety of investment positions. Later, we will discuss how they can be used as an alternative means of implementing the kinds of strategies investors now execute directly in the stock market—but with enhanced performance and reduced transaction costs. But more important, we'll discuss how they can be used to structure unique patterns of risks and returns that would have been impossible without them.

1. THE MENU:
AN INVENTORY OF INDEX OPTIONS AND FUTURES

The idea of index options and futures was born in 1977 in a committee of the Kansas City Board of Trade charged with developing new futures contracts. In October of that year the KCBOT submitted a proposal to the Commodities Futures Trading Commission to trade a futures contract based on the Dow Jones Industrial Average. It took more than four years for the CFTC to give its approval; the delay came not from the agency's doubts about the contract but rather from an interagency struggle for jurisdiction with the Securities and Exchange Commission. By the time the contract was approved it had been amended to be based on the Value Line Composite Index because the KCBOT could not reach an accord with Dow Jones & Company on the use of its famous index. Finally the new contract began trading on February 24, 1982.

On April 21, 1982, close on the heels of the KCBOT's introduction of the Value Line contract, the Chicago Mercantile Exchange introduced a contract based on the S&P 500 Index. A few weeks later, on May 6, the New York Futures Exchange introduced one based on the New York Stock Exchange Composite Index. During these heady days the Chicago Board of Trade, the elder statesman of the futures exchanges, was unable to bring out its own index futures contract. It was quagmired in the battle that the KCBOT thought it wiser to drop: litigation with Dow Jones & Company over the use of the Dow Jones Industrial Average.

In the following year the CFTC began a pilot program under which the exchanges could gradually introduce options-on-futures—that often-abused class of contract had been banned for many years. On January 28, 1983, the CME introduced options on its S&P 500 futures and the NYFE, on its NYSE Composite futures.

It was not until later the same year that the options exchanges began to get into the act. The Chicago Board Options Exchange was first when, on March 13, 1983, it introduced cash-settled options on the CBOE-100 Index, cooked up specifically for the occasion by the CBOE, selecting 100 stocks with CBOE-listed options. Cash-settled options were an immediate hit, eclipsing the earlier-established options-on-futures almost entirely, so other exchanges quickly mobilized to imitate the CBOE's success. The American Stock Exchange joined the fray on April 19 when it introduced options on the Major Market Index, an index of its own invention geared to mimic the Dow Jones Industrial Average but without the copyright problems. On July 3 the CBOE added options on the S&P 500 Index (and changed the name of the CBOE-100 to the S&P 100). And on September 23 the New York Stock Exchange traded the first option in its long and illustrious history when it introduced trading in options on the NYSE Composite. It wasn't until January 11, 1985, that the Philadelphia Stock Exchange introduced options on the Value Line Composite Index, a belated tribute to the first index to have futures contracts.

The venerable old Chicago Board of Trade finally got into the index business on July 23, 1984. Having been firmly rebuffed by Dow Jones (and the courts), the CBT struck a deal with the American Stock Exchange and introduced futures on the Major Market Index.

The index instruments mentioned so far have all consistently attracted sufficient investor interest to be considered successful. But along the way a number of other index instruments have not been so fortunate; for example, the Chicago Board Options Exchange, the American Stock Exchange, the Philadelphia Stock Exchange, and the Pacific Stock Exchange all listed options on industry-group indexes, many of which have now been delisted; those that remain can go weeks without trading a single contract.

The most conspicuous failure was the listing of options and futures on indexes of over-the-counter stocks. The Chicago Board of Trade and the Chicago Mercantile Exchange engaged in a pitched battle over their respective listings of futures on the NASDAQ-100 Index and the S&P 250 OTC Index. The internecine warfare was carried out very much in public, with each combatant vying to outspend and outhype the other in the media. Both exchanges sponsored seminars and road shows, published lavish brochures, and advertised heavily in the financial press. At one point the CBOT even ran television commercials for its NASDAQ-100 futures. The zenith of competitive zeal was reached when the CME arranged to have huge canvas banners advertising its S&P 250 futures hung from lamp posts on Jackson Boulevard in front of the CBOT building. The irony is that all this effort has so far been to utterly no avail—after an initial flurry of interest, trading in both exchanges' OTC index futures fell to almost zero in a matter of months. Attempts to trade companion options on the NASDAQ-100 Index through the National Association of Securities Dealers over-the-counter network, and on the S&P 250 Index on the CBOE, met even more severe fates—both have been delisted.

But these few failures have not prevented exchanges around the world from competing in the development of new index instruments. The Sydney Futures Exchange and the Sydney Stock Exchange list options, futures, and options-on-futures on the Australian Stock Exchanges All Ordinaries Price Index; the Hong Kong Futures Exchange lists futures on the Hang Seng Index; the Toronto Futures Exchange and the Toronto

Stock Exchange list options, futures, and "spot" futures on the Toronto Stock Exchange 300 Index; and the London International Financial Futures Exchange lists futures and options on futures on the Financial Times Stock Exchange 100 Index. The specter of 24-hour index trading looms in the Singapore International Monetary Exchange's plans to link trading in its futures electronically on the Nikkei 255 Average to the Chicago Mercantile Exchange, and in the plans of the European Options Exchange in Amsterdam to trade options on the Major Market Index.

A few years ago index options and futures did not exist. Today, they proliferate. In selecting the contract that best suits a particular investment application, investors must sort through a variety of obvious and not-so-obvious distinctions between the exchanges' various offerings. The most obvious distinguishing feature of an index contract is the underlying stock price index on which it is based. Although the various indexes are calculated in somewhat different ways, each is nothing more than a method of tracking the aggregate value of a portfolio of stocks meant to be representative of the market. The most famous of all, the Dow Jones Industrial Average, is little more than what its name suggests: a simple average of the prices of its component stocks.

Next, the contracts differ in terms of their basic type: options, futures, or options-on-futures. In addition, within options themselves there is a further distinction between American options that can be exercised at any time and European options that can be exercised only at expiration.

Beyond these broad distinctions the specifications of the various contracts differ in several details:

1. *Contract Multiplier.* The contract multiplier is the value times which the contract price is multiplied to determine its total value. We've seen an important difference in the size of the multiplier in the two examples we've already looked at: for S&P 500 futures this value is $500.00, while for S&P 100 options it is $100.00.

2. *Minimum Fluctuation.* The minimum fluctuation is the smallest permissible increment of price change. For index options this is usually expressed fractionally, generally $\frac{1}{16}$ or $\frac{1}{8}$; but for index futures and options-on-futures it is usually expressed decimally, generally 0.05.

3. *Expiration Terms.* These are the dates on which index options and futures expire. Generally, options expire on the Saturday following the third Friday in the expiration month; futures and options-on-futures expire simply on the third Friday. Index contracts are listed with either quarterly or consecutive monthly expirations, and in some cases both.

4. *Trading Hours.* Trading hours are those during which the exchange permits trading, expressed first in local time and then, parenthetically, in Eastern Standard Time.

5. *Speculative Position Limits.* These are the maximum number of contracts the exchanges will permit a single investor to control. In the futures and options-on-futures markets, investors can obtain an exemption from these limits if they can demonstrate to the satisfaction of the exchange that they are bona fide hedgers. For cash-settled options, no exemptions are permitted.

The contract specifications of the major currently listed options, futures, and options-on-futures on broad-based U.S. stock indexes are detailed on the following pages, ranked in alphabetical order by underlying index. Next, similar information for index instruments on non-U.S. indexes is listed. Bear in mind that these specifications are subject to revision by the exchanges and regulatory agencies. Investors should consult the exchanges or their brokers to obtain the most current contract specifications.

U.S. INDEXES

Institutional Index

Index Sample: 75 stocks most widely held by institutions, updated quarterly
Index Construction: Capitalization-weighted arithmetic average
Index Base: 250.00 in 1986

Contract Type: European cash-settled options
Exchange: American Stock Exchange
Quotation: Quoted in terms of the index
Contract Multiplier: $100.00
Minimum Fluctuation: 1/16 ($6.25) for contracts priced $3.00 or less, 1/8 ($12.50) for those higher than $3.00
Expiration Terms: Saturday following third Friday of the nearest three consecutive months, plus next two nearest of March, June, September or December
Trading Hours: 9:30 AM to 4:30 PM EST
Position Limits: 15,000 contracts on each side of the market in all months combined

Major Market Index

Index Sample: 20 NYSE blue-chip industrial stocks
Index Construction: Price-weighted, arithmetic average
Index Base: 200.00 in 1983

Contract Type: American cash-settled options
Exchange: American Stock Exchange
Quotation: Quoted in terms of the index
Contract Multiplier: $100.00
Minimum Fluctuation: ⅟₁₆ ($6.25) for contracts priced $3.00 or less, ⅛ ($12.50) for those higher than $3.00
Expiration Terms: Saturday following third Friday in nearest three consecutive months
Trading Hours: 9:15 AM to 4:10 PM EST
Position Limits: 15,000 contracts on each side of the market in all months combined

Contract Type: Cash-settled futures
Exchange: Chicago Board of Trade
Quotation: Quoted in terms of the index
Contract Multiplier: $100.00 (Mini contract)
Minimum Fluctuation: ⅛ ($12.50)
Expiration Terms: Third Friday in nearest three consecutive months, plus next nearest of March, June, September, or December
Trading Hours: 8:15 AM to 3:15 PM (9:15 AM to 4:15 PM EST)
Position Limits: 20,000 contracts net long or short in all months combined (consolidates with Maxi contract; two maxi contracts are deemed equivalent to five mini contracts)

Contract Type: Cash-settled futures
Exchange: Chicago Board of Trade
Quotation: Quoted in terms of the index
Contract Multiplier: $250.00 (Maxi contract)
Minimum Fluctuation: 0.05 ($12.50)
Expiration Terms: Third Friday in nearest three consecutive months, plus next nearest of March, June, September, or December
Trading Hours: 8:15 AM to 3:15 PM (9:15 AM to 4:15 PM EST)
Position Limits: 8000 contracts net long or short in all months combined (consolidates with Mini contract; five mini contracts are deemed equivalent to two maxi contracts)

New York Stock Exchange Composite Index

Index Sample: Approximately 1500 stocks; all common stocks listed on NYSE
Index Construction: Capitalization-weighted, arithmetic average
Index Base: 50.00 in 1965

Contract Type: American cash-settled options
Exchange: New York Stock Exchange
Quotation: Quoted in terms of the index
Contract Multiplier: $100.00
Minimum Fluctuation: $\frac{1}{16}$ ($6.25) for contracts priced $3.00 or lower, $\frac{1}{8}$
  ($12.50) for those higher than $3.00
Expiration Terms: Saturday following third Friday in nearest three consecutive
  months
Trading Hours: 9:30 AM to 4:15 PM EST
Position Limits: $300 million aggregate underlying value on each side of the
  market

Contract Type: Cash-settled futures
Exchange: New York Futures Exchange
Quotation: Quoted in terms of the index
Contract Multiplier: $500.00
Minimum Fluctuation: 0.05 ($25.00)
Expiration Terms: Third Friday in March, June, September, or December
Trading Hours: 9:30 AM to 4:15 PM EST
Position Limits: 5000 contracts net long or short, all months combined

Contract Type: American options-on-futures
Exchange: New York Futures Exchange
Quotation: Quoted in terms of the index
Contract Multiplier: $500.00
Minimum Fluctuation: 0.05 ($25.00)
Expiration Terms: Third Friday in March, June, September, or December
Trading Hours: 9:30 AM to 4:15 PM EST
Position Limits: 2000 net long or short, all months combined, calculated sepa-
  rately for puts and calls

Standard & Poor's 100 Index

Index Sample: 100 stocks with options listed on CBOE
Index Construction: Capitalization-weighted, arithmetic average
Index Base: 100.00 in 1983

Contract Type: American cash-settled options
Exchange: Chicago Board Options Exchange
Quotation: Quoted in terms of the index
Contract Multiplier: $100.00
Minimum Fluctuation: 1/16 ($6.25) for contracts priced $3.00 or lower, 1/8
  ($12.50) for those higher than $3.00
Expiration Terms: Saturday following third Friday in nearest four consecutive
  months
Trading Hours: 8:30 AM to 3:15 PM (9:30 AM to 4:15 PM EST)
Position Limits: 15,000 contracts on each side of the market

Standard & Poor's 500 Index

Index Sample: 500 listed and over-the-counter stocks: 400 industrials, 40 utilities, 20 transportations, and 40 financials

Index Construction: Capitalization-weighted, arithmetic average

Index Base: 10.00 in 1941–1943

Contract Type: European cash-settled options

Exchange: Chicago Board Options Exchange

Quotation: Quoted in terms of the index

Contract Multiplier: $100.00

Minimum Fluctuation: $\frac{1}{16}$ ($6.25) for contracts priced $3.00 or lower, $\frac{1}{8}$($12.50) for those higher than $3.00

Expiration Terms: Saturday following third Friday in nearest two consecutive months, plus next nearest three of March, June, September, and December

Trading Hours: 8:30 AM to 3:15 PM EST (9:30 AM to 4:15 PM EST)

Position Limits: 15,000 contracts on each side of the market

Contract Type: Cash-settled futures

Exchange: Index & Option Market division of the Chicago Mercantile Exchange

Quotation: Quoted in terms of the index

Contract Multiplier: $500.00

Minimum Fluctuation: 0.05 ($25.00)

Expiration Terms: Third Friday in March, June, September, or December

Trading Hours: 8:30 AM to 3:15 PM EST (9:30 AM to 4:15 PM EST)

Position Limits: 5000 contracts net long or short in all months combined (consolidated with options-on-futures by "IOM risk factor")

Contract Type: American options-on-futures

Exchange: Index & Option Market division of the Chicago Mercantile Exchange

Quotation: Quoted in terms of the index

Contract Multiplier: $500.00

Minimum Fluctuation: 0.05 ($25.00)

Expiration Terms: Third Friday in nearest three of March, June, September, and December

Trading Hours: 8:30 AM to 3:15 PM EST (9:30 AM to 4:15 PM EST)

Position Limits: 5000 contracts net long or short in all months combined (consolidated with futures, weighted by "IOM risk factor")

Value Line Composite Index

Index Sample: Approximately 1700 listed and over-the-counter stocks
Index Construction: Unweighted, geometric average
Index Base: 100.00 in 1961

Contract Type: American cash-settled options
Exchange: Philadelphia Stock Exchange
Quotation: Quoted in terms of the index
Contract Multiplier: $100.00
Minimum Fluctuation: 1/16 ($6.25) for contracts priced $3.00 or lower, 1/8 ($12.50) for those higher than $3.00
Expiration Terms: Saturday following third Friday in nearest three consecutive months, plus nearest three of March, June, September, and December
Trading Hours: 9:30 AM to 4:15 PM EST
Position Limits: $300 million aggregate underlying value on each side of the market

Contract Type: Cash-settled futures
Exchange: Kansas City Board of Trade
Quotation: Quoted in terms of the index
Contract Multiplier: $500.00
Minimum Fluctuation: 0.05 ($25.00)
Expiration Terms: Third Friday in March, June, September, or December
Trading Hours: 8:30 AM to 3:15 PM (9:30 AM to 4:15 PM EST)
Position Limits: 5000 contracts net long or short in all months combined

Contract Type: Cash-settled futures
Exchange: Kansas City Board of Trade
Quotation: Quoted in terms of the index
Contract Multiplier: $100.00 (Mini contract)
Minimum Fluctuation: 0.05 ($5.00)
Expiration Terms: Third Friday in March, June, September, or December
Trading Hours: 8:30 AM to 3:15 PM (9:30 AM to 4:15 PM EST)
Position Limits: 5000 contracts net long or short in all months combined

INTERNATIONAL INDEXES

Australian Stock Exchanges All Ordinaries Share Price Index

Index Sample: Approximately 280 Australian stocks listed on the Sydney and Melbourne stock exchanges

Index Construction: Capitalization-weighted, arithmetic average

Index Base: 500.00 in 1980

Contract Type: American cash-settled options

Exchange: Sydney Stock Exchange

Quotation: Quoted in terms of the index divided by 10

Contract Multiplier: $100.00 Australian per quoted point ($10.00 per full index point)

Minimum Fluctuation: 0.05 ($5.00 Australian)

Expiration Terms: Second to the last business day in nearest three of August, November, February, and May

Trading Hours: 10:00 AM to 12:15 PM and 2:00 to 3:15 PM (8:00 to 10:15 PM and 12:00 to 1:15 AM EST)

Contract Type: Cash-settled futures

Exchange: Sydney Futures Exchange

Quotation: Quoted in terms of the index

Contract Multiplier: $100.00 Australian

Minimum Fluctuation: 0.10 ($10.00 Australian)

Expiration Terms: 12:00 PM second to the last business day of March, June, September, and December, out to 18 months

Trading Hours: 9:30 AM to 12:30 PM and 2:00 to 3:15 PM (7:30 to 10:30 PM and 12:00 to 1:15 AM EST)

Contract Type: American options-on-futures

Exchange: Sydney Futures Exchange

Quotation: Quoted in terms of the index

Contract Multiplier: $100.00 Australian

Minimum Fluctuation: 0.10 ($10.00 Australian)

Expiration Terms: 12:00 PM second to the last business day of March, June, September, and December, out to 18 months

Trading Hours: 9:30 AM to 12:30 PM and 2:00 to 3:15 PM (7:30 to 10:30 PM and 12:00 to 1:15 AM EST)

Financial Times Stock Exchange 100 Index

Index Sample: 100 highest-capitalization stocks on London Stock Exchange, revised quarterly

Index Construction: Capitalization-weighted, arithmetic average

Index Base: 1000.00 in 1983

Contract Type: American cash-settled options

Exchange: London Stock Exchange

Quotation: Quoted in terms of the index divided by 10

Contract Multiplier: £100.00 per quoted point (£10.00 per full index point)

Minimum Fluctuation: ½ (£5.00)

Expiration Terms: Last business day in nearest four consecutive months

Trading Hours: 9:00 AM to 3:40 PM (3:00 to 9:40 AM EST)

Contract Type: Cash-settled futures

Exchange: London International Financial Futures Exchange

Quotation: Quoted in terms of the index divided by 10

Contract Multiplier: £250.00 per quoted point (£25.00 per full index point)

Minimum Fluctuation: 0.05 (£12.50)

Expiration Terms: Last business day in nearest three of March, June, September, and December

Trading Hours: 9:05 AM to 4:05 PM (3:05 to 10:05 AM EST)

Hang Seng Index

Index Sample: 33 stocks listed on the Hong Kong Stock Exchange
Index Construction: Capitalization-weighted, arithmetic average
Index Base: 100.00 in 1964

Contract Type: Cash-settled futures
Exchange: Hong Kong Futures Exchange
Quotation: Quoted in terms of the index
Contract Multiplier: HK$50.00
Minimum Fluctuation: 1.00 (HK$50.00)
Expiration Terms: Second to the last business day of nearest three consecutive
 months
Trading Hours: 10:00 AM to 12:30 PM and 2:30 to 3:30 PM; Wednesdays 10:00
 AM to 12:30 PM only (9:00 to 11:30 PM and 1:30 to 2:30 AM EST)

Nikkei 225 Stock Average

Index Sample: 255 Japanese stocks
Index Construction: Price-weighted, arithmetic average
Index Base: 225.00 in 1947

Contract Type: Cash-settled futures
Exchange: Singapore International Monetary Exchange
Quotation: Quoted in terms of the index
Contract Multiplier: ¥ 1000.00
Minimum Fluctuation: 5.00 (¥ 5000.00)
Expiration Terms: Third Wednesday of March, June, September, and December
Trading Hours: 8:00 AM to 2:15 PM (7:00 PM to 1:15 AM EST)

Toronto Stock Exchange 300 Index

Index Sample: 300 stocks listed on the Toronto Stock Exchange
Index Construction: Capitalization-weighted, arithmetic average
Index Base: 1000.00 in 1975

Contract Type: American cash-settled options
Exchange: Toronto Stock Exchange
Quotation: Quoted in terms of the index
Contract Multiplier: $100.00 Canadian
Minimum Fluctuation: 0.05 ($5.00 Canadian)
Expiration Terms: Saturday following the third Friday of the nearest three consecutive months
Trading Hours: 9:30 AM to 4:10 PM (9:30 AM to 4:10 PM EST)

Contract Type: Cash-settled futures
Exchange: Toronto Futures Exchange
Quotation: Quoted in terms of the index
Contract Multiplier: $10.00 Canadian
Minimum Fluctuation: 1.00 ($10.00 Canadian)
Expiration Terms: Third Friday of the nearest three consecutive months
Trading Hours: 9:30 AM to 4:15 PM (9:30 AM to 4:15 PM EST)

Contract Type: Cash-settled "spot" futures
Exchange: Toronto Futures Exchange
Quotation: Quoted in terms of the index
Contract Multiplier: $10.00 Canadian
Minimum Fluctuation: 1.00 ($10.00 Canadian)
Expiration Terms: Close of each trading day
Trading Hours: 9:20 AM to 4:10 PM (9:20 AM to 4:10 PM EST)

2. THE MECHANICS
OF INDEX OPTIONS AND FUTURES TRADING

CASH AND MARGIN REQUIREMENTS

Once the peculiar vocabulary of index options and futures is mastered, understanding their cash and margin requirements is really quite simple. But for those whose investment experience has been limited to the stock market, several unique accounting conventions will seem a bit unfamiliar.

For buyers of index options the requirements are quite simple—buyers are required to pay the full dollar value of their contracts. Because the buyer of an option cannot lose more than its initial cost, he is never required to deposit additional funds if the position moves against him. Conversely, if the position moves in his favor, he cannot withdraw his profits until the position is liquidated.

For sellers of index options the requirements are more complicated. As we discussed earlier, selling an option obligates the seller to pay in cash the difference between the option's strike-price and the price of the underlying index whenever the option buyer chooses; therefore the seller must post *margin*, a good-faith deposit of cash or securities to ensure eventual performance. In traditional stock market trading the term "margin" suggests a down payment on the full value of securities purchased, with the brokerage firm loaning the investor the balance. For index options it has a different meaning: margin is a performance bond, not a down payment.

There are two alternative formulas for determining the exact amount of margin to be deposited. Both are functions of the price of the underlying index, the market price at which the option is trading, and the strike-price of the option. The margin requirement is the greater of the results of the two formulas.

The first formula adds 5% of the price of the underlying index to the price of the option, and subtracts any amount by which the option is out of the money. The result is multiplied by $100.00, the contract multiplier, to determine the dollar requirement. As an example let's calculate the requirement for a call option on the S&P 100 Index, when the index is priced at 230.00, the market price of the option is 2.50, and the strike-price of the option is 240.00

5% of index price (230.00)	11.50
Market price of option	+ 2.50
Out-of-the-money amount	− 5.00
	9.00
Contract multiplier	× $100.00
Margin requirement	$900.00

This formula gives a margin requirement of $900.00, but we still must try the alternative formula to see if it gives a higher requirement. The alternative formula is simply 2% of the index price plus the option price.

2% of index price (230.00)	4.60
Market price of option	+ 2.50
	7.10
Contract multiplier	× $100.00
Margin requirement	$710.00

In this case the alternative gives a lower result: $710.00. Therefore the requirement would be the $900.00 given by the first formula. Note that the proceeds received from the sale of the option can be applied toward meeting the requirement. In this case, the seller would have received $250.00 and would only have to deposit an additional $650.00 to meet the requirement.

Because the prices of the index and the option change over time, the requirement is recalculated every day. Further deposits are necessary if subsequent calculations give higher requirements than were initially deposited. This would occur, of course, only if the position moved against the seller; as his risk of loss becomes greater, he must increase his performance bond.

Investors who sell index call options against a portfolio of stocks held by a custodian bank may meet the margin requirement by having the bank post a Market Index Option Escrow Receipt. The receipt must cover 100% of the value of the index, without adjustment for option price or any amount out of the money.

We've seen that for index options, margin requirements are very different for buyers and sellers. For futures contracts, on the other hand, they are identical for both. Both must post an *initial margin* deposit in cash or Treasury bills when the trade is initiated; the amount of the requirement is set by the exchanges and differs from contract to contract. When Treasury securities with maturities of over three months are posted as initial margin, only a portion of their market value can be applied against the requirement.

For each contract, there are two margin levels: one for speculators who take outright risk positions in the contracts and another for bona fide hedgers who use the contracts to offset risk in their overall portfolios. Following is a list of the speculative and hedge margins for the major contracts:

Contract	Initial speculative margin	Initial hedge margin
Major Market Index ($250.00 multiplier)	$3500.00	$1200.00
Major Market Index ($100.00 multiplier)	$1750.00	$500.00
NYSE Composite	$3500.00	$1500.00
S&P 500	$6000.00	$3000.00
Value Line Composite ($500.00 multiplier)	$6500.00	$2500.00
Value Line Composite ($100.00 multiplier)	$1800.00	$500.00

As the value of futures positions in an investor's account fluctuates, he is subject to another requirement: *variation margin*. This requirement calls for holders of futures positions to settle their realized and unrealized profits and losses in cash on a daily basis. Unrealized profits and losses are calculated by comparing an investor's trade price against the daily *settlement price* of the contract. Not necessarily an actual closing price, the settlement price is disseminated by the exchanges shortly after the daily close of trading and is broadly representative of pricing in the last 30 seconds of the trading day.

As an example of how this requirement works let's examine the account of an investor who buys one S&P 500 futures contract at 241.8C and deposits the $6000.00 initial margin requirement in cash. Let's say that at the close on day 1 the settlement price of the contract is 241.80, unchanged from when it was purchased. The investor's account would look like this:

Long 1	S&P 500 Index	Trade Price:	241.80
		Settlement price:	241.80
		Unrealized profit (loss):	None
		Cash	$6000.00

Now lets say that on day 2 the position begins to go against the investor:

the settlement price declines to 240.80. This 1.00 decline will result in a $500.00 unrealized loss, which has to be settled in cash immediately. Therefore the investor's cash balance declines from $6000.00 to $5500.00.

Long 1	S&P 500 Index		
		Trade price:	241.80
		Settlement price:	240.80
		Unrealized profit (loss):	($500.00)
		Cash	$5500.00

It is important to note that the initial margin requirement can be met by cash or Treasury securities but the variation margin requirement can be met only in cash. Because in our example the investor chose to meet the initial requirement with cash, he was able to meet the variation requirement simply by drawing on his initial $6000.00. But if the initial $6000.00 had been deposited in Treasury bills, the investor would have had to post an additional $500.00 in cash to meet the variation requirement.

If the position went against the investor much more seriously than we've looked at so far, the cash balance could fall below the *maintenance margin* level, at which point the investor would be required to deposit sufficient cash or Treasury securities to bring the cash balance back up to the *initial margin level*. Following is a list of the maintenance margin levels for the major index futures contracts:

Contract	Maintenance margin level
Major Market Index ($250.00 multiplier)	$1250.00
Major Market Index ($100.00 multiplier)	$500.00
NYSE Composite	$1000.00
S&P 500	$2500.00
Value Line Composite ($500.00 multiplier)	$2000.00
Value line Composite ($100.00 multiplier)	$400.00

In the case of S&P 500 futures the maintenance margin level is $2500.00, so a call for further deposits would be triggered if the futures contract showed an unrealized loss greater than $3500.00. Let's say that on day 3 the contract's settlement price is $227.00, bringing the investor's cash balance down to $2000.00.

Long 1	S&P 500 Index	Trade price:	241.80
		Settlement price:	233.80
		Unrealized profit (loss):	($4000.00)
		Cash	$2000.00

At this point the investor would have to deposit at least $4000.00 to bring the cash balance up to the initial margin requirement of $6000.00.

The flip side of the variation requirement can be seen if we suppose that the position had moved a similar amount in the investor's favor, up to 242.80 rather than down to 240.80. The investor's cash balance would have increased $500.00 to $6500.00 and he would be free to withdraw from the account the $500.00 excess above the $6000.00 margin requirement even though it would represent only an unrealized profit.

Long 1	S&P 500 Index	Trade price:	241.80
		Settlement price:	242.80
		Unrealized profit (loss):	$500.00
		Cash	$6500.00

Margin requirements for options-on-futures are a hybrid of the options and futures requirements. As with cash-settled options, the buyer of options-on-futures must pay the full market price of the options in cash. Sellers must deposit initial margin equal to the price of the option plus the initial margin that would be required on the underlying futures contract, minus half the amount by which the option is out of the money. As an example, let's look at the initial requirement for a 250.00 strike-price call option on S&P 500 futures when the futures contract is priced at 241.80 and the market price of the option is 2.50.

Initial margin for futures		$6000.00
Market price of option	2.50	
Contract multiplier	× $500.00	$750.00
Half out-of-the-money amount	4.10	
Contract multiplier	× $500.00	(2050.00)
Margin requirement		$4700.00

29

As an alternative to this formula the exchanges impose minimum margins for sellers of options-on-futures. For S&P 500 options the minimum is $1000.00 plus the price of the option; for NYSE Composite options it is $750.00 plus the price of the option. If the formula gives a requirement below these minimums, the minimums would be applied. It should be noted that just as with cash-settled options the proceeds collected from selling options-on-futures can themselves be used to meet the margin requirements.

As with cash-settled options the margin requirements are recalculated every day on a mark-to-the-market basis. If subsequent calculations produce higher requirements, the seller must deposit additional margins.

An important aspect of the margin requirements for options-on-futures, as distinct from those for the underlying futures, is that there is no variation margin requirement. Although sellers must deposit additional margins if recalculations on a mark-to-the-market basis require it, neither buyers nor sellers are permitted to withdraw and reinvest profits until the position is liquidated.

TRANSACTION COSTS

Any time investors trade securities they pay two types of transaction costs. First, they pay an explicit *commission* to a broker for executing and clearing the trade. Second, they pay an implicit *market impact cost* because their bids will inevitably drive prices marginally higher when they wish to buy and their offers will drive prices marginally lower when they wish to sell.

One of the great attractions of index options and futures is that their use can drastically reduce transaction costs compared with other means of achieving similar investment goals. First, let's look at the transaction costs associated with trading index futures contracts.

Index futures commissions, the first component of transaction costs, are fully negotiable between the investor and the broker. As a rule of thumb, an institutional investor can expect to pay approximately $25.00 per contract, varying with the investor's volume of trading and the kind of support services he requires. In keeping with the tradition of the futures markets, this $25.00 fee covers both the opening and liquidating sides of the transaction—it is a *round-turn* charge, collected at the time of the liquidating transaction.

How does this compare with the commissions associated with buying actual shares of stock? Because stock commissions are charged as cents per share, we'll have to estimate how many shares of stock it would take to create a position with a value equivalent to one S&P 500 futures contract.

First we must determine the underlying dollar value of an S&P 500 futures contract by multiplying the index price by its contract multiplier. For this example we assume a price of 240.00.

Underlying value		Index price		Contract multiplier
$120,000.00	=	240.00	×	$500.00

By dividing the underlying value of $120,000.00 by an estimated average price of $50.00 per share we can determine that one contract is equivalent to 2400 shares of stock.

Number of shares		Underlying value		Average price per share
2400	=	$120,000.00	÷	$50.00

An institutional commission rate roughly equivalent to $25.00 per contract would be $0.05 per share (stock commissions are typically charged on a one-way basis; to convert $0.05 into a futures-type round-turn charge we simply double it to $0.10). At this rate the total round-turn charge for 2400 shares is $240.00.

Total cost		Number of shares		Round-turn commission
$240.00	=	2400	×	$0.10

The commission associated with trading S&P 500 Index futures—$25.00—is about one-tenth that of trading an equivalent number of shares of stock—$240.00.

In terms of market impact, the second type of transaction cost, index futures enjoy an even greater advantage over stocks. Although it varies, it is usually possible to transact S&P 500 futures contracts within 0.05 of the last sale quotation—an investor wishing to buy could do so 0.05 higher than the last sale and an investor wishing to sell could do so 0.05 lower. Multiplying 0.05 by the contract multiplier yields the dollar value of the market impact cost per contract: $25.00.

Dollar value of market impact cost		Market impact cost per contract		Contract multiplier
$25.00	=	0.05	×	$100.00

To estimate the market impact cost of trading the stocks that make up the index let us assume that on average they could be bought or sold ⅛ of a point, or 0.125, away from the last sale. Multiplying 0.125 by the number of shares required to create a position equivalent to one futures contract gives the dollar market impact cost: $300.00.

Total cost		Number of shares		Market impact cost per share
$300.00	=	2400	×	0.125

The market impact cost associated with trading S&P 500 Index futures—$25.00—is one-twelfth that of trading an equivalent number of shares of stock—$300.00.

Strictly speaking, it is impossible to make these simple comparisons for index options because there is no single position in stocks or futures that is ever truly comparable to an option contract. Accepting this limitation, we can nonetheless consider approximations that will give us an intuitive grasp of the transaction costs associated with options. Let's consider options on the S&P 500 Index—this way our calculations will be roughly comparable to our examination of futures on the same index.

Like all commissions, options commissions are fully negotiable between an investor and his broker. As a rule of thumb, an institutional investor can expect to pay approximately $3.00 to $6.00 per contract, depending not only on his volume of trading and the kind of support services he requires, but also on the price of the option contracts being traded. To settle on a single figure as an example let's use $5.00. Like stocks, options commissions are charged on a one-way basis; therefore to make them comparable to round-turn futures commissions we'll double them to $10.00 per contract.

The contract multiplier for S&P 500 options is $100.00, as opposed to $500.00 for S&P 500 futures. So to establish an options position roughly comparable to a futures contract, an investor would have to trade at least five options contracts. Multiplying the $10.00 per contract round-turn commission by five gives $50.00—twice the $25.00 commission for trading futures, but still only about a fifth of the $240.00 cost of trading stocks.

In terms of market impact costs roughly the same relationship obtains. Depending on the price of the option in question, the difference between the last sale quotation and the price at which an investor can expect to buy or sell will be $1/16$ of a point ($6.25) or $1/8$ of a point ($12.50). Because we said that an investor would have to trade at least five options to create a position comparable to a single futures contract, we'll multiply these two possible market impact costs by five to get $31.25 and $62.50, respectively. Neither is so advantageous as the $25.00 market impact cost associated with futures, but both are still far superior to the $300.00 market impact cost associated with stocks.

For options-on-futures, commissions and market impact costs are identical to those of futures, with one exception. If the option-on-futures is exercised, an additional commission (although no market impact cost) must be paid on the futures transaction mandated by the exercise.

It is clearly good news for investors that index options and futures allow them to establish positions in the stock market with commission and market impact costs far lower than those associated with trading stocks. But the low transaction costs of index options and futures have another benefit as well, beyond merely lowering the cost of doing existing business. Just as important, these low costs mean that new strategies made possible for the first time by index options and futures can be economically implemented.

TAX TREATMENT

For tax purposes all index options, futures, and options-on-futures are treated alike under Internal Revenue Code §1256. As such, profits and losses arising from transactions in them are subject to some unusual regulations.

First, regardless of the holding period or whether the position was a purchase or a short sale, profits and losses from trading §1256 contracts are treated as 60% long-term capital gains or losses, and 40% short-term capital gains or losses.

To understand how this might affect an investor in 1987 consider an individual in the maximum 38.5% tax bracket with a $1000.00 profit from trading index futures. 60% of the gain, or $600.00, would be taxed at the maximum long-term capital gains rate of 28%

Total gain		Long-term portion		Long-term capital gains rate		Tax liability
$1000.00	×	60%	×	28%	=	$168.00

40% of the gain, or $400.00, would be taxed at the short-term capital gains, or ordinary income, rate, of 38-½%.

Total gain		Short-term portion		Short-term capital gains rate		Tax liability
$1000.00	×	40%	×	38.5%	=	$154.00

The total tax liability would be the sum of the long-term and short-term liabilities: $322.00. Under this regulation the maximum tax an individual would have to pay on profits from trading index futures, or any §1256 contract, would be 32.2%.

In 1988 long-term and short-term capital gains will be taxed at a maximum rate of 28%, but the division of §1256 contract profits or losses into 60% long-term and 40% short-term can remain quite important. This is especially true with respect to the limited deductability of losses, or when, in the same tax-year as §1256 contracts are traded, an investor is realizing or carrying forward capital gains or losses in other sectors of his portfolio.

Another special regulation governing taxation of §1256 contract profits and losses is the requirment that taxes be paid at the end of each investor's tax year on a mark-to-the-market basis, regardless of whether the positions have been closed out or remain outstanding. In other words, investors are required to pay taxes on both realized and unrealized profits. For outstanding positions the year-end mark-to-the-market becomes a new cost-basis against which next year's profits and losses are calculated.

The descriptions just provided are necessarily brief and cannot possibly describe all potentially applicable tax regulations or every possible tax consequence that may arise from trading index options, futures, or options-on-futures. Further, the tax regulations governing index instruments may be changed subsequent to this writing. It is imperative that every investor consult a tax advisor to determine the tax impact that may result from the interaction of index options, futures, or options-on-futures with his total investment portfolio.

TRADING ORDERS

In many ways trading index options and futures is just like trading stocks. But, because of the complexity of these instruments, a number of special trading orders have evolved so that investors can fine-tune their transactions. Following is a list of the trading orders most commonly used; some are officially recognized by the exchanges as bona fide orders; others exist only by custom. Because customs differ from broker to broker, an investor should consult his broker before trading to ascertain which orders will be honored.

Time Duration

1. *Day.* A day order remains in effect only for the duration of the trading day on which it is entered, unless it is canceled or executed. Unless otherwise specified, all orders are generally presumed to be day orders

2. *Good-Til-Canceled (Also GTC or Open).* A good-til-canceled order remains in effect until it is executed or explicitly canceled.

3. *Opening-Only.* An opening-only order is to be executed only at the opening of trading on the day on which it is entered. Opening-only orders for options must be executed in the opening rotation; for futures and options-on-futures opening-only orders must be executed in the first 30 seconds of trading.

Price Specification

1. *Limit.* A limit order specifies a maximum purchase price or a minimum sale price.

2. *Discretion.* A discretionary order is a limit order that permits the broker to execute at a specified price differential from the limit.

3. *Delta.* A delta order is an instruction to adjust a limit price in relation to movements in the underlying index from a specified reference point. This order is used only for options and options-on-futures, not for futures.

4. *Market.* A market order is to be executed immediately, not at a specified price level but at the best price then prevailing.

5. *Market-on-Close (Also MOC).* A market-on-close order is to be executed at the close of trading on the day on which it is entered. Although

a price is not specified, a market-on-close order should be executed at the closing price or in the closing range.

6. *Market-if-Touched (Also MIT or Board)*. A market-if-touched order is an order to buy or sell that becomes a market order when the option or future to be traded reaches a specified price. An MIT order to buy is entered when the option or future is trading *above* the specified purchase price; it becomes a market order when the option or future trades or is offered there. Conversely, an MIT order to sell is entered when the current price of the option or future is below the specified sales price; it becomes a market order when the option or future trades or is bid there.

Contingencies

1. *Contingent*. A contingency order is in effect when a specified condition is satisfied (for instance, that the underlying index be priced at or above a certain price).

2. *Stop*. Like a market-if-touched order, a stop order to buy or sell becomes a market order when the option or future to be traded reaches a specified price. Whereas an MIT order to buy is entered when the option or future is trading *above* the specified purchase price, a stop order to buy is entered when the option or future is trading *below* the specified purchase price. It becomes a market order when the option or future trades or is offered there. Whereas an MIT order to sell is entered when the current price of the option or future is *below* the specified sale price, a stop order to sell is entered when the current price of the option or future is *above* the specified sale price. It becomes a market order when the option or future trades or is bid there.

3. *Stop Limit*. A stop limit order operates much like a stop order except that it becomes a limit order, rather than a market order, working at a specified price when activated.

Special Instructions

1. *Immediate-or-Cancel (Also IOC or Immediate)*. An immediate-or-cancel order must be executed immediately in whole or in part after it is entered. If for any reason a portion of the order cannot be executed immediately, any unexecuted balance is automatically canceled.

2. *All-or-None*. An all-or-none order must be executed in its entire specified quantity or not at all.

3. *Fill-or-Kill (Also FOK)*. A fill-or-kill order combines the intent of an immediate-or-cancel order and an all-or-none order. It must be exe-

cuted immediately and in its entirety or it is automatically canceled.

4. *One-Cancels-the-Other (Also OCO).* A one-cancels-the-other order is more than one order entered at the same time with instructions that as soon as one is executed the other(s) will be canceled automatically.

5. *Not Held.* A not held order authorizes the broker to exercise personal judgment in regard to the price and time of the trade. The broker is not held responsible if the order goes unexecuted or is executed at a price or time unsatisfactory to the customer.

Cancellations

1. *Straight Cancel.* A straight cancel order is an instruction to cancel any unexecuted portion of a previously entered order.

2. *If-Nothing-Done-Cancel.* An if-nothing-done-cancel order is an instruction to cancel a previously entered order only if it remains entirely unexecuted. If it has been partially executed, it is permitted to remain in effect.

3. *Cancel-Former-Order (Also CFO or Cancel/Replace).* A cancel-former-order order replaces a previously entered order with entirely new instructions.

Multiple Contracts

1. *Spread.* A spread order is an instruction to execute a specified combination of options and futures (for instance, in different contract months or with different strike-prices). Spread orders can utilize all the duration, price specification, special, and cancellation orders just listed.

EXERCISE AND ASSIGNMENT

For cash-settled index options, orders to exercise must be tendered in writing to the exchanges by a member firm no later than the close of trading on the day of the exercise. Brokerage firms may apply earlier cutoff times for receipt of oral exercise instructions from their customers. At expiration, long customer positions in the money by 0.25 or more are automatically exercised, unless the customer specifically instructs that they not be.

A little-known Options Clearing Corporation regulation poses a most unusual risk for holders of long cash-settled index options. If, for any reason, an option holder exercises an out-of-the-money call or put, he or she must *pay to the seller* the difference between the index price and the strike-price. For example, suppose the holder of a 240.00 strike-price call issues instructions to exercise 10 minutes before the close of trading, when the index is at 241.50, in-the-money by 1.50. The holder expects to receive $150.00—the in the money amount times the contract multiplier. But suppose, in the final runoff, the index suddenly declines to 239.50, placing the option 0.50 *out*-of-the-money. Instead of simply receiving nothing, the investor must *pay* $50.00—the out of the money amount times the contract multiplier. Considering that no one would ever do this intentionally, that it virtually *must* be an accident whenever it occurs, and that it promotes misunderstanding by the public of the options markets, one must question the wisdom of this policy.

Once a contract has been exercised, the Options Clearing Corporation assigns it by random lottery among the universe of member brokerage firms carrying matching short positions. Once a brokerage firm has been assigned it follows its own procedures to determine which of its customers will, in turn, be assigned. Assignment policies vary among brokers; some are entirely random and some allocate on a first-in, first-out basis. Assignment notices are generally conveyed to customers before the opening of trading on the market day following the exercise date.

Exercises and assignments of options-on-futures work very much the same way. Exercise notices for S&P 500 index options-on-futures must be tendered in writing to the clearing house by 5:00 PM CST (6:00 PM EST), and for the NYSE Composite Index options-on-futures to the clearing house by 5:00 PM EST. For both contracts brokerage firms may apply earlier cutoff times. For the S&P 500 any in-the-money option-on-futures will be automatically exercised unless a customer instructs otherwise. For the NYSE Composite, only options-on-futures in-the-money by 0.25 or more will be exercised.

39

3. IT'S THE PITS:
THE WORLD OF THE FLOOR TRADERS

When one opens the Wall Street Journal and reads the preceding day's quotations and volume statistics for index options and futures, it's easy to take for granted the invisible mechanism that makes it all possible—the trading floors of the nation's options and futures exchanges. This book would not be complete without an exploration of how the floors operate; and this exploration would not be proper without paying homage to that unique creature known as the floor-trader.

The work of the men and women who populate the octagonal pits on the floors of the index options and futures exchanges is shot through with paradox and contradiction. The world of the floor-trader has the aura of excitement associated with any high-risk profession, yet the reality of the day-to-day work is almost comically unglamorous as they pack themselves into the pits shoulder to shoulder, shouting at the top of their voices, less concerned with making a fortune than they are with making it through the day. The exchanges maintain a staff of medics on call at all times to treat mishaps that include fainting, accidental pencil stabbings, ankles twisted on the deep steps that ring the pits, and even an occasional heart attack.

For floor-traders the fast track does not lead to Wall Street but to Chicago—to the S&P 100 Index options pit at the Chicago Board Options Exchange and the S&P 500 Index futures pit at the Index and Options Market division of the Chicago Mercantile Exchange. Taken together, these two pits can trade more than a million contracts on a good day, a volume that represents in equivalent terms more than three times the value of trading on the entire New York Stock Exchange. In the floor-trader's world these pits are the ultimate opportunity and the ultimate challenge.

Floor-traders are of two basic breeds: *market-makers* and *floor-brokers*. Floor-brokers act as agents, executing orders in the crowd on behalf of others. They earn their livelihoods by collecting commissions on the trades they execute; thus, like other salespeople, their incomes are determined (and ultimately limited) by the volume of transactions they complete. Market-makers, or locals, as they are called on the floor, put their own capital at risk in the trading crowd. Their only source of income is the profit they can derive from their trading and its only limit is the risk they're willing to bear.

All it really takes to trade in the S&P pits is the courage to do it. A reasonable amount of financial backing is probably a good idea, too, but less money is required to get started than one might think. Exchange memberships—seats on the exchange (a ridiculous misnomer because members never get to sit down)—trade in an auction market, priced recently around $300,000.00 for the CBOE and $100,000.00 for the IOM. But it is not necessary for a floor-trader actually to buy a membership; he can just as easily rent one for about $3500.00 a month for the CBOE and only $500.00 for the IOM. Before the exchanges will admit a new trader as a member they investigate his background and administer a test covering the details of floor procedure, but there is no formal educational requirement. For trading capital a new market-maker can start with almost nothing; a member clearing firm may demand as little as $10,000.00 in a new trader's account before it will put its name behind his trades.

These low barriers to new entrants lend a Horatio Alger quality to the trading crowds. The crowds are made up of entrepreneurial self-starters, many without much money or any other qualification for being there other than the dream of getting rich quick. Of course there is a core of calloused survivors in the crowds who've learned that if anything is likely to happen quickly there, it won't be getting rich. But they are surrounded by an ever-changing stream of newcomers, whose faces are as fresh and agonizingly innocent as the face of a would-be starlet stepping off the bus from Iowa at the corner of Hollywood and Vine.

The floors also support another entirely different class of hopefuls: platoons of young girls hoping to hitch their wagons to a star. Working for minimum wages as clerks, runners, and trade-checkers for the opportunity to husband-hunt among the fast-money set, the "optionettes," as they are called on the CBOE, swarm to the floor-traders like groupies to rock stars. The flaw in their game plan is that floor-traders, like rock stars, are not the marrying kind.

For the majority of traders, as for the majority of the young girls who pursue them, the exchange floors will prove to be places of broken dreams, for despite the apparent ease of entry into the pits the standards of success are rigid and unforgiving. The fluctuating daily value of a trader's account—the net liquidating balance or "net lick"—is an unmistakable record of triumphs and failures delivered every morning on the clearing firm's computer, an irrefutable report card, a judgment of professional merit for which there is no court of higher appeal. For most newcomers the net lick will gradually—or just as likely with horrible suddenness—diminish to the point at which they will finally have to be honest with themselves and admit that their experiences in the pits were just interludes on the way to becoming accountants, salespeople or taxi-drivers, an easily glorified memory about which they will someday say wistfully, "So near and yet so far."

There are few professions that are so emphatically *not* a team effort, in which success is so directly and visibly tied to individual performance day in and day out. Despite the oppressive proximity of hundreds of bodies—or perhaps because of it—the S&P trading floors may be among the loneliest places in the world. In one sense floor-traders compete together against forces outside the pits that could be thought of as a common enemy—public customers, upstairs traders at member firms, or just a global abstraction of "the market." Yet, ultimately, thoughts of tomorrow morning's net lick will crowd out any natural tendency to form working alliances and personal loyalties to colleagues, for in the last analysis trading is a zero-sum game: any money in one trader's pocket comes out of another's.

Paradoxically, because this very solitariness is common to all floor-traders, it creates its own strange sense of camaraderie among them. One of its manifestations is the colorful language heard in the pits. For the index futures, S&P 500s are called "Spooze" after their Quotron symbol "SPU.Z"; Major Market Index futures are called "Missiles" after their symbol "MX"; and NYSE Composite futures are called "Knifes" after the acronym for the exchange on which they trade(the *New York Futures Exchange*). For the trading increments, 1/16 is a "teenie" or a "steenth," 1/4 is a "quack," 1/2 is a "laugh.", 5/8 is "fried eggs," 3/4 is "the orders," and an even dollar is a "bone." The expiration months are reduced to their first syllable; for instance, April is "Ape" and December is "Deece." Options with a strike-price of 25.00 are the "quarters," of 55.00, the "doubles," and of 100.00, the "pars."

When this jargon is combined into whole sentences, the results can be somewhat surreal, especially for visitors who had expected the official language of trading to be English. For instance, a CBOE trader wishing to pay 1/2 for the S&P 100 Index December 225.00 calls might say, "Deece quarters:pay a laugh!" A market-maker responding that he would sell them at 5/8 would quickly reply, "At fried eggs! At fried eggs!"

In the S&P 500 Index futures pit an entirely different communications protocol has evolved: an official language of hand signals (diagrammed in Figure 3.1). Designed for use in an environment of such intense noise pollution that it is almost impossible to distinguish words being spoken more than a few feet away, the signals are used to communicate all the essential information of a trade: buy or sell, expiration month, quantity, and price.

The dress code in the pits calls for tie and jacket—but the ties are often ties in name only, frequently worn so loosely knotted as to look more like lariats thrown around the traders' torsos. Many traders wear the same "lucky tie" every day, fearing to change it or launder it at the cost

Price quotations:

Palm out indicates sell, palm in indicates buy.
Integer of price is assumed.
Decimal indicated by fingers; add .05 if fingers half-extended.

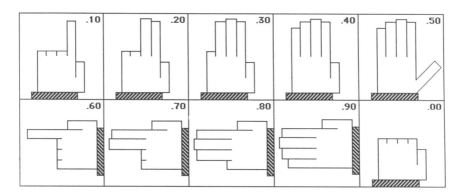

FIGURE 3.1. Hand signals in the S&P 500 index futures pit

of losing the benefit of its mystical influence. One well-known CBOE trader, now on the IOM trading S&P 500 futures, is famous for sucking on his lucky tie during moments of tension and adversity; of course, it long ago devolved into a filthy shred, but it is still worn and sucked to this day.

And the jackets are no better, for an ordinary suit jacket wouldn't last a day under the onslaught of perspiration and pencil stabbings it would receive in the crowds. Veterans from the early days of the CBOE still fondly recall one husband-and-wife team of traders who wore matching black leather trading jackets, but most traders wear loose-fitting, light cotton smocks, color-coded by special contrasting collars, piping, or epaulets to identify affiliations with the various clearing firms.

Many traders encrust their jackets with a galaxy of buttons. Some feature color photographs of wives or children, others the logos of sports teams, promotional slogans of the exchanges such as "The CBOE loves its customers!," or various "in" jokes such as "Spooze Don't Lie" or "Bored of Trade."

The functional decoration all personnel in the pits must wear is a badge designating their floor function. The badges of market-makers and floor-brokers bear the traders' acronyms, brief letter codes unique to each trader allowing other traders to correctly identify opposing parties on transaction tickets. Most will simply select their initials as their acronyms, but others use the opportunity for self-expression. Some acronyms are chosen to express a trader's attitude like "JET," "JOK," "KIL" or "WOW." Others express trading styles like "BET," "BUY," or "MKT." Others abbreviate nicknames, such as "USA " for a trader known as Uncle Sam, or "RKT" for Rocket.

The most profound element that binds the floor-traders together into a common culture is the absolutely indispensable requirement of mutual trust. In a trading crowd in which transactions valued in the millions of dollars are routinely consummated with hand signals or slang, a trader's word must, quite literally, be his bond. To appreciate how easily one could take advantage of the trust implicit in the structure of the crowd consider what would happen if an unscrupulous trader chose to "DK" a losing trade (claim he *didn't know* it): the winning trader on the other side of the transaction could be cheated of his profit. It would be one trader's word against the other's because it would be unlikely that anyone else in the crowd would happen to remember the trade reliably enough to act as a witness. It is the singular beauty of the pits that the enormous energies and naked greed of their participants are harnessed productively by a rigid code of honor that makes abuses of this type almost unheard of. Traders who practiced such methods would quickly find themselves DKed by the rest of the trading crowd.

FLOOR STRATEGIES

The Scalpers. Market-makers in the trading crowds fall into three broad categories: "scalpers," "shooters," and "spreaders." It is the scalpers whose strategy is most uniquely adapted to the environment of the pit. Scalpers exploit the fact that the price of any traded asset is quoted as a two-sided market comprised of the highest bid and the lowest offer. Scalpers will simultaneously make bids and offers, indifferent to whether they end up buying or selling. Their concern is that whenever they buy, they *buy on the bid* side of the market, and whenever they sell, they *sell on the offer* side of the market, thus earning as their profit the differential between the two. If prices remain generally stable and order flow into the crowd is fairly evenly divided between buys and sells, scalpers should be able to earn enough to see them through those times when prices move suddenly against them. The obvious drawback of this strategy is that a series of purchases on the bid will not be profitable if prices decline before the scalper has a chance to sell at the offer.

Competition among scalpers to buy the bid and sell the offer is a powerful mechanism for keeping the markets fair, liquid, and efficient for public investors. And it is one of the elements that give the trading crowds their sense of urgency. As public orders are brought into the trading crowd for execution, the floor-brokers representing the orders will call for a market; for example, in the S&P 100 crowd a floor-broker might represent an order to buy May 225.00 calls by shouting, "How now May quarters?" He is not revealing whether his order is to buy or sell; the call is for a two-sided market. Almost before the words are out of his mouth all the scalpers within earshot will scream out bids and offers. If the prevailing bid were 2.00 and the offer 2 1/16, the scalpers would shout back, "Two bid, at a teenie!" But the scalpers are not the only ones screaming; other market-makers pursuing other strategies or floor-brokers representing limit orders may join in as well; for instance, another floor-broker, this one holding an order to sell May 225.00 calls at 2 1/16, would shout, "At a teenie! At a teenie!"

The trader who responds first will be awarded the trade; the floor-broker who asked for the market will reveal the size of his order and whether he is a buyer or seller and then he and the trader deemed to have responded first will document their transaction on trading tickets. The need to respond first leads traders into all manner of histrionics; if one can't be the first, one can at least be the loudest, and that is often quite enough to get the trade.

Proximity is an advantage, too; it helps to be standing near floor-brokers who tend to handle many public market orders. The best position of all for the scalpers in the S&P 500 futures pit is to be near floor-brokers holding *stop orders*. Stops are orders to buy or sell at the market if the futures trade at a specified trigger price; for example, a "buy stop" might be entered at 236.00 when the futures are trading at 235.50; if the futures trade at 236.00, the buy stop becomes a market order, authorizing the floor-broker to buy at the best price available. Stop orders are of special interest to market-makers because if they can find out at which prices the stops are placed, they can have what amounts to advance knowledge of upcoming market orders. This information can be abused by means of a procedure known in the pit as a *bag run*. If market-makers know that there are buy stops for 500 contracts at 236.00 (when the futures are only trading at $235.50), they can confidently bid the futures up in an attempt to move the market toward 236.00. As soon as futures trade at 236.00, the buy stop will be triggered and the floor-broker will have to pay any price to buy 500 contracts. The locals can then turn around and sell to the floor-broker, for prices probably higher than 236.00, all the contracts they just bought between 235.50 and 236.00.

This description should not be taken to mean that a seat on the Chicago Mercantile Exchange is a license to steal. On the contrary, even a trading stratagem like the bag run is fraught with risk for the locals. First, floor-brokers make every attempt to conceal their stop orders and may at times even provide "disinformation" to market-makers to secure a better execution for their public customers. Second, even if certain market-makers know exactly where stops are placed there is no assurance that they can move the market all the way to reach them. If competing orders blockade them just a tick away from the stops, the would-be bag run can leave the market-makers holding the bag to the tune of many thousands of dollars.

The Shooters. The shooter, another type of market-maker, tries to make purchases at the bid and sales at the offer, but, unlike the scalper, he is willing to inventory positions in anticipation of market moves. Whereas the scalper accumulates profits one tick at a time, earning a gradual return on his labors, the shooter is in the game for the big score. The basic approach is not unlike that of any speculator, but, by virtue of being located in the trading crowd, the shooter has the luxury of extremely short time horizons—a shooter's idea of a long-term investment is an hour and a half.

To form the basis of opinion necessary to make trading decisions, shooters keep their eyes on the market quotations ringing the ceiling of the cavernous exchange floor and displayed on screens above the pits. They continously monitor the Dow Jones news ticker, price changes in the underlying indexes and in the most heavily weighted stocks, and trading in T-bond, currency, energy, and other index options and futures. They are voracious consumers and profligate distributors of the latest rumors about any event—political, economic, or otherwise—that might affect the stock market. Their antennas constantly monitor the "feel" of the pit, waiting for the "tone change" that will signal the next turn in the market. Some rely on technical analysis, a system of theories for interpreting index price charts that includes "Elliot waves," "Fibonnacci series," and "two-thirds speed-resistance lines." There is even one shooter, legendary on the CBOE as the "Moon Man," who makes no secret of trading by the stars.

By virtue of the liberal margins granted to exchange members, shooters can trade positions of extraordinary size and risk; as a result, their net licks are notoriously unstable. Every few months, when an unusually large rally or decline in the market takes place—a "lights-out move"— the classified ad section of the Chicago Sun-Times is filled with a disproportionate number of Rolls Royces and diamond pinky rings offered at fire-sale prices.

The most dangerous species of shooter—dangerous to himself, at any rate—is the *teenie seller*. He believes that most options end up expiring worthless, especially the extremely low-priced ones trading for the minimum increment of 1/16, or $6.25 per contract (a teenie, in the parlance). Indeed, the probability of such options ever attaining any value before they expire is extremely small; since only a fool would buy them, the teenie seller reasons, perhaps selling them isn't such a bad idea.

A teenie seller may go for months without a hitch; at expiration the "junk" he sold dutifully expires worthless. With an expiration every month, the sale of thousands of contracts at a time for $6.25 each can be an extraordinarily lucrative enterprise. The trouble with this strategy is that even long shots pay off every once in a while, and when the time to pay off finally comes, the teenie seller realizes that although his earnings were limited to $6.25 per contract, losses are potentially infinite

The Spreaders. The spreader's approach is entirely different from that of the scalper or the shooter. Whereas the scalper earns a return on labor and the shooter earns a return on risk, the spreader seeks out and exploits minute inefficiencies in the pricing structure of the options market. Armed with pocket calculators programmed for options pricing models or with reams of dog-eared computer printouts, spreaders scan the video screens above the pits for combinations of options or options-on-futures that their mathematics reveals to be out of line. For example, a spreader might, according to statistical analysis, determine that a particular S&P 100 call option is severely overpriced in relation to other available options. By selling the overpriced options and simultaneously buying other more fairly priced options, he establishes a *neutral spread*, immune from changes in the price of the underlying index because of being both long and short. If the spreader has correctly identified a market inefficiency in the overpriced options he has sold, they will eventually deflate to a more normal price range, whereas the fairly priced options he bought can be expected to hold their value. When this revaluation is complete, he unwinds his position and starts looking for a new opportunity.

A DAY IN THE PITS

The daily cycle of the Exchange floors begins early, at 7:20 AM CST, as the pits of the Chicago Mercantile Exchange's International Monetary Market division begin trading futures and options-on-futures on foreign currencies, Eurodollar deposits, and Treasury bills. Trading begins this early so that European traders, six to eight hours ahead of the local time zone, can participate in the opening.

At this early hour the S&P 500 futures and the S&P 100 options pits are almost deserted, except for a few clerks beginning to cross-compare records of the preceding day's trading. These records, often reflecting trading volume that can run to more than 1 million contracts a day, are generated by the unsung heroes of the world of index options and futures—the clearing houses, the ultimate issuers and guarantors of all contracts. For any given buyer, a clearing house is the seller; for any given seller a clearing house is the buyer. Because they interpose themselves between all pairs of buyers and sellers, the clearing houses allow investors to trade without concern for the specific identity or creditworthiness of the opposing side of the transaction. The clearing houses accept as members only those firms that demonstrate substantial financial strength and business integrity. They maintain elaborate safeguards against defaults, including special funds to be used in the event of losses, to which member firms must contribute.

The Chicago Board of Trade, the Chicago Mercantile Exchange, and the Kansas City Board of Trade maintain their own exclusive clearing houses. The options exchanges share a common clearing house, the Options Clearing Corporation. A new division of OCC, the Intermarket Clearing Corporation, offers clearing house services for futures and options-on-futures, but so far, among the futures exchanges that list index futures, only the New York Futures Exchange has elected to use it.

The clerks poring over the clearing houses' records at this early hour are seeking to resolve *out-trades*, transactions the computers have been unable to clear. Many are simply the result of input errors made by keypunch operators, and the clerks can easily resolve them among themselves. A significant number every day, however, are actual trading errors which can be enormously costly and must usually be resolved by the traders themselves when they begin to arrive at around 8:00 AM.

Out-trades fall into three major categories, each generally the result of legitimate misunderstandings. First is the *price out*, in which the buyer and the seller dispute the price at which they thought they had traded. Second is the *size out*, in which the buyer and seller dispute the number of contracts in the trade. Third is the *buy-versus-buy out* or the *sell-versus-sell out*, in which both parties to the trade thought they were the buyer or both thought they were the seller. With options there are two kinds of out-trades that result from misunderstanding which option is to be traded: *strike outs* and *put-versus-call outs*.

When events can be reconstructed adequately to determine which party to these disputes is in the right, the erring party is held responsible. Unfortunately it is often not possible to ascertain exactly why the errors take place or which party is at fault. Because the money at stake can be substantial, the traders have evolved by custom a simple system of justice for handling out-trades. If the disputing parties are both market-makers, trading for their own risk, they usually split the cost of the out-trade evenly. If both parties are floor-brokers, handling public orders as agents, the cost will again usually be split evenly; but if one party is a market-maker and the other is a floor-broker, the market-maker usually bears the entire cost. That this system is rarely abused is a striking example of the mutual trust shared by the traders. Those who would take unfair advantage of the system are swiftly punished and reformed by intense social pressure. In the hectic world of the pits there is no room and no time for a trader whose word cannot be taken as his bond.

Overlaying the customs and folkways of the floor-traders is an elaborate set of exchange rules geared to ensuring fair and orderly markets for public customers. These rules include provisions for arbitration of disputes that cannot be solved informally. But whether floor disputes like out-trades are solved by handshake or by arbitration, and regardless of their outcome, they are strictly a family affair. They do not affect public customers' orders in any way.

After out-trades are resolved the traders begin to prepare for the opening bell at 8:30. Because the stock market often seems to take its cues from the bond market, the tone for the day is generally set by the opening of T-bill futures trading at 7:30 and of Treasury bond futures trading at the Chicago Board of Trade at 8:00. By 8:05 the clerks representing brokerage firms on the floor begin to call their customers to give opening indications for S&P 500 futures based primarily on how the bond futures are trading. These calls help to stimulate the customer order flow that will ultimately determine how the futures actually open at 8:30.

At 8:15, in an attempt to compete with the S&P 500 futures by opening 15 minutes earlier, the Board of Trade begins trading futures on the Major Market Index. S&P 500 futures traders in the pit take note of the Board's opening but it has little influence on their outlook. They know that trading on the Board of Trade before 8:30 is generally thin and timid as they wait to see how the S&P 500 futures will open.

By 8:25 the trading crowds have assembled in full strength and the process of opening the markets gets ready to begin. In the S&P 500 futures pit on the IOM the process of determining the opening price is an unstructured negotiation that begins several minutes before the official opening. Slowly at first, the market-makers begin to shout out the prices at which they will buy or sell and the floor-brokers begin to vocalize their limit orders. It's like an auction, where bidders can outbid one another and where sellers can undercut one another as well. As it becomes clear whether buyers or sellers are in excess, a rough consensus emerges.

Until the opening bell rings at 8:30 no actual trades take place, but as soon as it is heard, the S&P 500 futures pit explodes in a frenzy of shouting. Exchange employees called Pit Observers, identifiable by their powder-blue jackets, listen to the action during the first 30 seconds and report the transactions to terminal operators via radio; the terminal operators in turn disseminate the transactions to quotation services around the world as the *opening range*. This procedure for price reporting, practiced throughout the day, results in last-sale quotations that are at least 15 seconds behind the action (and sometimes downright inaccurate).

Once trading has begun in the S&P 500 futures pit the crowd settles back from the frenzy of the opening into its usual pace of mere pandemonium. From now until the closing bell there will be no silence in the pit. Even during rare moments when no trades are being executed, traders continuously shout out competing bids and offers. Scores of crowd-clerks ringing the pit constantly hand signal the best bids and offers to phone-clerks manning the floor-booths of the member brokerage firms outside the pit. Telephone orders begin to pour in to the floor-booths. The phone-clerks hand signal the orders to the crowd-clerks, who in turn shout the orders to their floor-brokers in the trading crowd. Occasionally an order will be too large or complex to be hand signaled, in which case it will be jotted on a card. The crowd-clerks and the phone-clerks are astonishingly skilled at throwing these cards with great accuracy over surprising distances

Once the floor-broker in the crowd has an order it is executed by open outcry; the floor-broker simply shouts out the order to the crowd. If he were a buyer of 100 contracts at $230.60, the order would be "Sixty on a hundred!" The use of the expression "on" and putting the price before size identifies the broker as a buyer. If he were a seller, he'd shout "A hundred at sixty!" The expression is "at" instead of "on" and size is put ahead of price. The first trader in the crowd to respond executes the trade. After an order is executed in the crowd the floor-broker signals the crowd-clerk, who signals the phone-clerk, who informs the customer.

Discipline in the pit is provided by Pit Observers who monitor trading activity for accuracy and fairness throughout the day. One of their most important tasks is to make last-sale price reporting as accurate as possible. If they see a price reported at which contracts did not actually trade, the report is "whistled out" and will not be recorded in the records of the Exchange.

The entire process of trading S&P 500 futures takes place without the intervention of a "specialist" to maintain a book of public orders and ensure market continuity. All public orders are handled by floor-brokers, who represent them equally in the democracy of open outcry, and market continuity is provided by the presence of a large group of competing market-makers.

Trading in the S&P 100 pit at the CBOE works differently. On the CBOE a staff of exchange employees maintains a public book of limit orders and is loosely responsible for overseeing trading in the crowd. By regulation they are scrupulously impartial because they are prohibited from entering trades for their own accounts. When the opening bell rings at 8:30, the order-book officials, or OBOs, identifiable by their tan jackets, begin to supervise the day's *opening rotations*, one for the nearest two expiration months and another simultaneous rotation for the furthest two. Speaking into microphones attached to headsets like telephone operators wear, the OBOs are heard above the voices of the crowd through speakers ringing the pits. They begin by calling out the name of the longest term, lowest strike-price call options and their calls are met by a chorus of conflicting bids and offers from the crowd. When they have acquired a feeling for the highest bids and lowest offers, they disclose the public orders they are representing and a single opening price is negotiated that will allow the greatest number of contracts to be transacted. The OBO's public orders are given priority in the opening rotation and throughout the day: any transactions that occur at a given price must be made first with the OBOs before other orders at the same price can be filled. Next, the OBOs call out the names of the put options with the same expiration terms and strike-price, and so on through all the puts and calls, moving forward through the expiration terms and upward through the strike-prices. Anywhere from 10 to 30 minutes later the crowd is opening the last options: the nearest/term, highest strike-price puts. When the opening rotation is completed, the OBOs no longer trade one option at a time—any option can be traded by anyone in the crowd.

The trading day in the pit does not end when the New York Stock Exchange closes at 3:00 PM, Chicago time. Index options and futures trading on all the exchanges continues for 15 minutes, usually one of the busiest times of the day. On the IOM the momentum of the day's activity usually impels several traders to continue trading among themselves after the closing bell, "on the curb" as it's called, even as the majority is packing up and going home. Their reluctance to call it a day reminds one of an old joke is told in Chicago about the life of the floor-trader—sure it's tough, but the hardest part is figuring out what to do with evenings and weekends.

THE CBOE AND THE IOM: EVOLUTION BY ORDEAL

The success of index options and futures is challenging the CBOE and the IOM to evolve institutional structures capable of dealing with volume levels unprecedented in the history of the securities markets. The exchanges are taking very different approaches to the challenge—the CBOE stresses relatively tight structuring of the trading process for the protection of public investors (at the occasional expense of efficiency) and the IOM stresses ad hoc, free-market structuring geared to the fastest execution (at the occasional expense of accountability).

Throughout the market day trading on the CBOE is more rigidly regulated than on the IOM. This is evident from the moment the market opens, when the S&P 100 options conduct an opening rotation while the S&P 500 futures trade freely. The advantage of the rotation is that it focuses the entire trading crowd on establishing a single opening price for each option. The disadvantage is that, because the many different calls and puts spread out over various strike-prices and expiration terms have to be opened separately, the opening rotation can take 30 minutes on an extremely busy morning. Late-arriving orders for the options to be opened first have to wait for the entire rotation to conclude before they can be executed.

Whereas the IOM orders for S&P 500 futures can be hand-signaled or shouted into the crowd, S&P 100 options orders on the CBOE must be physically conveyed into the crowd in writing. This helps to produce an accurate record of an order's history in the event of a later dispute, but given the difficulty of penetrating into the center of a crowd as large as that of the S&P 100 this regulation can, at times, cause irritating delays in executions and reports.

Another major distinction between the methods by which the two exchanges conduct business is their procedures for price reporting. The IOM disseminates no official market information during the day, beyond the price of the last sale—no bids and offers and no cumulative volume; the only way to get this information is to telephone the floor and ask a phone-clerk. The CBOE, on the other hand, keeps an elaborate audit trail of *time and tape*, just like the New York Stock Exchange, and disseminates not only last-sale information but also bids and offers and cumulative trading volume. Because of the difficulties of discerning the highest bids and lowest offers of 500 screaming traders, the CBOE's market reporting is often wrong; and, given volume that can exceed 1 million contracts in a single day, the cumulative volume reporting is sometimes delayed up to 30 minutes. Sometimes it seems that the attempt to report this often faulty information achieves nothing but to raise investors' expectations for accuracy to unrealistic levels—and then, inevitably, disappoint them when they depend on the information to trade.

A similar conflict of the CBOE's high-minded motives of public service and the reality of what it can deliver is the OBO's book of public limit orders. By granting priority to customer orders in the book the CBOE is attempting to give an advantage to the unsophisticated public investor; the problem is that on the busiest days, just when the public most needs every advantage it can get, the physical task of getting orders into and out of the book becomes so congested that it can take hours to find any given order if the customer decides to change or cancel it.

Lest it seem that the CBOE's S&P 100 pit is coming in for more than its share of criticism, the special difficulty of its task deserves some emphasis. To put into perspective the volume of business that flows through the pit consider the information presented in Figure 3.2. In March 1983, the month in which S&P 100 options were first introduced, their average daily volume was 7620 contracts. At that time options on individual stocks, traded on four exchanges around the country, averaged 460,550 contracts. In February 1986 the average daily volume for S&P 100 options was 518,110 contracts, 12% higher than the entire options industry put together just three years earlier. Given these facts, the CBOE's

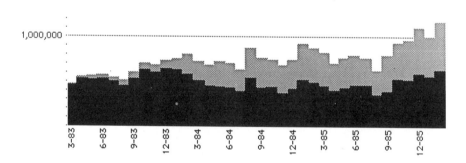

Source:
Chicago Board Options Exchange

FIGURE 3.2. Growth of S&P 100 index options trading

problems shrink into insignificance and one is overwhelmed with admiration and wonder that the system can be made to work at all.

Since its inception in 1973 the CBOE has consistently displayed a commitment to progress and modernization unique among exchanges, usually better known for their adherence to tradition at any cost. A new CBOE project that brings leading-edge electronic technology to bear on the problems produced by the S&P 100 pit's crushing trading volume is the Retail Automated Execution System. RAES—to use the inevitable acronym—allowing member brokerage firms to input customer market orders into a computer that randomly assigns them to participating market-makers and reports the trades instantaneously. It is currently by far the fastest way to get a customer order into the pit and onto the tape. As new technologies like RAES become integrated into the CBOE's trading process the exchange's goal of handling high volume without compromising customer accountability will come closer to attainment.

PRICES & VALUES

Oscar Wilde once defined a cynic as "A man who knows the price of everything, and the value of nothing." We may not be cynics, but this aptly describes a serious problem we encounter when we consider implementing strategies with index options and futures. We can easily see their *market prices* listed in the *Wall Street Journal*, but it is much more difficult to know their *"fair" prices*—their true *values*.

Our intuition gives us a natural sense of their values, but only in a very wide range. For example, we would certainly buy an in-the-money three-month call option on the S&P 100 index if it were offered to us for just a penny—and just as certainly we would scratch our heads in astonishment to learn that one had sold on the Chicago Board Options Exchange for a billion dollars. The most famous piece of investment advice in history must be, "Buy low, sell high." Unfortunately generations of investors have learned the hard way that for many types of investment there are no reliable benchmarks against which we can determine how low is low and how high is high. In the case of our S&P 100 call option a penny is obviously too low and a billion dollars is obviously too high—but how do we determine where in between these two extremes the fair price might lie?

Perhaps there is no reliable way of finding the value of a share of common stock, a piece of real estate, or a work of art, but index options and futures are different. Because they are tied to an underlying index, the current price of which is known with certainty, there are simple formulas for determining their values. These formulas can't determine whether an index itself is fairly priced, but given a known index price they can calculate a fair price—a *theoretical value*—for index options and futures with great precision.

As exchange markets in options, futures, and options-on-futures have developed and flourished over the last two decades the valuation of these instruments has been the subject of intense academic research. Although this research can be traced as far back as 1877, the first conceptually satisfying valuation model for options wasn't published until 1973, in a paper by Fischer Black and Myron Scholes called "The Pricing of Options and Corporate Liabilities." Their formulation, now widely known as the Black–Scholes model, is an elegant and extremely sophisticated piece of higher mathematics, but it has significant limitations in valuing the kinds of options that actually trade on exchanges. In 1978 John Cox, Stephen Ross, and Mark Rubinstein corrected these limitations in a brilliant but extraordinarily complicated paper ironically called "Option Pricing: A Simplified Approach." Both the Black–Scholes and Cox–Ross–Rubinstein models are so difficult for nonmathematicians to understand that most investors who use the models tend to treat them as "black boxes," relying on their output without really understanding how they work.

The purpose of this chapter is to outline the principles of options and futures valuation in intuitive, common sense language. Although basic arithmetic cannot be avoided entirely, the deliberately simple style of this chapter will unlock a doorway into a fascinating new world of useful ideas. For quantitatively oriented readers this chapter provides a refreshingly intuitive viewpoint that will remind them of the practical concepts that underlie the mathematical intricacies of the models.

Throughout this section we make no statements about the valuation of index options and futures that cannot be proved by simple logic. Therefore whenever we offer an important new principle we'll offer a proof as well. The proofs are quite simple and add a dimension of credibility to concepts that might otherwise be rather abstract. Nonetheless, for the reader who wishes to skip them we have bracketed them by the expressions *"Proof"* and *"End of Proof."*

Similarly, in a few cases an algebraic solution to an equation is presented. The solutions are simple to begin with and are explained step by step to help the most math-averse reader to follow along. Nonetheless, they, too, can be skipped by locating the expressions *"Solution"* and *"End of Solution."*

4. A FORMULA FOR THE VALUATION OF INDEX FUTURES

A common misconception about index futures is that their prices represent the market's best estimate of the price of the index at some point in the future; for example, if an index were priced at 240.00 and futures contracts with three months until expiration were trading at 241.78, this theory would hold that the futures market must be predicting that the index will be at 241.78 in three months. The flaw in this theory is that it fails to explain why investor expectations expressed in the higher futures price aren't expressed in the index itself. It is unlikely over the long run that futures investors could operate on information drastically better than, or even different from, that of stock investors.

If investor expectations are not at work, how do we explain the fact that index futures generally trade at prices somewhat different than the prices of their underlying indexes? Would an intelligent investor ever pay the higher futures price in the example just given when he might just as easily buy the index itself 1.78 cheaper? Or, if the prices were reversed, would any investor not prefer to buy the cheaper futures? In practice, choosing between an investment in an index futures contract versus an investment in the underlying index is a little more complicated than selecting the one with the lower price. In fact, we can objectively prove, in many circumstances, that it would be more economical to select the one with the higher price.

Let's imagine a situation in which an investor is choosing between an investment in a three-month futures contract versus a three-month investment in the index itself when *both are at the same price*. If the investor chooses to buy the index (by buying all of its component stocks), he will have to invest a dollar amount equal to the index price, today. His account balance in three months will be equal to the index price at that time plus any dividends he has received. If we call today's index price "index price$_1$" and the index price in three months "index price$_2$," we can set up a simple formula for determining the results of this investment:

Investment required today		Result in three months
Index price$_1$	$\rightarrow$	Index price$_2$ + Dividends

Now let's fill in some sample numbers. Let's say that the index is priced at 240.00 and that its yield is 4% annually—it will pay $2.40 in dividends, evenly over the three months. Because the investor can reinvest the dividends at the riskless interest rate as he receives them during the three months, their value will be somewhat greater than $2.40 at the end of the holding period. If we assume a yield of 1.75% on Treasury bills maturing at the end of the holding period (7% annualized, uncompounded), the instantaneous daily rate at which the investor could reinvest the dividends to arrive at a continuously compounded quarterly rate of 1.75% would be 0.019%. At this reinvestment rate the value of the $2.40 dividend payments at the end of three months would be $2.42.

By plugging these figures into the foregoing formula, we can determine how an investment of $240.00 in the index would fare in three months, assuming that the index is unchanged, up or down.

Investment required today		Result in three months				
Index price$_1$	$\rightarrow$	Index price$_2$	+	Dividends		
240.00	Unchanged	240.00	+	$2.42	=	$242.42
240.00	+10%	264.00	+	$2.42	=	$266.42
240.00	−10%	216.00	+	$2.42	=	$218.42

Alternatively, what would happen if the investor bought a three-month index futures contract instead, also priced at 240.00? Recall that buying a futures contract doesn't require the investor to *spend* its full value, but rather to post a small margin deposit. To keep the investor's initial cash flows equivalent between these two alternatives let's say he invests $240.00 in Treasury bills maturing in three months and deposits them in his futures account to meet the margin requirement. Now, his account balance at the end of the three-month holding period will be determined by somewhat different factors: first, any profit or loss in his futures contract, which will be equal to the index price in three months minus the 240.00 price at which he bought the contract today; second, the maturity value of the Treasury bills.

Investment required today	Result in three months
Index price$_1$ in T-bills $\rightarrow$	(Index price$_2$ − Futures price) + Mature T-bills

A 1.75% quarterly yield for a $240.00 investment in Treasury bills would result in a maturity value of $244.20. By plugging this value into the formula we can check the results of this alternative means of buying the index for three months.

Investment required today		Result in three months		
Index price$_1$ in T-bills	$\rightarrow$	(Index price$_2$ − Futures price)	+	Mature T-bills
$240.00	unchanged	(240.00 − 240.00) + $244.20		= $244.20
$240.00	+10%	(264.00 − 240.00) + $244.20		= $268.20
$240.00	−10%	(216.00 − 240.00) + $244.20		= $220.20

These two alternatives—investing $240.00 in Treasury bills while holding an index futures contract as opposed to investing $240.00 in stocks directly—are equivalent in terms of the initial investment required ($240.00 in both cases) and the amount of risk to be borne (any fluctuation in the price of the index in both cases). Yet, because holding the index futures contract allows the investor to earn $4.20 in interest while the stocks pay only $2.42 in dividends, in all circumstances the futures investment earns more or loses less. It is clear that the investor would always be better off with the futures contract *if it can be bought at the same price as the index.*

	Results of buying all stocks in index at 240.00	Results of buying futures contract at 240.00
Index unchanged	$242.42 (+2.42)	$244.20 (+4.20)
Index + 10%	$266.42 (+26.42)	$268.20 (+28.20)
Index − 10%	$218.42 (−21.58)	$220.20 (−19.80)

In fact, in this example the futures contract offers such an obvious advantage that it violates the "TANSTAAFL rule" (which states that There Ain't No Such Thing As A Free Lunch). In an efficient market an investor cannot reasonably expect to get something for nothing; free lunches do not last for long. Alert investors will bid up the "too low" price of this futures contract (or offer down the "too high" price of the index) until an equilibrium is established in which neither alternative presents an obvious advantage. If we can calculate this equilibrium point, we will have the *theoretical value* of the futures contract. Fortunately the algebra required to do so is quite simple.

Solution: The equilibrium point is the futures price at which the result of buying a futures contract is the same as the result of a direct investment in stocks.

Results of buying stocks in index	Results of buying futures contract
Index price$_2$ + Dividends	=	(Index price$_2$ − Futures price) + Mature T-bills

Before we solve for the futures price that satisfies this equation let's simplify it a little bit. "Index price$_2$" appears on both sides and can be dropped out. This simple algebraic step is more than a convenience—it confirms the statement we made earlier that the value of a futures contract is not contingent on the future price of the underlying index.

$$\text{Dividends} = (-\text{Futures price}) + \text{Mature T-bills}$$

It may appear at this stage that we have disposed of the initial price of the index as well, but we have not—it is implicit in the expression "Mature T-bills." Recall that the initial investment in Treasury bills was equal to the initial price of the index. Therefore the value of the mature T-bills must equal the initial index price, multiplied by 1 plus the interest rate.

$$\text{Dividends} = (-\text{Future price}) + [\text{Index price}_1 \times (1 + \text{Interest rate})]$$

Next we isolate the futures price on one side of the equation.

$$\text{Futures price} = [\text{Index price}_1 \times (1 + \text{Interest rate})] - \text{Dividends}$$

Finally we plug in the numbers from our example.

Futures price	=	[Index price$_1$	×	(1 + Interest rate)]	−	Dividends
$241.78	=	(240.00	×	1.0175)	−	$2.42
$241.78	=	244.20	−	$2.42		

We have solved for the equilibrium futures price of 241.78—the theoretical value of the futures contract. *End of solution.*

At this price the investor is paying a $1.78 premium to own the futures contract, a locked-in penalty that will offset the $4.20 interest to be earned on the Treasury bills. With this penalty the outcomes in all circumstances of buying a three-month futures contract will be exactly the same as an investment in the stocks that constitute the index.

Investment required today		Result in 3 months		
Index price$_1$ in T-bills	$\rightarrow$	(Index price$_2$ − Futures price)	+	Mature T-bills
$240.00	unchanged	(240.00 − 241.78)	+ $244.20	= $242.42
$240.00	+10%	(264.00 − 241.78)	+ $244.20	= $266.42
$240.00	−10%	(216.00 − 241.78)	+ $244.20	= $218.42

	Results of buying all stocks in index at 240.00	Results of buying futures contract at 241.78
Index unchanged	$242.42 (+2.42)	$242.42 (+2.42)
Index + 10%	$266.42 (+26.42)	$266.42 (+26.42)
Index − 10%	$218.42 (−21.58)	$218.42 (−21.58)

With the index priced at 240.00 and the futures contract priced at 241.78, an efficient investor would not be able to choose between them on the basis of price alone—neither one offers a relative price advantage. The simplest way of expressing the valuation formula, and the one that we use throughout this book, relates the interest-earning benefit of buying a futures contract to the dividend-earning benefit of owning the index itself:

Futures value		Index price		Interest		Dividends		Interest on dividends
241.78	=	240.00	+	$4.20	−	$2.40	−	$0.02

Strictly speaking, this formula treats futures contracts as though they were *forward* contracts. The technical difference is that a forward contract is settled only on expiration day, whereas a futures contract is settled daily through the mechanism of variation margin—investors settle profits and losses in cash on a daily basis even if the position is left outstanding. If a futures position moves in favor of the investor, he can reinvest the cash inflow from the daily settlement at the riskless rate; conversely, if it moves against him, he will have to finance the cash outflow. We will explore this distinction no further here because it has no practical impact on valuation, but it does have a fundamental impact on futures trading strategies. In that context the importance of daily settlement is discussed later in great detail.

The theoretical value of an index futures contract is more than just an abstraction. If an investor's effective price for trading the index is truly 240.00, if he can really borrow and lend at the riskless rate of 7% annually, and if the index can be depended on to pay $2.40 in dividends, then any deviation from the theoretical value of 241.78 represents a riskless arbitrage opportunity returning greater than the riskless interest rate.

Proof. If the futures were trading precisely at their theoretical value of 241.78, an investor who sold them, while simultaneously buying the index itself, would establish a riskless position yielding the riskless rate of 7% annually. At expiration, any profit or loss in the index would be perfectly offset by a corresponding profit or loss in the futures contract, but the investor would earn $2.42 in dividends and the $1.78 premium in the futures—a riskless profit of $4.20 in three months, a simple annualized rate of return of 7% on the $240.00 investment required to establish the position.

If the futures were trading above their theoretical value of 241.78, an investor establishing this position would be taking no more risk, yet he would lock in a profit above the riskless rate of 7%; for example, if he could sell the futures 1.00 higher than their theoretical value, his profit would rise from $4.20 to $5.20—a simple annualized return of 9%. With this kind of riskless return available an alert investor would borrow all the money he could find at 7% and invest it in this position to earn 9%.

Underpricings in the futures contracts could be exploited the same way, but in reverse. A riskless position with no cash investment can be established by buying futures and short-selling the index itself. An investor with this position would have to make restitution for the dividends, which would cost him $2.42, but he could reinvest the proceeds of the short-sale in Treasury bills, earning $4.20. But this apparent net profit of $1.78 is precisely consumed by the 1.78 premium paid for the futures contracts at their theoretical value. To the extent that an investor could buy the futures below their theoretical value a riskless profit could be earned on a cash investment of zero. Later, in our exploration of index futures strategies, we discuss this opportunity in great detail. *End of Proof.*

When interest rates are higher than the dividend yield of the index during the life of the futures contract (as in our example), futures will be valued at a premium to the index price. In this state a futures contract will decrease in value as time passes, reflecting the diminishing dollar value of the relative advantage of earning interest as opposed to dividends. Consider the same futures contract, but with only one month till expiration rather than three; with only one month the interest that could be earned on $240.00 in Treasury bills would be only $1.40 and the dividends and reinvestment interest that could be earned on $240.00 in stocks yielding 4% would be only $0.79. By plugging these lower numbers into the valuation formula we can see that the theoretical value of the one-month futures contract would be 240.61.

Futures value		Index price		Interest		Dividends		Interest on dividends
240.61	=	240.00	+	$1.40	–	$0.78	–	$0.01

The premium in the one-month contract is 0.61 above the index price, whereas the premium in the three-month contract was about three times that—1.78 above the index price. Does this mean that a futures contract is a "wasting asset," that by holding the three-month contract for two months an investor will automatically lose $1.17? No, because the $240.00 invested in Treasury bills acting as margin for the contract over the intervening two months would have earned $2.78 interest, leaving the investor $1.61 ahead. It is no coincidence that this $1.61 is just what he would have earned in dividends had he opted to hold the stocks for two months instead of the futures contract.

Throughout most of recent history interest rates have tended to run above dividend yields; therefore most of the time we can expect that index futures will be valued at a premium. But because stock indexes do not pay dividends evenly over time there are occasions when a cluster of high payouts can raise the effective yield of an index to levels higher than prevailing interest rates, in which case futures will be valued at a discount to the index price.

In the preceding example we looked at our futures contract with only one month till expiration, implicitly assuming that the dividends paid during that month would be an even third of the total to be paid over three months. But now, because of extreme clustering of ex-dividend days in this particular index, let's assume that this month the payout is much higher than the average—let's say that with reinvestment an investor would receive $1.58 instead of $0.79. If we were to value this one-month futures contract now, during this high-payout month, the contract would be valued at 239.80—a discount to the index price because the month's dividend payout would be greater than the interest earned on Treasury bills.

Futures value		Index price		Interest		Dividends		Interest on dividends
239.80	=	240.00	+	$1.38	−	$1.57	−	$0.01

Before, when the futures were valued at a premium to the index, we saw that the passage of time caused the futures to decline in value. But, when dividend yields are above interest rates and index futures are valued at a discount to the index price, just the opposite occurs: the futures will increase in value with the passage of time to reflect the diminishing disadvantage of earning the interest rate as opposed to the relatively high dividend yield.

We can summarize what we have learned so far by reviewing the four simple factors that determine the value of an index futures contract. With each factor we present a table to demonstrate how the futures value of 241.78 would change, based on changes in that factor.

PRICE OF THE UNDERLYING INDEX. The *higher* the price of the underlying index, the *higher* the value of the futures contract. It is interesting to note that futures values do not change point for point with changes in the price of the underling index. Because futures values are determined, in part, by interest that can be earned by reinvesting the index price at the riskless rate, changes in the index price affect futures prices by 1 plus the riskless rate. Given the assumptions we've been using in this example, a 5.00 change in the index price would result in a futures value change of 5.0875.

Change in futures value		Change in underlying index price	1 plus periodic riskless rate
5.0875	=	5.00 ×	1.0175

	Time 3 Mo.	Interest 7%	Dividends 4%
Value 221.43 Index 220.00			
Value 226.52 Index 225.00			
Value 231.60 Index 230.00			
Value 236.69 Index 235.00			
Value 241.78 Index 240.00			
Value 246.87 Index 245.00			
Value 251.95 Index 250.00			
Value 257.04 Index 255.00			
Value 262.13 Index 260.00			

TIME REMAINING TILL EXPIRATION. The *more* time remaining till expiration, the *higher* the value of the futures contract if the riskless rate is *above* the dividend yield and the lower the value of the futures contract if the riskless rate is *below* the dividend yield. Note that if dividends are paid out evenly over time the futures value's premium or discount to the index price will change proportionately to time remaining till expiration; for example, if the value's premium to the index price with two months till expiration is 1.20, with one month till expiration it will be 0.60.

Index 240.00		Interest 7%	Dividends 4%
Value 240.02	Time 1 day		
Value 240.14	Time 1 wk.		
Value 240.60	Time 1 mo.		
Value 241.20	Time 2 mo.		
Value 241.78	Time 3 mo.		
Value 243.67	Time 6 mo.		
Value 245.57	Time 9 mo.		
Value 247.49	Time 1 yr.		
Value 255.44	Time 2 yr.		

THE RISKLESS INTEREST RATE. The *higher* the riskless interest rate, the *higher* the value of the futures contract. The rates quoted in the table that follows are annualized, uncompounded. The values for three-month contracts are based on dividing these rates by 4. Note that when the interest rate is lower than the dividend yield the future value is at a discount to the index price. When the interest rate is equal to the dividend yield, the futures value is identical to the index price, and when the interest rate is higher than the dividend yield the futures value is at a premium to the index price.

Index 240.00	Time 3 Mo.		Dividends 4%
Value 239.40		Interest 3%	
Value 240.00		Interest 4%	
Value 240.59		Interest 5%	
Value 241.19		Interest 6%	
Value 241.78		Interest 7%	
Value 242.38		Interest 8%	
Value 242.98		Interest 9%	
Value 243.58		Interest 10%	
Value 244.17		Interest 11%	

THE DIVIDEND YIELD OF THE UNDERLYING INDEX. The *higher* the dividend yield of the underlying index, the *lower* the value of the futures contract.

Index 240.00	Time 3 Mo.	Interest 7%	
Value 242.98			Dividends 2%
Value 242.69			Dividends 2.5%
Value 242.38			Dividends 3%
Value 242.08			Dividends 3.5%
Value 241.78			Dividends 4%
Value 241.48			Dividends 4.5%
Value 241.17			Dividends 5%
Value 240.87			Dividends 5.5%
Value 240.57			Dividends 6%

Over their history of trading since 1982 index futures have by and large been priced close to what the valuation formula would predict. Nonetheless, investors who watch the markets closely have often seen the futures priced quite erratically, swinging from a discount one day to a premium the next and then back again. Even more mystifying than the daily fluctuations (which might be excused by the frenzy of the marketplace) have been the long periods of persistent mispricing both above and below the formula's prices.

In one sense, perhaps, investors shouldn't be concerned with mispricings. After all, by knowing the formula an efficient investor never has to pay more than the price the formula calculates no matter how futures are priced in the marketplace. If futures are overpriced, the investor can choose to buy the stocks in the index instead, thus driving the price of the index up until the overpricing in the futures is justified. If futures are underpriced, they can be bought at an advantage, thus driving up their price until they reach the formula value. But just because mispricings may represent opportunities for arbitrage-minded investors does not mean that we should not be curious as to how they arise or how we might adapt our valuation formula in light of them.

First we must recognize that, like beauty, the valuation of index futures is in the eye of the beholder. For example, the valuation formula depends chiefly on the current index price; we are accustomed to thinking of this as a single number, but that is highly inaccurate mental shorthand that does not reflect where investors could actually hope to trade. In fact, an index—like any traded security—really has two prices; an offer price for buyers and a bid price for sellers. For the S&P 500, for instance, the spread between the bid and the offer is usually at least 1.00, which suggests that buyers typically would have to pay 0.50 higher than the last sale quotation to buy the index and sellers would have to take 0.50 less than the last sale price to sell it.

In our first example of index futures valuation we calculated a value of 241.78, based on an index price quotation of 240.00. If we were to adapt this calculation to reflect the fact that a buyer would actually have to pay 240.50 for the index, our valuation would rise to 242.29. Note that the amount of interest is adjusted upward to reflect the higher effective price of the index.

Futures value		Index price		Interest		Dividends		Interest on dividends
242.28	=	24.50	+	$4.21	−	$2.40	−	$0.02

Similarly, if we were to adapt this calculation to reflect the fact that a seller would actually receive only 239.50 for the index, our valuation would fall to 241.27.

Futures value		Index price		Interest		Dividends		Interest on dividends
241.27	=	239.50	+	$4.19	−	$2.40	−	$0.02

The value of index futures is even lower for those short-sellers who cannot earn interest on the proceeds of their sales—237.08, a 2.92 discount to the nominal index price.

Futures value		Index price		Interest		Dividends		Interest on dividends
237.08	=	239.50	+	0	−	$2.40	−	$0.02

These values are driven even further apart when brokerage commissions are factored into the calculation. From the buyer's perspective commissions effectively raise the price he must pay for the underlying index, so they raise the value of index futures contracts as well. Assuming a commission of 0.25, the index price is raised to 240.75 and the futures value to 242.54.

Futures value		Index price		Interest		Dividends		Interest on dividends
242.54	=	240.75	+	$4.21	−	$2.40	−	$0.02

For a seller or a short-seller, commissions would effectively reduce the effective index price to 239.25, and therefore the futures values as well, to 241.02 and 236.83, respectively.

Futures value		Index price		Interest		Dividends		Interest on dividends
241.02	=	239.25	+	$4.19	−	$2.40	−	$0.02

Futures value		Index price		Interest		Dividends		Interest on dividends
236.83	=	239.25	+	0	−	$2.40	−	$0.02

During periods when buyers strongly dominate the market the higher futures value derived from their viewpoint may make the futures trade consistently higher than would be expected on the basis of the nominal price of the index. Conversely, during periods of dominant selling the lower valuation derived from the sellers' viewpoint may make futures seem underpriced. This suggests that when futures prices reflect the high valuation placed on them by the buyers' perspective, sellers receive a pricing advantage. When prices reflect the sellers' perspective, buyers have a pricing advantage. Paradoxically, when prices are anywhere between the two extremes, both buyers and sellers have a pricing advantage. This logic leads to an astounding but accurate conclusion about the index futures markets: *there is no price at which futures do not offer some kind of advantage to someone.*

Just as the different perspectives of buyers and sellers lead to differing valuations of index futures, so do the various tax rates affecting particular investors, because taxation can have a profound impact on how investors value interest and dividend income effectively. In the initial example in which we valued the three-month futures contract at 241.78 our formula was seen from the viewpoint of a tax-exempt institution. But now let's look at it again through the eyes of a taxable corporation in the 35% bracket. This corporation would have to pay $1.48 in taxes on the interest income of $4.22 from Treasury bills and $0.02 from reinvestment of dividends, leaving after-tax interest income of only $2.28.

Tax on interest income		Pretax interest income		Tax rate
$1.48	=	$4.22	×	35%

After-tax interest income		Pretax interest income		Tax on interest income
$2.74	=	$4.22	−	$1.48

The corporation could exclude 75% of the $2.40 in dividend income, but it would have to pay taxes of $0.17 on the balance of $0.36, leaving after-tax dividend income of only $2.23.

Excluded dividend income		Total dividend income		Exclusion
$1.68	=	$2.40	×	75%

Unexcluded dividend income		Total dividend income		Excluded dividend income
$0.72	=	$2.40	−	$1.68

Tax on dividend income		Unexcluded dividend income		Tax rate
$0.25	=	$0.72	×	35%

After-tax dividend income		Pretax dividend income		Tax on dividend income
$2.15	=	$2.40	−	$0.25

When we plug the corporation's effective after-tax interest and dividend figures into the valuation formula, we get a futures value of 240.59, only 0.59 higher than the price of the index itself.

Futures value		Index price		After-tax interest		After-tax dividends
240.59	=	240.00	+	$2.74	−	$2.15

Now let's consider the individual investor taxed at the 28% maximum (1988) rate. This investor would have to pay $1.18 in taxes on the interest income of $4.22, leaving after-tax interest income of only $3.04.

Tax on interest income		Pretax interest income		Tax rate
$1.18	=	$4.22	×	28%

After-tax interest income		Pretax interest income		Tax on interest income
$3.04	=	$4.22	−	$1.18

An individual would have to pay taxes of $0.67 on the dividend income of $2.40, leaving after-tax dividend income of only $1.73.

Tax on dividend income		Pretax dividend income		Tax rate
$0.67	=	$2.40	×	28%

After-tax dividend income		Pretax dividend income		Tax on dividend income
$1.73	=	$2.40	−	$0.67

When we plug the taxable individual's effective after-tax interest and dividend figures into the valuation formula, we get a futures value of 241.31.

Futures value		Index price		After-tax interest		After-tax dividends
241.31	=	240.00	+	$3.04	−	$1.73

There is a substantial range in futures values among the various investors we have examined; it is illustrated graphically in Figure 4.1. The lowest and the highest both happened to be associated with tax-exempt investors. The lowest value is that of the tax exempt short-seller, after commissions, who cannot earn interest on the proceeds of the sale: 236.83, a 3.17 discount to the index price.

Futures value		Index price		Interest		Dividends		Interest on dividends
236.83	=	239.25	+	0	−	$2.40	−	$0.02

The highest value is that of the tax-exempt institution wishing to buy: 242.54, a 2.54 premium to the index price.

Futures value		Index price		Interest		Dividends		Interest on dividends
242.54	=	240.75	+ $4.21	−	$2.40	−		$0.02

The range between the tax-exempt short-seller's lowest value and the tax-exempt buyer's highest value is 5.72, or 2.38% of the index price. Given that any point in this range of valuation can be thought of as "fair" for certain types of investors, perhaps it is reasonable that futures pricing in the marketplace is as unstable as it appears.

Falling entirely outside the scope of the valuation model presented here are two other factors that can account for apparent mispricing of index futures, and both suggest that prices should be systematically lower than the valuation formula would otherwise calculate. One is the New York Stock Exchange's plus-tick rule, which requires that any short-sale of stock be executed only on a plus-tick or zero-plus-tick from the previous trade price. No such rule applies to index futures contracts, and because this effectively makes them easier to sell their prices might be expected to be marginally lower as a result. In addition, the plus-tick rule creates barriers for arbitrageurs who would otherwise exploit underpriced futures contracts by buying them and short-selling the stocks that make up their underlying index. The requirements to wait for plus-ticks makes simultaneous short-selling of a large number of stocks functionally impossible. Futures overpricings, on the other hand, are easy to exploit simply by

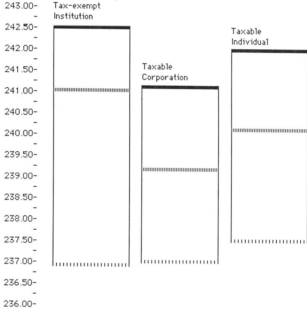

FIGURE 4.1. Theoretical value of index futures as a function of the investor's perspective.

selling the overpriced futures and buying the stocks at the market.

Another explanation for underpricing is the difference in the tax treatment of gains and losses in index futures versus the stocks that make up the underlying indexes. Profits and losses for futures are taxed at year-end on a mark-to-the-market basis, even if positions remain outstanding; stock profits and losses are not taxed until the positions are liquidated. Stocks therefore convey an opportunity to realize or defer taxable gains and losses by deciding whether to liquidate at year-end. This right amounts to a valuable "timing option." Because stocks convey this right and futures contracts do not, futures prices might be expected to be marginally lower as a result.

5. A PROCEDURE FOR THE VALUATION OF INDEX OPTIONS

We approach the valuation of index options in pretty much the same way we did index futures—with common sense and basic arithmetic. All four factors that contributed to futures valuation—the price of the underlying index, its dividend yield, the riskless interest rate, and the time remaining until expiration—contribute to options valuation as well. But for options there is a fifth factor: the *volatility* of the underlying index—how far and how fast it can be expected to move during the life of the option.

We didn't need to consider volatility in the valuation of futures because the risk of a futures contract is symmetrical between buyer and seller—neither should have to pay or be paid for expected volatility. But in buying an option, the most the investor can lose is the price paid for it. The buyer's gains—and the seller's losses—are potentially without limit. Therefore the *higher* the volatility of the underlying index, the more the buyer will have to compensate the seller, and the *higher* the value of *both* a *call* and a *put* option.

To integrate all five factors properly into a coherent options valuation formula will be a bit more difficult than it was for the four factors of futures valuation. In fact, there is no single *formula* for the valuation of index options. Instead, we'll have to build a valuation *procedure*. We begin by establishing the simplest possible rule about option valuation:

The value of an option is never less than zero.

Proof: Because an option contract conveys only the *right* (but *not the obligation*) to buy or sell an underlying index, the worst it can be is worthless—it can never be a liability. An option price of less than zero would require that the seller literally pay us to own the option. No matter what then happened to the price of the option's underlying index, in no possible scenario would we ever be forced to pay any money whatsoever to close the position; the worst thing that could happen would be for the option to expire worthless. Therefore any amount we received from the seller would be a certain profit with absolutely no cash investment and no risk, a violation of the TANSTAAFL rule. In the real world of efficient markets, watchful investors, competing ruthlessly with one another, would jump on rare opportunities like this one with sufficient enthusiasm to drive up the price of the option until it did not represent a free lunch anymore. *End of Proof.*

It may seem simple, but having established zero as an absolute lower boundary for options valuation will prove to be remarkably useful as we proceed. To build our options valuation procedure let's imagine a simple world where there are only two types of securities: indexes and options on the indexes. As with options in the real world, a *call* in our simple world conveys the right to receive in cash any amount by which the underlying index is *above* the option's strike-price, and a *put* conveys the right to receive in cash any amount by which the underlying index is *below* the option's strike-price. But our options have one special quality: they expire the moment they are purchased. This makes them similar to options in the real world during the last few minutes of trading on expiration day.

By using the TANSTAAFL rule it is possible to calculate prices for our simple options with great precision, knowing nothing more than the index price and the option's strike-price.

The price of an immediate-expiration call *option must equal the* index price minus the strike-price *(but cannot be less than zero).*

For example, if the index is priced at 240.00, a call option with a strike-price of 235.00 must be priced at 5.00.

Proof: If we could *buy the call for less than 5.00*, we would immediately exercise it, thus receiving $5.00 in cash, the amount by which the index price is above the call's strike-price. Therefore any amount below 5.00 paid for the call option would be an instantaneous riskless profit. Under the TANSTAAFL rule investors would compete so vigorously to put on this position that they would bid the calls up and offer the stock down until the position was no longer profitable.

If we could *sell the call for more than 5.00*, it would be exercised immediately and we would have to pay out $5.00 in cash, the amount by which the index price is above the call's strike-price. Any amount above 5.00 received when we initially shorted the option would be another instantaneous riskless profit and another violation of the TANSTAAFL rule. *End of Proof.*

The same kind of logic applies to put options, but in reverse:

The value of an immediate-expiration put *option must equal the* strike-price minus the index price *(but cannot be less than zero).*

Now that we've learned how to value the immediate-expiration options found in our simple world we can relax some of our simplifying restrictions and get closer to valuing options in the more complex real world. Let's start by saying that our options now don't expire immediately; we'll give them a lifetime of three months. Just to keep things manageable, though, we'll make the rule that they cannot be exercised prior to their expiration. Now we have to deal with some new complications. First, when we consider financial transactions that may tie up money over time, we must deal with the concept of interest rates. For now, let's say that the rate at which we can borrow and lend for three months is 1.75%, an uncompounded annual rate of 7%.

Second, because our options don't expire for three months we'll have to deal with the fact that, over time, index prices can fluctuate. Before, when our world was simpler, we were able to assume that index prices would never change during the life of our options—a functionally correct assumption because our simple options expired immediately after they were purchased. For now, let's use a very basic model of index price behavior, shown graphically in Figure 5.1. According to this simple model, the price of an underlying index can rally or decline by 7.5% over the three-month life of our options; for example, if the underlying index is priced at 240.00 today, it will be 258.00 or 222.00 three months from now.

The magnitude of the move we attribute to each branch of this simple tree is the way the valuation procedure incorporates the concept of volatility. When Modern Portfolio Theory enthusiasts speak of the volatility of an index, they are referring to its "annualized standard deviation of returns." 15% is a fair representative of the level of annual volatility currently associated with most stock indexes. As an intuitive approximation, if an index has an annual volatility of 15%, *two-thirds of the*

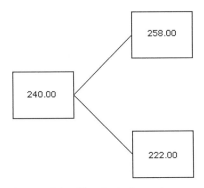

FIGURE 5.1. Simple index price tree

81

time its price can be expected to move by *less* than 15% annually; *one-third of the time* it will move *more* than 15%.

There is a simple statistical rule for transforming a given annual volatility into the percentage move that can be expected over the three-month life of our options. We simply divide the annual volatility by the square root of 4, the number of three-month periods in a year (the square root of a number is another number that, when multiplied by itself once, equals the first number; the square root of 4 is 2 because 2 multiplied by 2 equals 4).

Percentage change per period		Annual volatility		Square root of number of periods
7.5%	=	15%	÷	$\sqrt{4}$

Given this index price tree and an interest rate of 1.75%, how should we value three-month call options with a strike-price of 240.00? Believe it or not, using nothing but what we already know about options valuation and applying no economics theory other than the TANSTAAFL rule, we can prove with certainty that the value of such options under these simple conditions should be exactly 10.91.

At first it may seem incredible to claim that we can determine an exact value of 10.91 for our three-month, 240.00-strike-price call options. But as you'll soon see it's actually quite simple. In fact, we've already learned some principles of options valuation that can help us. Earlier we proved that the value of an immediate-expiration call must be the index price minus the option's strike-price (but not less than zero). Because we know how to value options that expire immediately, we know how our three-month options will be valued three months from today, at the moment that they expire; as shown in Figure 5.2, we know that the calls must either be valued at 18.00 (if the index moves up to 258.00) or at zero (if the index moves down to 222.00).

Now that we know how the calls will be valued at expiration we can use the TANSTAAFL rule to value them today, three months before expiration. All we have to do is to construct some other investment that has all the same characteristics as the calls, including the same value at expiration under all possible conditions. If we can do that and then determine *how that equivalent investment is valued today*, we can use the TANSTAAFL rule to prove that our *calls must be valued the same way*.

What investment could we possibly make that would look, act, and feel just like a three-month, 240.00-strike-price call option? In the simple

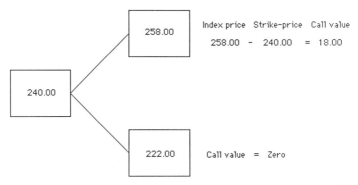

FIGURE 5.2. Call valuation at expiration with index price up and down

world we've created there's nothing to work with but the underlying index, call options on the index, and borrowing or lending at 1.75% interest—and because we're trying to price the call options we can't use the calls themselves in setting up this other equivalent investment. Our task, then, is to figure out how to make a *synthetic call* out of some combination of buying or selling the index and borrowing or lending at 1.75%.

Let's start by stating the problem two different ways, depending on whether the 240.00 index goes up to 258.00 or down to 222.00 over the three months. On the upside we are looking for a combination of some number of "shares" of the index and some amount of borrowing that will be worth 18.00 when the index price is 258.00 at the end of the three-month period, just as the calls would. To put this into a simple formula:

Shares of index	Index price	Amount of borrowing and interest	Call value at expiration
S	$\times$ 258.00 $-$	$(B + 1.75\% B)$ =	18.00

The difficulty is that the number of shares of the index, S, and the amount of borrowing, B, have to work on the downside as well; to act just like the calls, they have to be worth zero when the index is at 222.00 at the end of the three-month period, just as the calls would. To put this requirement into the same kind of formula:

Shares of index	Index price	Amount of borrowing and interest	Call value at expiration
S	$\times$ 222.00 $-$	$(B + 1.75\% B)$ $=$	0

There is but a single combination of number of shares of the index and amount of borrowing that works in both formulas.

Solution: We'll begin by solving for S. As a first step, we'll relate these two formulas in terms of the 18.00 difference between the two call values at expiration:

$$(S \times 258.00) - (B + 1.75\% B) = (S \times 222.00) - (B + 1.75\% B) + 18.00$$

We can immediately simplify this equation by dropping out the references to B appearing on both sides:

$$(S \times 258.00) = (S \times 222.00) + 18.00$$

To isolate S on just one side of the equation we subtract $S \times 258.00$ and 18.00 from both sides:

$$-18.00 = (S \times 222.00) - (S \times 258.00)$$

Multiplying both sides of the equation by -1 and simplifying:

$$18.00 = S \times (258.00 - 222.00)$$
$$18.00 = S \times 36.00$$

Dividing both sides of the equation by 36.00 finally solves for S:

$$18.00 \div 36.00 = S$$
$$S = 0.50$$

Now that S is solved as 0.50 it is relatively easy to solve for B by plugging 0.50 into one of the initial equations. Let's start by examining the equation used when the stock goes up to 258.00:

$$(0.50 \times 258.00) - (B + 1.75\% B) = 18.00$$

This can be simplified by combining the B terms:

$$(0.50 \times 258.00) - (1.0175 \times B) = 18.00$$

We can isolate B on one side of the equation by adding $(1.0175 \times B)$ to both sides and subtracting 18.00 from both sides:

$$(0.50 \times 258.00) - 18.00 = 1.0175 \times B$$

We can isolate B entirely by dividing both sides of the equation by 1.0175:

$$[(0.50 \times 258.00) - 18.00)] \div (1.0175) = B$$
$$(129.00 - 18.00) \div 1.0175 = B$$
$$111.00 \div 1.0175 = B$$
$$B = \$109.09$$

B is then easily solved as \$109.09. *End of solution.*

Now that S has been solved as 0.50 and B as \$109.09 let's plug these solutions into the two formulas to make sure they're the right numbers:

Shares of index		Index price		Amount of borrowing and interest		Call value at expiration
0.50	×	258.00	−	($109.09 + $1.91)	=	18.00

Shares of index		Index price		Amount of borrowing and interest		Call value at expiration
0.50	×	222.00	−	($109.09 + $1.91)	=	0

All that remains to determine the initial price of our synthetic call three months before expiration is to plug 0.50 and \$109.09 into the formula by using the initial index price of 240.00. We don't include the interest on the borrowing because that doesn't have to be paid until the loan is retired in three months. The result is 10.91, as promised:

Shares of index		Index price		Amount of borrowing		Value of synthetic call
0.50	×	240.00	−	$109.09	=	10.91

Under the TANSTAAFL rule perfectly equivalent investments must be valued identically. Therefore by deriving the value of a synthetic call we automatically determine the value of a real call as well.

Proof: If perfectly equivalent synthetic calls and real calls were priced differently, we could buy the less expensive one and simultaneously short-sell the more expensive. We've just seen that on expiration day the two options must have identical values, so any difference in price that we initially collect represents a riskless profit with no cash investment (a serious violation of the TANSTAAFL rule). *End of Proof.*

The same simple technique for valuing three-month call options can apply just as easily to put options. We know that the value of an immediate-expiration put must be the option's strike-price minus the index price (but cannot be less than zero). By using this valuation formula in the context of our index price tree we know that three-month put options must be valued at zero (if the index moves up to 258.00) or at 18.00 (if the index moves down to 222.00) at the moment they expire (Figure 5.3).

To set up the synthetic put necessary to value the real put we use the same procedure we used for calls to find a number of shares of the index and an amount of borrowing or lending that will satisfy these two formulas:

Shares of index		Index price		Amount of borrowing and interest		Put price at expiration
S	$\times$	258.00	$-$	$(B + 1.75\%B)$	$=$	0

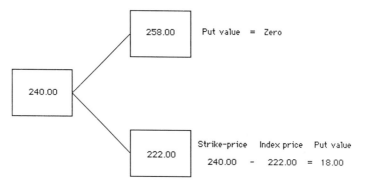

FIGURE 5.3. Put valuation at expiration with index price up and down

86

Shares of index		Index price		Amount of borrowing and interest		Put price at expiration
S	×	222.00	−	$(B + 1.75\% B)$	=	18.00

Once again there is but a single combination of shares of the index (0.50 or one-half share) and borrowing ($126.78) that will work in both formulas. But in this case both numbers are negative, which indicates that we would short-sell the shares of the index rather than buy them and lend rather than borrow.

Plugging these negative numbers into the formula using the initial index price of 240.00 reveals that the value of a three-month synthetic put—and consequently the value of a real put as well—is 6.78:

Shares of index		Index price		Amount of borrowing		Value of synthetic put
−0.50	×	240.00	−	−$126.78	=	6.78

The valuation model we've developed here works quite well in its own primitive way, although it is limited by the simplicity of the world we've created for it. Fortunately we can add realistic complexity to this world without fundamentally changing our technique for valuing options. Let's begin by creating a more complex index price tree, one that can move twice during the three-month period instead of just once.

In each of the two iterations of movement, percentage price changes up and down will be of equal magnitude, as shown graphically in Figure 5.4. Because each iteration now represents one-eighth of a year rather than one quarter, we now determine the percentage move associated with each iteration by dividing the 15% annual volatility by the square root of 8 rather than of 4:

Percentage change per period		Annual volatility		Square root of number of periods
5.3%	=	15%	÷	2.828

It may seem that there's something wrong with this method because the two-iteration tree shows that the index price at the end of the three months varies between a high of 266.13 and a low of 215.22, as opposed to 258.00 and 222.00 in the one-iteration free (Figure 5.1). But bear in mind that now there is a third possible outcome, 239.32, and that this outcome is twice as likely as either of the other two. From the initial price of 240.00 the index can only get to 266.13 by first going up and

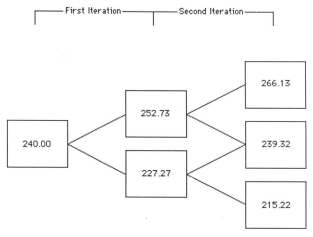

FIGURE 5.4. Two-iteration index price tree

then up again; and it can only get to 215.22 by first going down and then down again. But it has two ways of getting to 239.22—by first going up, then down, or by first going down, then up. Given this, the distributions of index prices in both the one-iteration and two-iteration trees conform to the definition of an annual volatility of 15%, seen over three months: that two-thirds of the possible outcomes fall within 7.5% of the initial price. As we add more iterations this conformity will become increasingly precise.

We are faced with a problem when we try to value our 240.00-strike-price, three-month call options using our new, two-iteration index price tree: the primitive option valuation model we've developed so far is only capable of dealing with a one-iteration tree. The solution is to break up the index price tree into segments that the valuation model can easily digest (Figure 5.5). As before, we'll start by applying the rule that the value of an immediate-expiration call must be the index price minus the option's strike-price (but cannot be less than zero). This rule will tell us what a call will be worth at the moment it expires, given the two possible expiration index prices in the isolated segment.

Once again, we set up a synthetic call, but this time it is as though the three-month option has only a month and a half left and the initial index price is 252.73. Just as we did before, we'll find a number of shares of the index and an amount of borrowing or lending that will satisfy these two formulas:

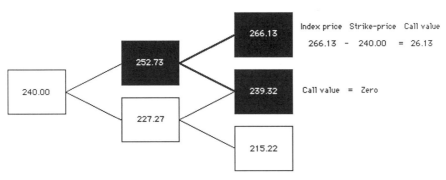

FIGURE 5.5. Call valuation at expiration in the first isolated segment of the two-iteration index price tree

Shares of index	Index price	Amount of borrowing and interest	Call value at expiration
S	$\times$ 266.13 $-$	$(B + 0.87\% B)$ $=$	26.13

Shares of index	Index price	Amount of borrowing and interest	Call value at expiration
S	$\times$ 239.32 $-$	$(B + 0.87\% B)$ $=$	0

Note that the interest rate has been reduced to reflect the one and a half month duration of the isolated segment. The reduced rate of 0.87% is the rate that, if compounded twice, would produce the same effective rate as 1.75% uncompounded.

Once again, there is but a single combination of shares of the index (0.9746 of a share) and borrowing ($231.23) that will work in both formulas. Plugging these numbers into the formula using the mid-point index price of 252.73 reveals that the value of the one and a half month synthetic call—and consequently the value of the corresponding real call as well—is $15.08.

Shares of index	Index price	Amount of borrowing	Value of synthetic call
0.9746	$\times$ 252.73 $-$	$231.23 $=$	15.08

Next we'll isolate another segment of the index price tree and repeat the procedure, as illustrated in Figure 5.6. This time we set up a synthetic call as though the three-month option has only one and a half months

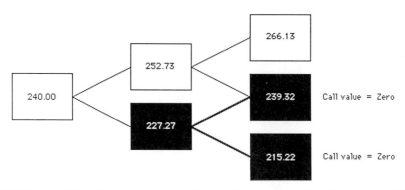

FIGURE 5.6. Call valuation at expiration in the second isolated segment of the two-iteration index price tree

left and the initial index price is 227.27. Just as we did before we'll find a number of shares of the index and an amount of borrowing or lending that will satisfy these two formulas:

Shares of index		Index price		Amount of borrowing and interest		Call value at expiration
S	×	239.32	−	$(B + 0.87\%\,B)$	=	0

Shares of index		Index price		Amount of borrowing and interest		Call value at expiration
S	×	215.22	−	$(B + 0.87\%\,B)$	=	0

This time the single combination of shares of the index and borrowing that will work in both formulas is zero. In other words, the synthetic call consists of taking no position at all in the index or borrowing.

The result is obvious, but let's plug these zeros into the formula using the mid-point index price of 227.27. As you might have expected, the value of the one and a half month synthetic call—and consequently the value of the corresponding real call as well—is zero.

Shares of index		Index price		Amount of borrowing		Value of synthetic call
0	×	227.27	−	0	=	0

Having established the value of the three-month calls at the one-and-a-half months point, both when the index rises to 252.73 and falls to 227.27, we are ready to isolate the final single segment of the index price tree and calculate the value of the calls with three months till expiration.

Once again, we set up a synthetic call as though the three-month option has only one and a half months left (Figure 5.7). But this time we use the mid-point index prices of 252.73 and 227.27 instead of the expiration index prices and we use the mid-point call prices of 15.08 and 0 instead of expiration call prices.

Just as we did before, we'll find a number of shares of the index and an amount of borrowing that will satisfy these two formulas:

Shares of index		Index price		Amount of borrowing and interest		Call value at expiration
S	$\times$	252.73	$-$	$(B + 0.87\%\,B)$	$=$	15.08

Shares of index		Index price		Amount of borrowing and interest		Call value at expiration
S	$\times$	227.27	$-$	$(B + 0.87\%\,B)$	$=$	0

Once again there is but a single combination of shares of the index (0.5919 of a share) and borrowing ($133.35) that will work in both formulas.

Plugging these numbers into the formula using the initial index price of 240.00 reveals that the value of the three-month synthetic call—and consequently the value of the corresponding real call as well—is 8.70.

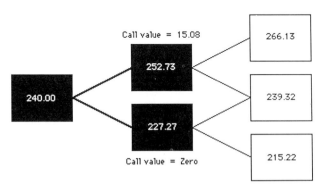

FIGURE 5.7. Call valuation at mid-point in the final isolated segment of the two-iteration index price tree

91

Shares of index		Index price		Amount of borrowing		Value of synthetic call
0.5919	×	240.00	−	$133.35	=	8.70

This iterative procedure—*breaking the index price tree into single segments, applying the primitive options valuation model to each segment, and working back to a final option value*—seems almost ridiculously simple. It may surprise you, then, to know that *this exact procedure is the mechanism of the Cox–Ross–Rubinstein options valuation model,* considered by most professional options traders to be the state of the art.

But we still have a very obvious problem with our procedure. We obtained very different answers—10.91 and 8.70—depending on whether we used one or two iterations. This is because we have yet to take a sufficiently large sample of possible index prices diffused through the index price tree. As a rule, as Figure 5.8 illustrates, the more iterations in the tree, the more accurate the option value; but beyond about 50 iterations the improvement is hardly noticeable. In the case of our 240.00-strike-price, three-month calls the option value stabilizes within one-half penny of 9.37 after 40 iterations. In the case of the otherwise identical puts that we valued earlier at 6.78 using only one iteration the value after 40 iterations stabilizes at 5.24.

The academics call the iterative procedure a *discrete-time* model, because it breaks up time into discrete segments. The famous Black–Scholes model, on the other hand, is a *continuous-time* model; it uses advanced statistical methods to simulate an index price tree with an infinite number of iterations, one that is smooth and continuous over time. For the kind of options we've tried to value so far the iterative model and the Black–Scholes model are substantially identical: both come up with exactly the same 9.37 value for our calls and 5.24 for our puts. If there is any reason to prefer one model over the other at this point, perhaps the elegant mathematics of Black–Scholes gives this model a certain advantage. It avoids the repetitive calculations of the iterative model, so computers can run it very quickly.

But unfortunately for the computers, many exchange-traded index options have one particular quality that makes valuation by the Black–Scholes model completely inadequate: they are American options that can be *exercised at any time during their lifetimes,* not European options that can be exercised only on expiration day, as we've been assuming so far. As we demonstrate in a moment the effects of the right of premature exercise arise only at certain discrete points in the index price tree, and must be properly evaluated one by one as they occur. The seamless,

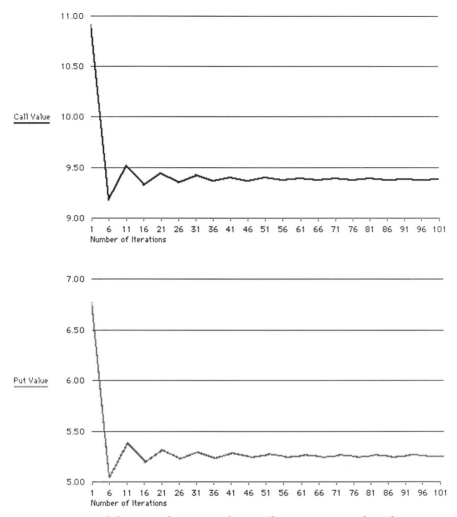

FIGURE 5.8. Stabilization of options values with increasing number of iterations in the index price tree

continuous Black–Scholes model cannot be adapted to this requirement, but our iterative, discrete-time model *can*.

The TANSTAAFL rule suggests that options that convey the right of premature exercise must be worth more than options that don't; because it cannot be adapted to evaluate this crucial feature, the Black–Scholes model systematically undervalues American options, sometimes in ridiculously extreme ways. As an example, consider a 240.00-strike-price, three-month, American put option (with the index price at 227.00, an annual volatility of 15%, and a three-month interest rate of 1.75%). For this deeply in-the-money put, the Black–Scholes model gives a value of 12.24. This would be the right value if the put could *not* be exercised early. But we've already learned enough about options valuation to prove that if the put *can* be exercised early it can't possible be priced lower than 13.00.

Proof: A put that can be exercised at any time can't be worth less than the amount by which the index price is below the option's strike-price, in this case 13.00. If we could buy this put for less than that, we would immediately exercise it and receive $13.00 and any difference would be an instantaneous riskless profit (and a violation of the TANSTAAFL rule). *End of Proof.*

This proof can be used to adapt for American options the rules we learned earlier for our simple immediate-expiration options.

The value of an American call *option cannot be less than the* index price minus the strike-price *(or less than zero).*

The value of an American put *option cannot be less than the* strike-price minus the index price *(or less than zero).*

The difference is that for *immediate*-expiration options, these rules give the *exact price* of the option, while for *premature*-exercise American options, they only set a *minimum*.

Proof: Owners of American options can effectively convert them into immediate-exercise options simply by exercising, so they can never be worth less than immediate-exercise options. On the other hand, American options convey the right to defer exercise if the owner wishes, potentially making them more valuable. For example, an out-of-the-money immediate-exercise option is worthless, but an option that need not be exercised immediately may have value if there is any chance that the index price may fluctuate enough to put the option in the money. *End of Proof.*

All we have to do to adapt our iterative model to the requirements of American options is to apply these simple minimum-value rules. As we work backward through the index price tree, we check the results of each single segment to make sure that these rules are not violated. If we find that they are, we replace the violating result with the minimum value specified in the rules.

Let's use these minimum-value rules to value the 240.00-strike-price, three-month, American puts (with a 227.00 index price, 15% annual volatility, and 1.75% quarterly interest rate) that the Black–Scholes model incorrectly valued at 12.24 We begin by setting up an index price tree and valuing the two single segments that make up the second iteration, as shown graphically in Figure 5.9.

The upper single segment of the second iteration produces a value of 5.65, based on selling short 0.54 share of the index and lending $134.27— no problem, because the minimum-value rules require only that the put value be greater than 0 when the index price is at 239.04.

The result of the lower single segment of the second iteration is 22.96, based on selling short one share of the index and lending $237.97, and this *is* a violation of the minimum value rules. Under the rules it cannot be less than 25.04, the strike-price (240.00) minus the index price (214.96). The violating result of 22.96 would have been perfectly correct if the put could not be exercised prior to expiration. But since it *can* be exercised prematurely, its owner can always guarantee himself the minimum value given in the rules simply by exercising. For this reason, we must replace the violating result of 22.96 with the minimum value of 25.04. Then, having adjusted the intermediate results of the second iteration to reflect the realities of early exercise, we can work back through the first iteration, as illustrated in Figure 5.10, to determine the final put value: 13.63.

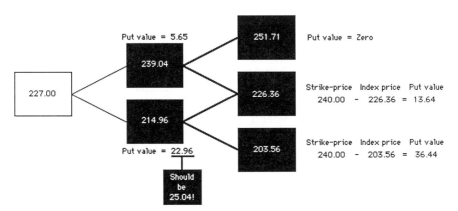

FIGURE 5.9. Checking for minimum-value rule violations in the first two segments of the two-iteration index price tree

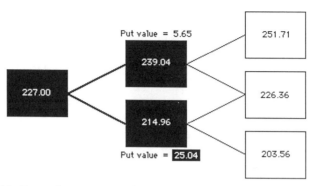

FIGURE 5.10. Put valuation at mid-point, with minimum value correction, in the final isolated segment of the two-iteration index price tree

This correction for premature exercise could never be performed within the continuous-time structure of the Black–Scholes model; there would be no way to examine a single moment in time, even to determine if this correction were necessary. With the iterative model time can be broken up into discrete steps, each one evaluated and corrected on its own. We proved before that the Black–Scholes value of 12.24 couldn't possibly be right for American puts; according to the minimum-value rules, the put could never be valued lower than 13.00, and, in fact, may well be valued higher. Now, using what seemed just a few moments ago to be a primitive model, we've produced a more accurate put value. By a rather amazing coincidence, it happens in this case that adding more iterations to the index price tree will not improve this put value. After 40 iterations, the value stabilizes right where it was with only two iterations—at 13.63.

There is one more simplifying restriction we will have to dispense with before our iterative model is ready to be used in the real world: we'll have to take into account the fact that indexes pay dividends. When an index pays a dividend, its price is marked down on the ex-dividend day by the amount of the dividend. To account for this fact, index prices must be adjusted downward in the iterations of the index price tree in which ex-dividend days fall.

The resulting downward bias to the index price tree tends to lower the value of calls. As ex-dividend days are encountered in the iterative procedure, call values are sometimes even lowered below the minimum values required by the rules. When these situations are encountered, the violating values must be replaced by the minimums given in the rules.

Here again, the fact that the iterative model can be adapted piece by piece gives it an unbeatable advantage over the Black–Scholes model.

Just as the downward bias of the index price tree tends to lower call values, it will raise put values. To fully adjust our model for this effect, we will have to modify our minimum-value rule with respect to puts. We already know that the value of an American put option cannot be less than the strike-price minus the index price (or less than zero). But now, given the payment of dividends, we have to look at an alternative minimum as well.

The value of an American put *option cannot be less than the* maximum present value of the strike-price plus accumulated dividends *at any time during the option's life,* minus the index price.

Proof: Consider again our 240.00-strike-price, three-month, American put (the index price is 227.00 and the quarterly interest rate is 1.75%). We know with certainty that an unusually large $50.00 dividend will be paid on expiration day, in three months. According to our minimum-value rule, this put cannot be priced below 13.00 (the strike-price of 240.00 minus the index price of 227.00).

If we were to buy this put for 13.00, we could simultaneously buy all the stocks that comprise the index for 240.00, for a combined investment of $253.00. If, at expiration, the index (now trading ex-dividend) were priced below 240.00, we would sell our stocks and exercise the put (thus making in cash any difference between the price at which we sold the stocks and 240.00). Given that we collected the dividend of $50.00, we now have $290.00, a 14.6% return on a riskless investment of $253.00 just three months earlier. If the index price were above 240.00 at expiration, we would earn even more by selling the stocks and letting the put expire unexercised: the 14.6% return is just a minimum.

Under the TANSTAAFL rule it is impossible for a riskless three-month investment to yield 14.6% (or more!) when funds can be borrowed at 1.75%. Every alert investor would borrow all the money possible at 1.75% and put it to work to earn 14.6%. Soon the puts would be bid up until the position yielded only 1.75%, at which point there would be no motive for additional borrowing to finance it.

Because the minimum value of the position at expiration is 290.00—the strike-price plus the dividends—this point of equilibrium would be reached when the cost of the combined position of stock and put was exactly 285.01—*the present value of the strike-price plus the dividend.* In this case the riskless profit of $4.99 would represent a reasonable 1.75% return. As long as the index remains priced at 227.00 the put price that satisfies this condition is 58.01, not 13.00 as given in the initial minimum-value rule. *End of Proof.*

At every single segment of the iterative procedure both minimum-value rules will have to be applied. If the option value is lower than the greater of the two alternative minimums, the greater minimum must be substituted in the iterative procedure before working back to the next iteration.

With this final adaptation in place our options valuation procedure is complete. It is not unlike the approach we developed earlier for futures valuation, where we learned that a futures contract's value is not determined by predictions of market trends, earnings forecasts, investor expectations, or other familiar staples of the investment analyst's trade. Rather it is determined by objective evaluation of five factors that can be determined with reasonable certainty, even if they differ somewhat among various investors or may be unstable through the life of the option—the price of the underlying index, its volatility, its dividend yield, the riskless interest rate, and the time remaining till expiration.

As we did earlier with futures, let's review the factors contributing to the valuation procedure one by one. With each factor, we will present a table showing its effect on three-month American and European calls and puts with the index price at 240.00, strike-price at 240.00, annual volatility of 15%, annual dividend yield of 4%, and annual riskless interest rate of 7%.

PRICE OF THE UNDERLYING INDEX. A *call* option entitles its holder to receive in cash any amount by which the underlying index is *above* the option's strike-price. Therefore the higher the price of the underlying index, the *higher* the value of the call option.

A *put* option, on the other hand, entitles its holder to receive in cash any amount by which the underlying index is *below* the option's strike-price. Therefore the *higher* the price of the underlying index, the *lower* the value of the put option.

An option's sensitivity to a marginal change in the price of the underlying index is called its *delta* or *hedge ratio*; for example, the value of a call option with a delta of 0.50 will change by 50% of a marginal change in the index; a delta of 0.25 by 25% of a marginal change, and so on. Put options, of course, always have negative deltas—the value of a put with a delta of −0.35 will change by 35% of a marginal change in the index, but in the opposite direction. It is interesting to note that the delta derives explicitly from the number of shares prescribed for the synthetic option in the valuation procedure.

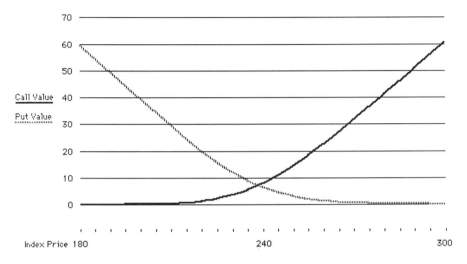

Strike-price: 240.00   Exercise policy: American
Volatility: 15%   Time till expiration: 3 months
Interest: 7%   Yield: 4%

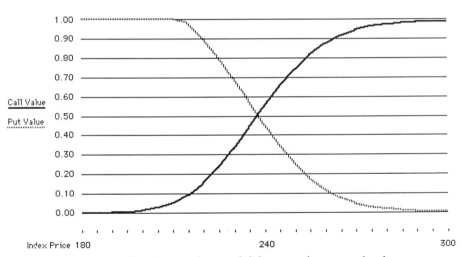

FIGURE 5.11. Call and put values and deltas as a function of index price

As changing the price of the underlying index changes the theoretical values of options, deltas change as well. Out-of-the-money options will have small deltas, limiting to zero; they are relatively unresponsive to small moves in the underlying index. In-the-money options, on the other hand, have large deltas, limiting to 1.00; they are very responsive to small moves. Figure 5.11 plots the values and deltas of a three-month, American, 240.00-strike-price call and put against an extreme range of prices in the underlying index, from 180.00 to 300.00. Note that, for the call, when the underlying index price is *low* and the call delta is near zero, the value rises only gradually; then, as the index price becomes *higher* and the call's delta limits to 1.00, the call value finally begins to track the index point for point. Precisely the reverse is the case for the put value. When the index price is *high* and the put delta limits to zero, the put value responds slowly to declines in the index. But when the index is *lower* and the put delta limits to 1.00 the put value finally begins to track the index point for point.

Strike 240	Time 3 Mo. Interest 7% Dividends 4% Volatility 15%

Amer call 1.24   Index 220
Euro call 1.24
Amer put 20.24
Euro put 19.35

Amer call 2.18   Index 225
Euro call 2.18
Amer put 15.95
Euro put 15.34

Amer call 3.59   Index 230
Euro call 3.58
Amer put 12.19
Euro put 11.79

Amer call 5.50   Index 235
Euro call 5.49
Amer put 9.01
Euro put 8.75

Amer call 7.97   Index 240
Euro call 7.96
Amer put 6.41
Euro put 6.27

Amer call 10.98 Index 245
Euro call 10.96
Amer put 4.42
Euro put 4.33

Strike 240	Time 3 Mo. Interest 7% Dividends 4% Volatility 15%
Amer call 14.46 Index 250	
Euro call 14.44	
Amer put 2.91	
Euro put 2.85	
Amer call 18.37 Index 255	
Euro call 18.35	
Amer put 1.85	
Euro put 1.82	
Amer call 22.63 Index 260	
Euro call 22.60	
Amer put 1.14	
Euro put 1.12	

TIME REMAINING UNTIL EXPIRATION. Because an option is a right and not a liability, common sense would seem to dictate that one would always prefer more time until expiration. Therefore, for most exchange-traded index options, the *longer* the time remaining till expiration, the *higher* the value of both a *call* and a *put* option. This suggests that, all else remaining equal, the theoretical value of an option relentlessly decays as time passes; indeed, options are often thought of as "wasting assets."

The periodic attrition of value as time passes is called an option's *theta* or *time decay*. Figure 5.12 plots the theoretical values of a three-month, American, 240.00-strike-price call and put against time remaining till expiration, from zero to one year. Note that the theta is steepest as the time remaining approaches zero and is almost negligible as time remaining approaches two years.

Another dimension of this same effect is that, as time until expiration increases, the divergence between American and European put values becomes wider. This is clearly evident in the accompanying table of values. As time increases there are more occasions on which a put is "worth more dead than alive"; that is to say, its leverage value is overcome by the value of exercising it and reinvesting the strike-price. Therefore an American put that allows an investor to act on this fact by premature exercise becomes increasingly valuable over a European put

101

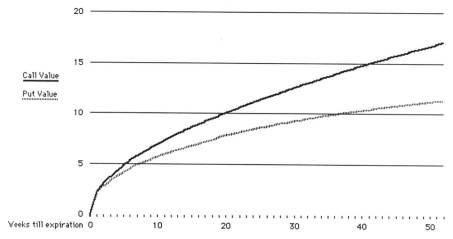

Index price : 240.00
Strike-price : 240.00   Exercise policy : American
Volatility : 15%
Interest : 7%   Yield : 4%

FIGURE 5.12. Call and put values as a function of time remaining until expiration

that does not. The precise reasons for this effect and its implications for strategic uses of index options are discussed in detail in the section on portfolio insurance.

Strike 240	Index 240		Interest 7%	Dividends 4%	Volatility 15%
Amer call 0.76	Time 1 day				
Euro call 0.76					
Amer put 0.74					
Euro put 0.74					
Amer call 2.06	Time 1 wk.				
Euro call 2.05					
Amer put 1.93					
Euro put 1.92					
Amer call 4.40	Time 1 mo.				
Euro call 4.39					
Amer put 3.88					
Euro put 3.83					

102

Strike 240	Index 240		Interest 7%	Dividends 4%	Volatility 15%
Amer call 6.36	Time 2 mo.				
Euro call 6.35					
Amer put 5.33					
Euro put 5.23					
Amer call 7.97	Time 3 mo.				
Euro call 7.96					
Amer put 6.41					
Euro put 6.27					
Amer call 11.64	Time 6 mo.				
Euro call 11.61					
Amer put 8.65					
Euro put 8.29					
Amer call 14.59	Time 9 mo.				
Euro call 14.55					
Amer put 10.21					
Euro put 9.63					
Amer call 17.12	Time 1 yr.				
Euro call 17.06					
Amer put 11.41					
Euro put 10.58					
Amer call 25.06	Time 2 yr.				
Euro call 24.94					
Amer put 14.57					
Euro put 12.69					

THE RISKLESS INTEREST RATE. A *call* option entitles its holder to benefit from appreciation in the underlying index, but without tying up all the cash that would be required to buy the index itself. Because the call holder has the opportunity to invest the difference at the riskless rate during the life of the call, the *higher* the riskless rate, the *higher* the value of the call option.

A *put* option, on the other hand, entitles its holder to benefit from depreciation in the underlying index, but without receiving the proceeds of selling the index itself. Because the put holder foregoes the opportunity to invest the proceeds at the riskless rate during the life of the put, the *higher* the riskless rate, the *lower* the value of the put option.

Note that the divergence between the American and European values for puts widens as the riskless rate increases, but for calls the divergence remains stable. This is because the higher the riskless rate, the greater the advantage of being able to exercise a put prematurely to reinvest the strike-price. For calls, on the other hand, premature exercise only conveys the opportunity to avoid markdowns in the underlying index on ex-dividend days, so the value of this opportunity does not increase with the riskless rate.

Strike 240	Index 240	Time 3 Mo.		Dividends 4%	Volatility 15%
Amer call 6.85		Interest 3%			
Euro call 6.78					
Amer put 7.44					
Euro put 7.43					
Amer call 7.09		Interest 4%			
Euro call 7.06					
Amer put 7.14					
Euro put 7.12					
Amer call 7.36		Interest 5%			
Euro call 7.35					
Amer put 6.88					
Euro put 6.83					
Amer call 7.66		Interest 6%			
Euro call 7.64					
Amer put 6.64					
Euro put 6.54					
Amer call 7.97		Interest 7%			
Euro call 7.96					
Amer put 6.41					
Euro put 6.27					
Amer call 8.26		Interest 8%			
Euro call 8.25					
Amer put 6.20					
Euro put 5.98					
Amer call 8.57		Interest 9%			
Euro call 8.56					
Amer put 6.00					
Euro put 5.72					
Amer call 8.89		Interest 10%			
Euro call 8.87					
Amer put 5.81					
Euro put 5.47					
Amer call 9.21		Interest 11%			
Euro call 9.19					
Amer put 5.63					
Euro put 5.22					

THE DIVIDEND YIELD OF THE UNDERLYING INDEX. The price of an underlying index is marked down on the ex-dividend day by the amount of dividends paid. Because dividend payments effectively lower the price of the underlying index, the *higher* the dividend yield, the *lower* the value of a *call* option and the *higher* the value of a *put* option.

Note that the divergence between American and European put values narrows as the dividend yield increases. The higher the dividend yield, the more the underlying index can be expected to be marked down due to dividend payments, thus creating an incentive not to exercise puts prematurely; therefore the right is of little value. For calls the divergence barely widens as the dividend yield increases. Because we have assumed that dividends will be paid smoothly over time, there are no large ex-dividend day gaps to create an incentive for premature exercise, so for calls as well the right is of little value.

Strike 240	Index 240	Time 3 Mo.	Interest 7%		Volatility 15%
Amer call 8.66			Dividends 2%		
Euro call 8.65					
Amer put 6.02					
Euro put 5.74					
Amer call 8.48			Dividends 2.5%		
Euro call 8.47					
Amer put 6.11					
Euro put 5.87					
Amer call 8.31			Dividends 3%		
Euro call 8.30					
Amer put 6.21					
Euro put 5.99					
Amer call 8.13			Dividends 3.5%		
Euro call 8.12					
Amer put 6.31					
Euro put 6.13					
Amer call 7.97			Dividends 4%		
Euro call 7.96					
Amer put 6.41					
Euro put 6.27					
Amer call 7.78			Dividends 4.5%		
Euro call 7.76					
Amer put 6.52					
Euro put 6.38					
Amer call 7.61			Dividends 5%		
Euro call 7.59					

Strike 240	Index 240	Time 3 Mo.	Interest 7%		Volatility 15%
Amer put 6.63					
Euro put 6.53					
Amer call 7.45				Dividends 5.5%	
Euro call 7.43					
Amer put 6.76					
Euro put 6.68					
Amer call 7.30				Dividends 6%	
Euro call 7.28					
Amer put 6.89					
Euro put 6.84					

VOLATILITY OF THE UNDERLYING INDEX. The most the buyer of an option can lose is the price he pays for it, but in the event of a dramatic move in the underlying index his profits are potentially unlimited. Because large adverse moves hurt him much less than large favorable moves help him, high volatility of the underlying index on balance works to his advantage. Therefore the *higher* the volatility of the underlying index, the *higher* the value of both a *call* and a *put*.

Strike 240	Index 240	Time 3 Mo.	Interest 7%	Dividends 4%	
Amer call 4.23					Volatility 7%
Euro call 4.22					
Amer put 2.69					
Euro put 2.53					
Amer call 5.15					Volatility 9%
Euro call 5.14					
Amer put 3.62					
Euro put 3.45					
Amer call 6.07					Volatility 11%
Euro call 6.06					
Amer put 4.54					
Euro put 4.48					
Amer call 7.01					Volatility 13%
Euro call 7.00					
Amer put 5.47					
Euro put 5.31					

Strike 240	Index 240	Time 3 Mo.	Interest 7%	Dividends 4%
Amer call 7.97				Volatility 15%
Euro call 7.96				
Amer put 6.41				
Euro put 6.27				
Amer call 8.90				Volatility 17%
Euro call 8.88				
Amer put 7.36				
Euro put 7.20				
Amer call 9.84				Volatility 19%
Euro call 9.83				
Amer put 8.30				
Euro put 8.14				
Amer call 10.78				Volatility 21%
Euro call 10.77				
Amer put 9.24				
Euro put 9.09				
Amer call 11.73				Volatility 23%
Euro call 11.71				
Amer put 10.19				
Euro put 10.03				

With futures we proved that if we discovered mispricings in the marketplace we could establish simple offsetting positions in the index itself to earn riskless arbitrage profits in excess of the riskless rate. The ease with which this simple arbitrage can be implemented can be expected to keep futures prices pretty much in line with their theoretical values.

FIGURE 5.13. Volatility: annual percentage standard deviation of monthly returns; S&P 500 Index 1883 to 1984

But with options an apparent mispricing may be due to our own misestimation of the volatility of the underlying index. If we attempt to exploit it by creating offsetting synthetic options, we may only be locking in a loss because the structuring of a synthetic option is a function of our possibly erroneous volatility estimate. This means that we can never be entirely sure whether options are truly *mispriced* by the marketplace or just *misvalued* by us.

This matter is of no small consequence, both because option values are sensitive to volatility changes and because, historically, volatilities have fluctuated over a broad range. Figure 5.13 is a graph of the annual volatility of the S&P 500 Index, calculated at each year-end from monthly prices from 1883 to 1984. The all-time high of 51.4% was achieved in 1932 and the all-time low of 4.7%, in 1963.

There may be as many ways—scientific and unscientific—to estimate future volatility as there are ways to predict the weather. The most popular method is to examine several months of historical prices and measure the volatility that has been experienced recently, and then to assume that the near future will be reasonably similar. This is like predicting it will rain today because it rained yesterday—not perfectly reliable but probably a reasonable guess in the absence of better information. To see how this measurement is accomplished let's consider 10 days of hypothetical index prices:

Day 1	50.00
Day 2	50.31
Day 3	50.31
Day 4	49.75
Day 5	50.12
Day 6	50.62
Day 7	50.25
Day 8	49.75
Day 9	49.63
Day 10	49.88

Because we're trying to measure total returns, not just price changes, we assume that these prices have been adjusted to include any dividends paid out during the 10 days. First, we divide each day's price by the preceding day's price to produce a list of nine *price relatives*—the ratios of each day's price to the preceding day's.

Day 1	$50.31 \div 50.00 = 1.0062$
Day 2	$50.31 \div 50.31 = 1.0000$

Day 3	49.75 ÷ 50.31 = 0.9889
Day 4	50.12 ÷ 49.75 = 1.0074
Day 5	50.62 ÷ 50.12 = 1.0100
Day 6	50.25 ÷ 50.62 = 0.9927
Day 7	49.75 ÷ 50.25 = 0.9900
Day 8	49.63 ÷ 49.75 = 0.9976
Day 9	49.88 ÷ 49.63 = 1.0050

Next, we take the natural logarithm of each price relative.

Day 1	Natural log of 1.0062 = 0.0062
Day 2	Natural log of 1.0000 = 0.0000
Day 3	Natural log of 0.9889 = −0.0112
Day 4	Natural log of 1.0074 = 0.0074
Day 5	Natural log of 1.0100 = 0.0100
Day 6	Natural log of 0.9927 = −0.0073
Day 7	Natural log of 0.9900 = −0.0101
Day 8	Natural log of 0.9976 = −0.0024
Day 9	Natural log of 1.0050 = 0.0050

Next, we square the logs and add up the squares.

Day 1	Square of 0.0062 = 0.00003844
Day 2	Square of 0.0000 = 0.00000000
Day 3	Square of −0.0112 = 0.00001258
Day 4	Square of 0.0074 = 0.00005476
Day 5	Square of 0.0100 = 0.00019853
Day 6	Square of −0.0073 = 0.00005329
Day 7	Square of −0.0101 = 0.00010000
Day 8	Square of −0.0024 = 0.00000573
Day 9	Square of 0.0050 = 0.00002500
	0.00050184

Next, we divide the sum by the number of price relatives (for larger samples, it is customary to divide by the number of relatives minus one).

$$0.00050184 \div 9 = 0.0000558$$

Next, we take the square root of the result.

$$\sqrt{0.0000558} = 0.00746723$$

This is the daily standard deviation of returns of the index. To annualize it, we multiply this number by the square root of 240 (the number of market days in a year).

$$0.00746723 \times \sqrt{240} = 0.115681830$$

The result—the index volatility or annualized standard deviation of daily returns for the 10 days of prices we examined—is 0.115681830 or about 11%. This means that *about two-thirds of the time* the index's price will change by *less* than 11% per year, up or down; *about one-third of the time* it will change by *more* than 11%.

Another way to estimate future volatility is to examine options in the marketplace and determine by a process of inference the volatility that is implicit in their prices—their so-called implied volatility. This is like predicting whether it will rain today by counting how many people are carrying umbrellas to work in the morning. For example, let's assume that the index is priced at 240.00, its annual dividend yield is 4%, and the riskless interest rate is 7%. If the six-month, 240.00-strike-price European call options are priced in the marketplace at 13.26, we can determine by trial and error that the volatility implied by that price is 17.5%. In other words, by plugging a volatility estimate of 17.5% into our options valuation procedure, we would get an option value of 13.26.

One problem with this approach is choosing from among the various slightly different implied volatilities derived from an underlying index's many puts and calls spread out among various strike-prices and expiration months. Only one volatility estimate will prove to be the right one as the future unfolds; therefore a rationale must be developed for deciding which of the many implied volatilities is most accurate. One common technique is to create an average of the implied volatilities weighted by measures deemed to be indicative of potential accuracy; for example, if one believed that liquidity might make options more effective indicators of future volatility, one could weight the implied volatilities by volume or open interest. One interesting approach suggested in academic writings weights the implied volatilities by each option's sensitivity to changes in volatility, on the assumption that the most sensitive options should carry superior information about volatility.

Another problem with implied volatilities is that, in calculating them from options prices, one assumes implicitly that all the other factors contributing to valuation—index price, dividends, interest, and time till expiration—are known with certainty and that volatility is the only unknown. To see how this assumption can occasionally distort the calculation of implied volatilities consider a case in which an excess of bullish sentiment in the marketplace has caused all call options to be upwardly mispriced in relation to put options, almost as though the marketplace were using an "implied index price" higher than the actual index price. Naive calculation in this circumstance will show all the calls with high implied volatilities and all the puts with relatively low implied volatilities. Ideally, we might wish to filter out the bullish sentiment by plugging the higher implied index price into the valuation procedure before calculating the implied volatilities.

Figure 5.14 shows the changing values of implied and historical volatilities of the S&P 100 Index during 1985 and how they might have been used to predict future volatility. The lightest line represents the target "perfect prediction"—the 90-day historical volatility that will occur three months in the future. An intuitive scan of the chart suggests that neither implied nor historical volatility was a particularly efficient predictor.

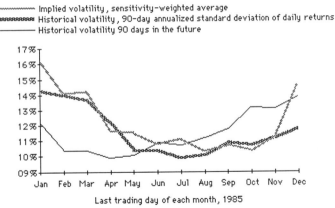

FIGURE 5.14. S&P 100 Index: implied and historical volatilities

ADAPTING THE PROCEDURE FOR INDEX OPTIONS-ON-FUTURES

In most respects options-on-futures are much like cash-settled options, so most of what we've learned about options valuation applies directly. But, because options-on-futures result in the delivery of futures contracts rather than in cash settlement, we must take into account all that we've learned about the valuation of futures as well. The surprising element of the valuation of options-on-futures is that, although it depends on the *valuation* of the underlying futures contracts, it almost completely ignores their *price*.

Let's return to the extremely simple world we developed earlier in which the index (which pays no dividends) is priced at 240.00 and the quarterly interest rate is 1.75%. We can use the futures valuation formula to calculate that three-month futures on the index should be priced at 244.20:

Futures value		Index price		Interest		Dividends
244.20	=	240.00	+	$4.20	–	0

Earlier, we proved that the value of a 240.00-strike-price, European call option in this simple world should be 10.91. At first intuition appears to argue that an otherwise similar option-on-futures would have to be valued higher because the futures contract is priced 4.20 higher than the index. But if exercise prior to expiration is not allowed, the difference between cash-settled options and options-on-futures is one of perception, not substance. In fact, we can make the following rule about this relationship:

The value of a European option-on-futures is identical to the value of an otherwise similar cash-settled option.

Proof: On the basis of our one-iteration model of index price movement, in which the index can only move up or down by exactly 7.5%, one might suppose—erroneously—that the 244.20 futures contract could move up to 262.51 or down to 225.88, as illustrated in Figure 5.15. But, because of the cash-settlement mechanism, futures prices must converge precisely with the underlying index at the moment they expire. A more accurate one-iteration index price tree, as illustrated in Figure 5.16, reflects this convergence—the 244.20 futures contract can move either up to 258.00 or down to 222.00, just as the index itself would.

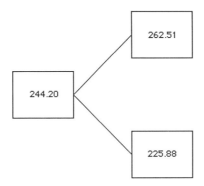

FIGURE 5.15. Erroneous futures price tree

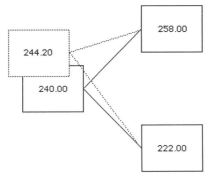

FIGURE 5.16. Correct futures price tree reflecting convergence with index price at expiration

Because the futures contract will always have the same value as the underlying index on expiration day, a European option-on-futures will always have the same expiration value as a European cash-settled option. Since their expiration values must be identical, their current values will be identical as well. *End of Proof.*

To demonstrate, let's work through the valuation procedure for three-month 240.00-strike-price, European call option-on-futures. First, we calculate the exercise values of the call at expiration with the index both up and down, as illustrated in Figure 5.17.

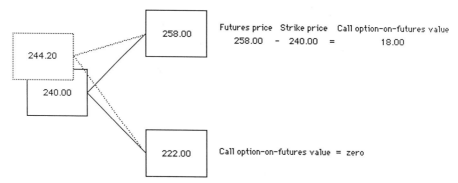

FIGURE 5.17. Call option-on-futures valuation at expiration with futures price up and down

For valuing the cash-settled call we set up a synthetic option consisting of a particular combination of *shares of the index* and borrowing. This time we set up a "synthetic option-on-futures" that consists of a combination of *futures contracts* and borrowing. We must find the combination that satisfies both equations:

Number of futures	Expiration futures P/L	Borrowing and interest	Call value at expiration
S	× (258.00 − 244.00) −	(B + 1.75% B) =	18.00

Number of futures	Expiration futures P/L	Borrowing and interest	Call value at expiration
S	× (222.00 − 244.20) −	(B + 1.75% B) =	0

Note that there is a subtle difference in the way we have constructed the equations this time. Instead of using the *futures price* at expiration, we have used the profit or loss at expiration from trading the futures with a cost basis of 244.20. Recall from our earlier discussion of cash and margin requirements that an investor never actually has to pay cash for the full market value of futures contracts—the only time cash payments are required is for settlement of variation margin on unrealized profits and losses. So the liquidating value of the synthetic option-on-futures consists only of borrowing and either the profit or the loss on the futures position.

The number of futures contracts is the same as the number of index shares required when we used this method to value cash-settled options: 0.50 or half a contract. But the amount of borrowing required is quite different—*lending* $10.91 instead of *borrowing* $109.09.

Number of futures	Expiration futures P/L	Borrowing and interest	Call value at expiration
0.50	$\times$ (258.00 − 244.20) −	($10.91 + $0.19) =	18.00

Number of futures	Expiration futures P/L	Borrowing and interest	Call value at expiration
0.50	$\times$ (222.00 − 244.20) −	($10.9 + $0.19) =	0

The $10.91 lending in the synthetic option-on-futures is the only cash commitment required to establish the position—no cash is required to buy half a contract. Therefore the value of the synthetic option-on-futures, and consequently of the real option-on-futures, is equal to the amount of lending: $10.91, the same value we calculated earlier for cash-settled calls.

As with cash-settled options, to value options-on-futures in the more complex real world, where they can be exercised at any time before expiration, we must use a more complex index price tree. Let's revisit the problem of calculating the value of an American, 240.00-strike-price put when the index is at 227.00. But this time we treat it as a put option-on-futures, so we'll have to add a new factor to the list of the determinants of value—the price of the underlying futures contract. According to the futures valuation formula, when the index price is 227.00 the underlying futures contract has a value of 230.97; we treat this value as the futures price.

Earlier we established the rules that the value of a cash-settled American put cannot be less than the strike-price minus the *index price*. For put options-on-futures a similar rule sets minimums below which values may not fall:

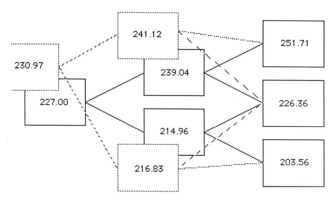

FIGURE 5.18. Two-iteration futures price tree, reflecting convergence with index price at expiration

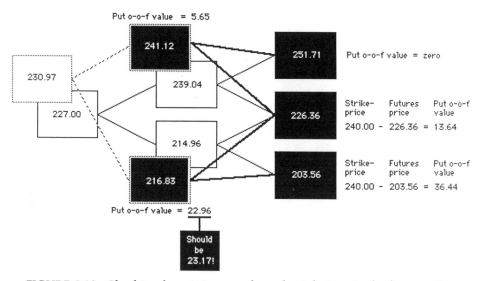

FIGURE 5.19. Checking for minimum-value rule violations in the first two isolated segments of the two-iteration futures price tree

The value of an American put *option-on-futures cannot be less than the* strike-price minus the current futures price *(or less than zero).*

Under this rule our 240.00-strike-price put options-on-futures cannot be

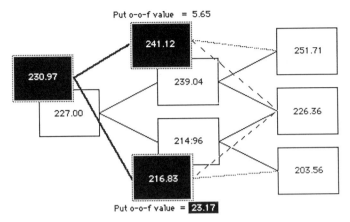

FIGURE 5.20. Put option-on-futures (o-o-f) valuation at midpoint, with minimum value correction, in the final isolated segment of the two-iteration futures price tree

valued lower than 9.03—240.00 minus 230.97.

Proof: If we could buy the put option-on-futures for less than 9.03, we would simultaneously sell the futures at 230.97 and then immediately exercise the put. Exercising effectively sells at 240.00 the futures contract we just bought for 230.97, producing a positive cash flow of 9.03. So any amount below 9.03 paid for the put option would be an instantaneous riskless profit (prohibited under the TANSTAAFL rule). *End of Proof.*

Of course, a simple adaptation of the same rule, and the same proof, applies to *call* options-on-futures, as well:

The value of an American call *option-on-futures cannot be less than the* current futures price minus the strike-price *(or less than zero).*

Having set 9.03 as a minimum value for the put option-on-futures we make no further use of the futures *price* in our calculations. From here on in we are concerned only with futures *values*. The only futures price we know with certainty is the current one; over the life of the put, the futures may be priced at any level the market dictates, regardless of how fairly or unfairly they are priced today. Therefore, as we attempt to apply our new minimum-value rules throughout the index price tree, we use futures values as our best estimates of upcoming futures prices.

To begin our valuation of the 227.00 strike-price put option-on-futures, as before, we create a two-iteration index price tree. But this time, because we are to value a put option-on-futures, not a cash-settled put, we overlay each index price with its corresponding futures value (Figure 5.18). Next, we isolate the first two segments of the index price tree and solve for the mid-year put values (Figure 5.19). As with cash-settled put, we encounter no problem in the first segment—the value of the put option-on-futures is the same as for the cash-settled put, 5.65. But in the second segment we calculate a value of 22.96, just as for the cash-settled put, and this violates our new minimum-value rule. With the index price at 214.96 at that point in the index price tree the futures value would be 218.63. Because 22.96 is less than the strike-price of 240.00 minus the futures value of 218.63—a difference of 23.17—we must substitute the minimum value before moving on to subsequent calculations.

Having corrected the minimum-value violation, we can proceed to calculate the put option-on-futures value in the final segment of the tree (Figure 5.20). The result is 12.85, somewhat lower than our earlier two-iteration value for the cash-settled put of 13.63. The value is lower than that of the cash-settled option, for whenever a minimum-value violation is corrected in a tree, it is replaced with the *strike-price minus the futures value* rather than the *strike-price minus the index price*. Because the futures are valued at a premium to the index, these replacement values will be systematically lower than they would have been for a cash-settled option. For call options the situation is reversed: call options-on-futures will be valued *higher* than cash-settled calls, because the premium in the futures values will cause all the correction values to be *higher* than they would be for cash-settled calls.

As we discussed earlier in our exploration of futures valuation, when the index dividend yield exceeds the riskless interest rate, futures will be valued at a discount to the index. Under such conditions we would expect to see put options-on-futures with higher values than those for cash-settled puts and call options-on-futures with lower values. Because during the life of an option it is possible for futures to be valued sometimes at a premium and other times at a discount, the relative valuation of options-on-futures and cash-settled options can be an unpredictable function of the precise timing of alternating premium and discount conditions.

6. COMPUTER PROGRAMS FOR THE VALUATION OF INDEX OPTIONS AND FUTURES

For readers who would like to experiment with the valuation of index options and futures the computer programs in this chapter are designed to produce values and deltas in accordance with the procedures we have discussed. There are four programs, one each for futures and options-on-futures and two for options (one using the iterative procedure we examined earlier and the other using the Black–Scholes model).

For each program a sample output is given, followed by the program itself. To run the programs on a wide variety of computers, they are written in the generic form of the computer language BASIC. Readers expert in programming will be able to optimize these programs to run more efficiently on a particular computer.

INDEX FUTURES VALUATION PROGRAM

Current date (YYMMDD):	860219
Maturity date (YYMMDD):	860620
Current index price:	142.35
Dividends through maturity:	1.66
Instantaneous interest rate:	.06939
Annualized periodic interest rate:	.07

	Value	Delta
Futures	143.9744	1.02322

```
100 REM ***********************************************
110 REM ***                                        ***
120 REM ***        Futures Valuation Routine        ***
130 REM ***                                        ***
140 REM ***      Written by Patrick Carlyle         ***
150 REM *** Copyright 1986 Luskin Carlyle Corp ***
160 REM ***********************************************
170 PRINT
180 INPUT "Current Date (YYMMDD):           ",A
190 GOSUB 430 : DATE=A : REM <<< Convert to Days <<<
200 INPUT "Maturity Date (YYMMDD):          ",A
210 GOSUB 430 : EXPD=A : REM <<< Convert to Days <<<
220 INPUT "Current Index Price:             ",X
230 INPUT "Dividends Through Maturity:      ",DM
240 INPUT "Instantaneous Interest Rate:     ",R
250 INPUT "Annualized Periodic Interest Rate: ",RP
260 GOSUB 360 : REM <<< Compute Future Value <<<
270 PRINT
280 PRINT "            Value       Delta"
290 PRINT "Futures       "; : PRINT USING " ####.####";FV,FD
300 PRINT
310 END
320 REM ***********************************
330 REM *** Futures Model Subroutine   ***
340 REM ***********************************
350 REM
360 ND=EXPD-DATE
370 AD=DM/ND : RD=1.+R/365.
380 TD=AD+AD*(RD-RD^ND)/(1.-RD)
390 FD=1.+RP*ND/365. : FV=X*FD-TD
400 RETURN
410 END
420 REM *********************************
430 REM *** Date to Days Subroutine ***
440 REM *********************************
450 REM
460 D=A : M=INT(A/100) : Y=INT(M/100)
470 D=D-100*M : M=M-100*Y : Y=Y+1900
480 T=D+(M-1)*31+Y*365
490 IF M>2 THEN T=T-INT(M*.4+2.3) ELSE Y=Y-1
500 A=T+INT(Y/4)-INT(.75*(INT(Y/100)+1))
510 RETURN
520 END
```

INDEX OPTIONS VALUATION PROGRAMS

Black–Scholes Model

Current rate (YYMMDD):		860401
Expiration date (YYMMDD):		860620
Current index price:		230
Index annual percent volatility:		.15
Dividends through expiration:		1.90
Instantaneous interest rate:		.06939

	Value	Delta
Call	7.1836	0.5531
Put	5.6120	−0.4469

INDEX OPTIONS VALUATION PROGRAM

Iterative Procedure

Current date (YYMMDD):	860915
Expiration date (YYMMDD):	861219
Current index price:	351.25
Index annual percent volatility:	.16
Dividends through expiration:	3.00
Instantaneous interest rate:	.075
Option strike price:	345
American/European option (A,E):	A
Number of iterations (1–100):	50

	Value	Delta
Call	16.8935	0.6457
Put	6.9331	−0.3449

121

```
100 REM ***********************************************
110 REM ***                                        ***
120 REM ***     Index Option Valuation Routine      ***
130 REM ***          Black-Scholes Model            ***
140 REM ***                                        ***
150 REM ***       Written by Patrick Carlyle        ***
160 REM *** Copyright 1986 Luskin Carlyle Corp ***
170 REM ***********************************************
180 PRINT
190 INPUT "Current Date (YYMMDD):              ",A
200 GOSUB 690 : DATE=A : REM <<< Convert to Days <<<
210 INPUT "Expiration Date (YYMMDD):           ",A
220 GOSUB 690 : EXPD=A : REM <<< Convert to Days <<<
230 INPUT "Current Index Price:                ",X
240 INPUT "Index Annual Percent Volatility: ",V
250 INPUT "Dividends Through Expiration:        ",DX
260 INPUT "Instantaneous Interest Rate:        ",R
270 INPUT "Option Strike Price:                ",K
280 GOSUB 400 : REM <<< Compute Option Value <<<
290 PRINT
300 PRINT "            Value       Delta"
310 PRINT "Call  "; : PRINT USING " ####.####";CW,CD
320 PRINT "Put   "; : PRINT USING " ####.####";PW,PD
330 PRINT
340 END
350 REM **********************************************
360 REM *** Black-Scholes Subroutine ***
370 REM **********************************************
380 REM
390 REM >>> Set Constants for C.N.D.F. <<<
400 B0=.2316419 : B1=.31938153 : B2=-.356563782 : B3=1.781477937
410 B4=-1.821255978 : B5=1.330274429 : B6=.39894228
420 REM >>> Compute Values for Option Computation <<<
430 T=(EXPD-DATE)/365.
440 X0=X-DX : KEX=K*EXP(-R*T)
450 V0=V*SQR(T) : Q1=(LOG(X0/K)+R*T)/V0 : Q2=V0/2.
460 D1=Q1+Q2 : D2=Q1-Q2
470 REM >>> Compute Call Value and Delta <<<
480 D= D1 : GOSUB 590 : CD= ND : D= D2 : GOSUB 590
490 CW=X0*CD-KEX*ND
500 REM >>> Compute Put Value and Delta <<<
510 D=-D1 : GOSUB 590 : PD=-ND : D=-D2 : GOSUB 590
520 PW=X0*PD+KEX*ND
530 RETURN
540 END
550 REM **********************************************
560 REM *** Cumulative Normal Density Function ***
570 REM **********************************************
580 REM
590 Q=1./(1.+B0*ABS(D))
600 Q=Q*(B1+Q*(B2+Q*(B3+Q*(B4+Q*B5))))
610 ND=B6*EXP(D*D/-2.)*Q
620 IF D>0. THEN ND=1.-ND
630 RETURN
640 END
650 REM **********************************************
660 REM *** Date to Days Subroutine ***
670 REM **********************************************
680 REM
690 D=A : M=INT(A/100) : Y=INT(M/100)
700 D=D-100*M : M=M-100*Y : Y=Y+1900
710 T=D+(M-1)*31+Y*365
720 IF M>2 THEN T=T-INT(M*.4+2.3) ELSE Y=Y-1
730 A=T+INT(Y/4)-INT(.75*(INT(Y/100)+1))
740 RETURN
750 END
```

```
100 REM ***********************************************
110 REM ***                                        ***
120 REM ***    Index Option Valuation Routine       ***
130 REM ***          Iterative Model                ***
140 REM ***                                        ***
150 REM ***     Written by Patrick Carlyle          ***
160 REM *** Copyright 1986 Luskin Carlyle Corp ***
170 REM ***********************************************
180 REM
190 DIM S(100),C(100),P(100)
200 PRINT
210 INPUT "Current Date (YYMMDD):           ",A
220 GOSUB 960 : DATE=A : REM <<< Convert to Days <<<
230 INPUT "Expiration Date (YYMMDD):        ",A
240 GOSUB 960 : EXPD=A : REM <<< Convert to Days <<<
250 INPUT "Current Index Price:             ",X
260 INPUT "Index Annual Percent Volatility: ",V
270 INPUT "Dividends Through Expiration:    ",DX
280 INPUT "Instantaneous Interest Rate:     ",R
290 INPUT "Option Strike Price:             ",K
300 INPUT "American/European Option (A,E):  ",AE$
310 INPUT "Number of Iterations (1-100):    ",N
320 IF AE$="e" THEN AE$="E" : IF AE$<>"E" THEN AE$="A"
330 GOSUB 450 : REM <<< Compute Option Value <<<
340 PRINT
350 PRINT "            Value      Delta"
360 PRINT "Call  "; : PRINT USING " ####.####";CW,CD
370 PRINT "Put   "; : PRINT USING " ####.####";PW,PD
380 PRINT
390 END
400 REM ***********************************
410 REM *** Iterative Model Subroutine   ***
420 REM ***********************************
430 REM
440 REM >>> Initialize Values for Option Model <<<
450 ND=EXPD-DATE : TIME=ND/365. : TN=TIME/N
460 DIVT=1.-DX/X : DIV=1./DIVT^(1./N)
470 VO=V*SQR(TN) : RO=EXP(R*TN)
480 U=1.+VO : D=1.-VO
490 DU=D/U : UR=1./U
500 A=(RO-D)/(U-D) : Q1=A/RO : Q2=(1.-A)/RO
510 REM >>> Set Expiration Values for Stock, Call, and Put <<<
520 S(N)=X*U^N*DIVT
530 FOR I=N TO 0 STEP -1
540    A=S(I)-K
550    C(I)=0. : IF C(I)< A THEN C(I)= A
560    P(I)=0. : IF P(I)<-A THEN P(I)=-A
570    IF I>0 THEN S(I-1)=S(I)*DU
580 NEXT I
590 REM >>> Initialize Values for Present Value of Dividend <<<
600 Y=DX/X/TIME : TO=0. : RKM=1. : PDM=1.
610 REM >>> Begin N Iterations of the Model <<<
620 FOR N=N TO 1 STEP -1
```

```
630    IF DX=0. OR AE$="E" THEN 750
640       REM >>> Adjust for Dividend Payment <<<
650       FOR I=0 TO N
660          S(I)=S(I)*DIV
670          A=S(I)-K
680          IF C(I)<A THEN C(I)=A
690          A=K*RKM-S(I)*PDM
700          IF P(I)<A THEN P(I)=A
710       NEXT I
720       REM >>> Compute New Present Value of Dividend <<<
730       TO=TO+TN : RKM=1.-(1.+R)^TO : PDM=1.-Y*TO
740    REM >>> Do Nth Iteration of Model <<<
750    FOR I=0 TO N-1
760       C(I)=Q1*C(I+1)+Q2*C(I)
770       P(I)=Q1*P(I+1)+Q2*P(I)
780       IF AE$="E" THEN 840
790          S(I)=S(I+1)*UR
800          A=S(I)-K
810          IF C(I)<A THEN C(I)=A
820          A=K*RKM-S(I)*PDM
830          IF P(I)<A THEN P(I)=A
840    NEXT I
850    REM >>> If N=2, Use Values to Compute Deltas <<<
860    IF N<>2 THEN 880
870       A=X*(U-D) : CD=(C(1)-C(0))/A : PD=(P(1)-P(0))/A
880 NEXT N
890 CW=C(0) : PW=P(0)
900 RETURN
910 END
920 REM ********************************
930 REM *** Date to Days Subroutine ***
940 REM ********************************
950 REM
960 D=A : M=INT(A/100) : Y=INT(M/100)
970 D=D-100*M : M=M-100*Y : Y=Y+1900
980 T=D+(M-1)*31+Y*365
990 IF M>2 THEN T=T-INT(M*.4+2.3) ELSE Y=Y-1
1000 A=T+INT(Y/4)-INT(.75*(INT(Y/100)+1))
1010 RETURN
1020 END
```

124

INDEX OPTIONS-ON-FUTURES VALUATION PROGRAM

Current date (YYMMDD):		860219
Expiration date (YYMMDD):		860620
Current index price:		142.35
Current futures price:		144.50
Index annual percent volatility:		.15
Dividends through expiration:		1.66
Instantaneous interest rate:		.06939
Annualized periodic interest rate:		.07
Option strike price:		145
American/European option (A,E):		A
Number of iterations (1–100);		50

	Value	Delta
Call	4,4255	0.4814
Put	5.4276	−0.5151

```
100 REM ********************************************
110 REM ***                                      ***
120 REM ***    Options-on-Futures Valuation Routine ***
130 REM ***        Using an Iterative Model       ***
140 REM ***                                      ***
150 REM ***       Written by Patrick Carlyle       ***
160 REM ***    Copyright 1986 Luskin Carlyle Corp  ***
170 REM ********************************************
180 REM
190 DIM S(100),C(100),P(100)
200 PRINT
210 INPUT "Current Date (YYMMDD):            ",A
220 GOSUB 1000 : DATE=A : REM <<< Convert to Days <<<
230 INPUT "Expiration Date (YYMMDD):         ",A
240 GOSUB 1000 : EXPD=A : REM <<< Convert to Days <<<
250 INPUT "Current Index Price:              ",X
260 INPUT "Current Future Price:             ",F
270 INPUT "Index Annual Percent Volatility:  ",U
280 INPUT "Dividends Through Expiration:     ",DX
290 INPUT "Instantaneous Interest Rate:      ",R
300 INPUT "Annualized Periodic Interest Rate ",RP
310 INPUT "Option Strike Price:              ",K
320 INPUT "American/European Option (A,E):   ",AE$
330 INPUT "Number of Iterations:             ",N
340 IF AE$="e" THEN AE$="E" : IF AE$<>"E" THEN AE$="A"
350 GOSUB 470 : REM <<< Compute Option Values <<<
360 PRINT
370 PRINT "          Value      Delta"
380 PRINT "Call   "; : PRINT USING " ####.####";CW,CD
390 PRINT "Put    "; : PRINT USING " ####.####";PW,PD
400 PRINT
410 END
420 REM ************************************
430 REM ***   Iterative Model Subroutine  ***
440 REM ************************************
450 REM
460 REM >>> Initialize Values for Option Model <<<
470 ND=EXPD-DATE : TIME=ND/365. : TN=TIME/N
480 DIUT=1.-DX/X : DIV=1./DIUT^(1./N)
490 VO=V*SQR(TN) : RO=EXP(R*TN)
500 U=1.+VO : D=1.-VO
510 DU=D/U : UR=1./U
520 A=(RO-D)/(U-D) : Q1=A/RO : Q2=(1.-A)/RO
530 REM >>> Set Expiration Values for Stock, Call, and Put <<<
540 S(N)=X*U^N*DIUT
550 FOR I=N TO 0 STEP -1
560    A=S(I)-K
570    C(I)=0. : IF C(I)< A THEN C(I)= A
580    P(I)=0. : IF P(I)<-A THEN P(I)=-A
590    IF I>0 THEN S(I-1)=S(I)*DU
600 NEXT I
610 REM >>> Initialize Values for Futures Valuation <<<
620 RD=1.+R/365. : AD=DX/ND
```

```
630 FF=1.-AD/X : TO=0.
640 REM >>> Begin N Iterations of the Model <<<
650 FOR N=N TO 1 STEP -1
660     IF DX=0. OR AE$="E" THEN 730
670         REM >>> Adjust for Dividend Payment <<<
680         FOR I=0 TO N
690             S(I)=S(I)*DIV
700             A=S(I)*FF-K
710             IF C(I)<A THEN C(I)=A
720         NEXT I
730     IF AE$="E" THEN 780
740         TO=TO+TN : RF=1.+RP*TO
750         TD=AD+AD*(RD-RD^(TO*365.))/(1.-RD)
760         FF=RF-TD/X
770     REM >>> Do Nth Iteration of the Model <<<
780     FOR I=0 TO N-1
790         C(I)=Q1*C(I+1)+Q2*C(I)
800         P(I)=Q1*P(I+1)+Q2*P(I)
810         IF AE$="E" THEN 860
820             S(I)=S(I+1)*UR
830             A=S(I)*FF-K
840             IF C(I)< A THEN C(I)= A
850             IF P(I)<-A THEN P(I)=-A
860     NEXT I
870     REM >>> If N=2, Use Values to Compute Deltas <<<
880     IF N<>2 THEN 900
890         A=X*(U-D)*(1.+RP*TIME) : CD=(C(1)-C(0))/A : PD=(P(1)-P(0))/A
900 NEXT N
910 REM >>> Check Parity of Current Future Price <<<
920 CW=C(0) : A=F-K : IF CW<A THEN CW=A
930 PW=P(0) : A=K-F : IF PW<A THEN PW=A
940 RETURN
950 END
960 REM ********************************
970 REM *** Date to Days Subroutine ***
980 REM ********************************
990 REM
1000 D=A : M=INT(A/100) : Y=INT(M/100)
1010 D=D-100*M : M=M-100*Y : Y=Y+1900
1020 T=D+(M-1)*31+Y*365
1030 IF M>2 THEN T=T-INT(M*.4+2.3) ELSE Y=Y-1
1040 A=T+INT(Y/4)-INT(.75*(INT(Y/100)+1))
1050 RETURN
1060 END
```

7. THE CONSTRUCTION OF THE UNDERLYING INDEXES

A stock price index is a simple way of answering the perennial question, "How's the stock market doing?" Economists are interested in this question because many believe that the aggregate performance of the stock market—as opposed to the performance of specific issues—is an indicator of the state of the overall economy. Investors are interested because measuring and monitoring the performance of the market as a whole provides a benchmark against which they can rank their own investment performance and anticipate future performance.

To the extent that a stock price index can represent the entire stock market, index options and futures allow an investor to effectively buy and sell the broad stock market in a single transaction—without ever actually trading a single share of stock.

Stock price indexes are constructed by *sampling*; in other words, selecting some manageable number of stocks to act as a proxy for the universe of all stocks. The sample is then *weighted* in some way, assigning different levels of importance to various component stocks. Next, the weighted sample is *averaged*, arithmetically or geometrically, to produce a single summary number. Finally the weighted average of the sample is *indexed*; in other words, it is divided by a constant to relate it to an arbitrary but intuitively meaningful *base value*.

The indexes on which options and futures are traded take a variety of approaches to sampling, weighting, averaging, and indexing. Because no single approach can ever be definitively ideal, each index should be understood as presenting a uniquely distorted portrait of the stock market. The best investors can do is understand the distortions of all the indexes and to use this understanding to select the indexes most appropriate to their particular investment applications.

PRICE-WEIGHTED ARITHMETIC AVERAGE INDEXES

Price-weighting is the simplest of all the ways of calculating stock price indexes. All that is required is to average the prices of the component stocks.

To see how this index construction works, and to understand why it results in effective weighting of the component stocks by price, let's construct a price-weighted index with a sample of just two stocks: ABC, priced at 50.00 per share, and DEF, priced at 100.00. First we add the prices of the two stocks and then divide the sum by 2, the number of stocks in the sample. The result is the arithmetic average of the prices of the two stocks: 75.00.

Price of ABC		Price of DEF		Sum of prices
50.00	+	100.00	=	150.00

Sum of prices		Number of stocks		Average
150.00	÷	2	=	75.00

To make this average into a useful stock price index we may wish to give it a more appropriate scale or base value; for example, we may wish to make the 75.00 average more easily comparable to the S&P 500, which is priced closer to 240.00. To achieve this we divide the sum of the prices by a number other than 2, one that makes the average price come out where we want it. In this case we would set the divisor at 0.625.

Sum of prices		Divisor		Index
150	÷	0.625	=	240.00

As the prices of the two stocks change, the price of the index changes: when ABC rises by 10% from 50.00 to 55.00, the index rises from 240.00 to 248.00.

Price of ABC		Price of DEF		Sum of prices
55.00	+	100.00	=	155.00

Sum of prices		Divisor		Index
155.00	÷	0.625	=	248.00

This chain of calculations can be simplified into a single formula for determining the effect on the index of any given change in a component stock: when ABC rises 10% from 50.00 to 55.00, the index rises 8.00.

Price change in index		Price change in stock		Divisor
8.00	=	5.00	÷	0.625

Now let's examine the effect on the index price if the other stock, DEF, rises 10% from 100.00 to 110.00. Because DEF is twice the price of ABC, a 10% rise in its price is twice as great: 10.00 rather than 5.00. The effect on the index is therefore also twice as great: 16.00 rather than 8.00. This is why this method of constructing an index can be thought of as price-weighted. The higher the price of a stock, the more a given percentage change in its price will affect the price of the index.

Price change in index		Price change in stock		Divisor
16.00	=	10.00	÷	0.625

The Major Market Index is the only price-weighted index on which options and futures are actively traded. Following is a list of the 20 stocks of which it is comprised, ranked by their closing prices on the New York Stock Exchange on Friday, August 1, 1986. After the closing price for each stock is the percentage weighting assigned to it by the price-weighting method. After the individual weighting is a running, cumulative weighting for the index as a whole.

	Stock	Price	Percent Weighting	Cumulative Percent Weighting
1	IBM	131-3/8	10.451	10.451
2	MMM	109-7/8	8.724	19.174
3	MRK	107-7/8	8.565	27.739
4	PG	77-1/4	6.143	33.883
5	DD	75-3/4	6.014	39.897
6	GE	72	5.726	45.623
7	MO	70-3/4	5.607	51.231
8	GM	67-5/8	5.369	56.600
9	JNJ	67-1/2	5.359	61.959
10	IP	63	5.002	66.961
11	XON	60-1/2	4.803	71.765
12	AXP	58-3/4	4.665	76.429
13	EK	56-1/8	4.456	80.885
14	DOW	53-1/8	4.218	85.103
15	S	43-1/8	3.424	88.527
16	KO	38-1/4	3.037	91.564
17	CHV	36-5/8	2.908	94.472
18	MOB	30-3/8	2.412	96.884
19	T	23-5/8	1.876	98.759
20	X	15-3/4	1.241	100.000

Note that by accident of its high price of 109-7/8 MMM (Minnesota Mining and Manufacturing) is the second most heavily weighted stock in the index. Because of its lower price of 23-5/8, T (American Telephone and Telegraph) is the second most lightly weighted; MMM, at 8.724%, has more than four times the weighting of T, at 1.876%. It could be argued that this ranking is inappropriate in light of the fact that T is a vastly larger company than MMM (about twice as large in terms of total market value).

One of the peculiarities of the price-weighted method is the effect of stock splits on the relative weightings of the component stocks. To see this unusual effect in operation let's reset the prices of ABC and DEF to their original values of 50.00 and 100.00 and set the index price back to 240.00. If DEF declares a two-for-one stock split, its nominal price would be reduced from 100.00 to 50.00. But this has no real economic effect, because the share position of each investor is automatically doubled. If no adjustment were made, the apparent 50.00 drop in DEF would cause the index price to fall by $80.00.

Price change in index		Price change in stock		Divisor
80.00	=	50.00	÷	0.625

Obviously the purposes of creating a stock price index would be ill served by allowing the index to fall 80.00 in response to a development that has no economic effect. Thus the divisor will have to be adjusted so that DEF's stock split will have no effect on the index price. It turns out that the number that works is 0.4167.

Price of ABC		New price of DEF		Sum of prices
50.00	+	50.00	=	100.00

Sum of prices		Divisor		Index
100.00	÷	0.4167	=	240.00

With the divisor reduced to 0.4167, any given price change in ABC and DEF will have a very different effect on the index than it would have had before DEF's stock split. Now a 10% rise in ABC from 50.00 to 55.00 will cause the index price to rise by 12.00 rather than by 8.00, as before.

Price change in index		Price change in index		Divisor
12.00	=	5.00	÷	0.4167

Also, because ABC and DEF are now the same price, identical percentage price moves in the two stocks will produce identical price moves, hence identical changes in the index price. Before DEF's stock split, a given percentage move would have had twice the effect on the index as the same percentage move in ABC—16.00 as opposed to 8.00 in the examples we used.

Although the relative weightings of ABC and DEF are changed by DEF's stock split, the combined effect of the two stocks on the index price is not. If both stocks had risen 10% before the split, the index would have risen 24.00 (the sum of 16.00 and 8.00); after the split a 10% rise in both stocks would have the same effect (the sum of 12.00 and 12.00).

CAPITALIZATION-WEIGHTED ARITHMETIC AVERAGE INDEXES

Capitalization-weighted indexes are calculated the same way as price-weighted indexes, but with one additional step: the component stocks are weighted by the number of their shares outstanding. Because of factoring both price and shares outstanding into the weighting process, these indexes represent component stocks in proportion to their total market values.

To see how this works we convert our price-weighted two-stock index to a capitalization-weighted index. Let's assume that ABC, priced at 50.00 per share, has 1000 shares outstanding; DEF, priced at 100.00, has only 100 shares outstanding. We begin by multiplying the stock prices by the numbers of shares outstanding to calculate the total market values of the two companies.

	Price		Shares outstanding		Market value
ABC	50.00	×	1000	=	$50,000.00
DEF	100.00	×	100	=	$10,000.00
			Total market value	=	$60,000.00

If we wanted to, we could use the total market value of $60,000.00 as our index number. But if we want to scale the index to 240.00, we'll have to use a divisor of 250.00.

Sum of weighted prices		Divisor		Index
$60,000.00	÷	250.00	=	240.00

The effect on the index price of a given price change in one of the stocks is calculated just as it would be for a price-weighted index, but the price change is first multiplied by the number of shares outstanding; for example, a 10% rise in ABC from 50.00 to 55.00 would result in a $5000.00 increase in total market value; when this is divided by 250.00, the resulting index price is 260.00

	Price		Shares outstanding		Market value
ABC	55.00	×	1000	=	$55,000.00
DEF	100.00	×	100	=	$10,000.00
			Total market value	=	$65,000.00
			Divisor		÷250.00
			Index	=	260.00

This chain of calculations can be simplified into a single formula for determining the effect on the index of any given change in a component stock; for example, when ABC rises 5.00, the index rises 20.00.

Price change in index		Price change in stock		Shares outstanding		Divisor
20.00	=	5.00	×	1000	÷	250.00

On the other hand, a 10% rise in the price of DEF, from 100.00 to 110.00, would have a smaller effect on the price of the index because DEF has significantly fewer shares outstanding, even though the price change in DEF is twice as great as that in ABC.

Price change in index		Price change in stock		Shares outstanding		Divisor
4.00	=	10.00	×	100	÷	250.00

Capitalization-weighted indexes do not need to be adjusted for stock splits because stock splits do not fundamentally affect the capitalization of a company; for example, if DEF declared a two-for-one split, its price would be halved and its shares outstanding doubled. These changes would be mutually offsetting and would require no adjustment to the divisor to keep the index priced at 240.00.

	Price		Shares outstanding		Market value
ABC	50.00	×	1000	=	$50,000.00
DEF	50.00	×	200	=	$10,000.00
			Total market value	=	$60,000.00
			Divisor		÷ 250.00
			Index	=	240.00

Although stock splits require no adjustment, economically significant changes in the capitalization of a company, such as in the number of shares outstanding, would necessitate a new divisor.

UNWEIGHTED GEOMETRIC AVERAGE INDEXES

There is only one unweighted geometric average stock index on which options and futures are traded: the Value Line Composite Index. To understand its construction we return to our two stocks, ABC (priced at 50.00) and DEF (priced at 100.00). To treat price changes in the component stocks without weighting by stock price or shares outstanding we look only at percentage changes, regardless of a stock's price or market value.

Let's say that both stocks rise by 5.00. First we convert the increase into percentage terms. For ABC, it would take the stock to 55.00, 110% of its earlier price of 50.00. For DEF, it would take the stock to 105.00, 105% of its earlier price of 100.00 (110% and 105% are called *price relatives*).

	Price		Price change		New price	Price relative
ABC	50.00	+	5.00	=	55.00	1.10
DEF	100.00	+	5.00	=	105.00	1.05

Next we'll multiply the two price relatives (105% and 110%) to get 115.5%.

ABC price relative		DEF price relative		Product of price relatives
1.05	×	1.10	=	1.155

Then we'll take the square root of 115.5%, to get 107.4709%, the geometric average of the price relatives. If we'd been working with three price relatives, we'd have taken the cube root; if we'd been working with n price relatives, we'd have taken the nth root.

Square root of product of price relatives		Geometric average of price relatives
$\sqrt{1.1555}$	=	1.074709

Now that we have the geometric average of the price relatives we can adjust our index value by the percentage given in the average. But before we can do this we must invent an arbitrary base value for our index to represent its value when the two stocks are unchanged; we use 240.00, as we have all along. We multiply our base value of 240.00 by the average price relative, 107.4709%, to find the new index value of 257.93.

New index value		Base value		Geometric average of price relatives
257.93	=	240.00	×	1.074709

Tomorrow the procedure would be repeated with new price relatives, based on changes from ABC and DEF's new prices of 55.00 and 105.00. The geometric average of the price relatives would then be multiplied by today's new base value of 257.93 to determine tomorrow's index value, which in turn would become tomorrow's base value.

Stock splits are easy to account for appropriately; the prices for split stocks are adjusted so that the price relatives are based on post-split prices.

Any geometric average index will suffer from an unavoidable side effect of the method itself—namely, a downward bias to the index relative to what would have been achieved with arithmetic averaging. This can be seen in the two-stock example just used. When the price relatives of the two stocks are arithmetically averaged, that is, when the two relatives of 105% and 110% are added together and divided by 2, the result is 107.5%.

ABC price relative		DEF price relative		Arithmetic average of price relatives
$\dfrac{1.05}{}$	+	$\dfrac{1.10}{2}$	=	1.075

Yet, as we've seen, when the price relatives are geometrically averaged, the average is 107.4709%—slightly but perceptibly lower. This will also be true when both stocks decline in price. Let's reset ABC and DEF to their respective original prices of 50.00 and 100.00 and assume that instead of both rising by 5.00 they fall 5.00, in which case their respective price relatives will be 90% and 95%. With arithmetic averaging the average is 92.5%.

ABC price relative		DEF price relative		Arithmetic average of price relatives
$\dfrac{0.90}{}$	+	$\dfrac{0.95}{2}$	=	0.925

To determine the geometric average we first multiply the two price relatives and then take the square root of the result—92.4662%.

ABC price relative		DEF price relative		Product of price relatives
0.90	×	0.95	=	0.8555

Square root of product of price relatives		Geometric average of price relatives
$\sqrt{0.8555}$	=	0.924662

Again, the geometric average is slightly but perceptibly lower than the arithmetic average.

What happens when the price of ABC rises and that of DEF declines by the same percentage amount? Intuitively, we would expect an unweighted index of the two stocks to be unchanged because, in a portfolio consisting of equal dollar amounts in both stocks, the rise in one would perfectly offset the decline in the other. The arithmetic average method bears this out; if the price of ABC rises by 10%, its price relative would be 110%, and if the price of DEF declines by 10% its price relative would be 90%. With arithmetic averaging the average is 100.00%; an average price relative of 100% means no net price change occurred for the two stocks taken together.

ABC price relative		DEF price relative		Arithmetic average of price relatives
$\dfrac{1.10 \quad + \quad 0.90}{2}$			=	1.00

To determine the geometric average we first multiply the two price relatives and then take the square root of the result—99.4987%.

ABC price relative		DEF price relative		Product of price relatives
1.10	×	0.90	=	0.99

THE CONSTRUCTION OF THE UNDERLYING INDEXES

Square root of product of price relatives		Geometric average of price relatives
$\sqrt{0.99}$	=	0.994987

The geometric average of the two price relatives suggests that the net value of the two stocks taken together has fallen to 99.4987% of its base value. But we know this would not be true in an actual portfolio that consisted of equal dollar investments in the two stocks. The actual portfolio would be unchanged, just as the arithmetic average suggests. In fact, investors always experience profits and losses in their portfolios consistent with arithmetic averaging. This is a boon to investment managers whose performance is measured against the Value Line Composite with its built-in downward bias. But on the other hand, it is a nuisance to index fund managers or arbitrageurs who wise to replicate the Value Line precisely—there is no way to construct a portfolio that will duplicate the performance of any geometric average index.

HOW THE INDEXES TREAT DIVIDEND PAYMENTS

All the stock price indexes on which options and futures are traded ignore the payment of dividends, focusing on price fluctuations as the exclusive source of value change: they are *price indexes,* not *total return* indexes. This means that actual portfolios made up of the same stocks would show higher returns than the indexes because the investor owning the portfolios would earn dividends ignored in the calculation of the index.

The failure to include the payment of dividends results in a downward bias to all price indexes, regardless of whether they are based on arithmetic or geometric averages. This is because, as stocks go ex-dividend, their prices are marked down by the amount of the dividend to reflect the partial liquidation of the company that the dividend represents. Investors don't mind the marking down of prices because it is perfectly offset by dividend checks. But for indexes, marking down for dividend payments is treated like any other price decline.

To see this process in action consider an index made up of a single stock—ABC, priced at 50.00 per share. Let's say that this index is calculated very simply; its value is always equal to the price of ABC, so at the outset the index is also priced at 50.00.

If ABC pays a $1.00 dividend, its price will be marked down to 49.00 to reflect the payment. A shareholder in ABC won't mind because his total wealth still equals 50.00: 49.00 in stock plus 1.00 in cash.

But because ABC's price is now 49.00, the index—the price of which is always equal to the price of ABC—will also be 49.00. Although accurately reflecting the nominal price of ABC, the index no longer reflects the total return of actually holding ABC. In fact, as time goes by and ABC pays more $1.00 dividends, the index could eventually fall to zero, even though an ABC shareholder will have experienced no change in total wealth.

Because dividend payments are expressed in indexes as price declines, it is important that investors be aware of dividend payments that will fall during the lifetimes of their index options and futures. The effort of monitoring the effect of dividend payments is complicated by the fact that the magnitude of the effect differs from day to day depending on the amount of the dividends being paid and the relative weighting of the stocks that are paying. Because most companies pay dividends quarterly, the pattern of effect on index prices repeats itself approximately every three months. Figure 7.1 shows the annual pattern of daily dividend payments for three indexes as of May 2, 1986. Note that because of the many overlaps in their composition the S&P 500, S&P 100, and Major Market

140

Hundredths of one percent

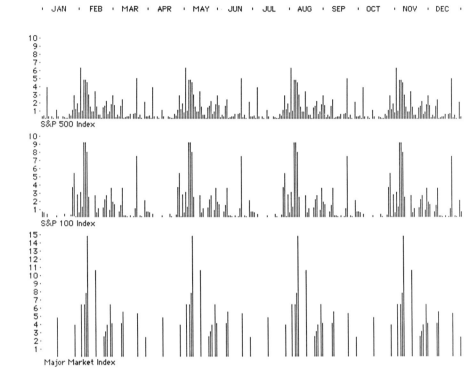

FIGURE 7.1. Daily dividend payouts as of May 2, 1986

Index exhibit a similar pattern—a concentration of payments in February, May, August, and November.

STRATEGIES & TACTICS

index options and futures can be used by institutional and individual investors to achieve an astonishingly broad spectrum of goals, from the most daring speculation to classic riskless arbitrage. This chapter is a detailed exploration of every strategy and tactic along this spectrum.

Throughout this chapter we rely on a number of assumptions and conventions. Unless we specify otherwise, the reader can assume that they are in force for any given example. To avoid repetition later we discuss them all here.

First, we use charts as a means of illustrating the pattern of risks and returns associated with each strategy. Figure 8.1 is an example of the charts we will use, depicting the risks and returns of owning a $120,000.00 portfolio of the stocks that comprise the S&P 500 Index, purchased when the index is at 240.00 and held for three months. The horizontal axis represents a range of possible prices for the index, centered around its current price. The vertical axis represents profit or loss in the strategy, expressed either in dollars or as an annualized rate of return, centered around the break-even level. Taken altogether, such a chart is a snapshot of an investor's *profit or loss as a function of the price of the underlying index, as of the end of the holding period* (usually the expiration of the options or futures employed in the strategy).

Second, a few words about interest rates. When we speak of the *riskless rate* or simply the *interest rate*, we mean the yield of default-free debt securities, such as Treasury bills, with maturities coinciding with the maturities of the options or futures in the examples. The rates that we quote are annualized, simple interest rates for the period being discussed, generally three months. So when we quote an annual rate of 7% for a three-month period, we mean a *simple periodic rate* of 1.75%. In other words, $100.00 invested for three months at 7% would grow to $101.75.

Because the options valuation procedure compounds continuously, it requires instead an *instantaneous interest rate*. Continuously compounded, $100.00 invested for three months at 7% grows to $101.76. The difference in this case is only a penny, but in the strategic examples we explore later this effect can make an important difference. Consequently, we adjust the interest rates used in options valuation slightly downward. In this case we would adjust 7% to 6.94%, the rate at which, continuously compounded, $100.00 grows to $101.75.

Third, when we quote dividend yields or dollar amounts of dividends received, we are making the simplifying assumption that *dividends cannot be reinvested* over the period; for example, $100.00 invested for one year in an index priced at 100.00 with a 4% yield would pay $4.00. In reality, if the dividends were paid out evenly over the year and reinvested at an instantaneous rate of 7%, the $100.00 investment would have paid $4.14.

Fourth, we frequently assume that *options and futures can be traded precisely at their theoretical values;* for example, when we speak of an option traded at 5.79, we are overlooking the fact that, in practice, such a trade could occur only in even increments of ⅛ of a point at 5¾ (5.75) or 5⅞ (5.875).

Fifth, along similar lines, we frequently assume that *fractional options and futures contracts can be traded.* When we speak of buying 147.34 option contracts, we are overlooking the fact that, in practice, we would have to buy either 147 or 148 contracts.

Finally, we assume that the *strategies discussed can be implemented perfectly*, with no brokerage commissions, market impact costs, or execution blunders. From time to time we pause to examine the effects of these and other cost factors and offer tactics for measuring, minimizing, or hedging them.

8. USING INDEX OPTIONS AND FUTURES IN MARKET RISK POSITIONS

First we look at one of the simplest and most direct uses of index options and futures—as alternatives to buying or selling stocks to take outright risk positions in the broad market.

Investors face two kinds of risk: *the risks of individual issues in their portfolios* and *the risk of the stock market as a whole*. The risk of individual issues, called unsystematic or firm-specific risk, derives from uncertainties associated with the prospects of particular companies. It can be diversified away by including a large number of issues in a portfolio. Certain investors prefer to take only firm-specific risk, selecting portfolios on the basis of fundamental research into what they hope are superior individual issues. For these investors, for whom the performance of the broad market is merely a distraction, index options and futures can isolate and remove the market component of portfolio risk. Later we discuss hedging strategies of this type in great detail.

This section concentrates on the second type of risk, that of the stock market as a whole. Called systematic or market risk, it cannot be diversified away because it derives from uncertainties associated with the entire economy, affecting all companies. In this section we examine how index futures can be used by investors who prefer to take only systematic risk, thinking only in terms of the broad market without regard to individual issues. For these investors index options and futures can provide a simple, cost-effective, and potentially highly levered means of tracking the world's most widely recognized market barometers without the necessity of dealing with selection and management of individual stocks.

BUYING INDEX FUTURES AS AN ALTERNATIVE TO BUYING PORTFOLIOS OF STOCKS

Let's consider the case of a bullish investor with $120,000.00 to invest. He is anticipating a 10% up-move in the broad market but has no interest in selecting individual stocks. To establish a background let's assume that the S&P 500 Index is at 240.00, its dividend yield is 4%, and the riskless interest rate is 7%.

One approach the bullish investor might take would be to buy a portfolio of stocks as a surrogate for the broad market. To safeguard against the risk that his portfolio might underperform the market when the anticipated move occurs, he would have to go to the trouble of buying every stock in whichever index he chooses as his benchmark of market performance—in this case, the S&P 500.

Figure 8.1 illustrates the pattern of risks and returns associated with this strategy. Three months later, if the index is unchanged from where the position was initiated, on liquidating the 500 stocks, the investor's only profit is $1200.00 in dividends.

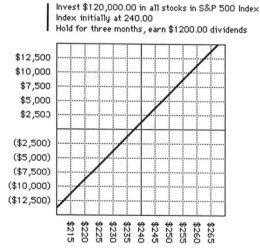

FIGURE 8.1. Buying the S&P 500 Index

	Index Unchanged
Initial cost of stocks	($120,000.00)
Sale of stocks	$120,000.00
Profit from stocks	0
Dividend income	$ 1,200.00
TOTAL PROFIT	$ 1,200.00

If the investor's forecast is correct, the S&P 500 Index will advance 10% from 240.00 to 264.00. in which case, on liquidation of the 500 stocks, the total profit is $13,200.00—$12,000.00 from appreciation in stocks and $1200.00 in dividends.

	Index + 10%
Initial cost of stocks	($120,000.00)
Sale of stocks	$132,000.00
Profit from stocks	$ 12,000.00
Dividend income	$ 1,200.00
TOTAL PROFIT	$ 13,200.00

If the investor's forecast is drastically incorrect and the S&P 500 Index declines by 10% from 240.00 to 216.00, his total loss is $10,800.00—$12,000.00 from loss in stocks, cushioned by $1200.00 received in dividends.

	Index − 10%
Initial cost of stocks	($120,000.00)
Sale of stocks	$108,000.00
Loss from stocks	($ 12,000.00)
Dividend income	$ 1,200.00
TOTAL LOSS	($ 10,800.00)

A 10% decline is large enough to cause a significant loss, but because of the cushion provided by dividend income the portfolio could come

through a small decline unscathed, from 240.00 to 237.60. The 237.60 is
the position's *down-side tolerance point*—the point in Figure 8.1 at which
the risk/reward line passes down through the center of the chart into the
region representing losses. To calculate it we begin by determining the
percentage dividend yield over the holding period:

Holding period dividend yield		Intial cost of stocks		Dividends
1%	=	$120,000.00	÷	$1200.00

The down-side tolerance point—237.60—is the current index price minus
the percentage dividend yield:

Down-side tolerance point		Index price		Holding period dividend yield
237.60	=	240.00	–	1%

As an alternative means of achieving the same investment pattern, the
investor could simply buy one three-month S&P 500 Index futures contract, and instead of using the $120,000.00 to pay for stocks, he could
invest it in three-month Treasury bills yielding 7%. According to the
futures valuation formula, the theoretical value of the futures is 241.80.

If the index is unchanged after three months, the investor's profit is
$1200.00, just as it was when the portfolio of 500 stocks was purchased—
but the profit accrues in a somewhat different way. Instead of earning
dividends, the investor earns interest on the Treasury bills. But the interest income is offset somewhat by losses in the futures contract, representing erosion of its premium.

	Index Unchanged
Initial contract value of futures (241.80 × $500.00)	($120,900.00)
Expiring value of futures (240.00 × $500.00)	$120,000.00
Loss from futures	($ 900.00)
Interest income from T-bills (7% on $120,000.00 for 3 months)	$ 2,100.00
TOTAL PROFIT	$ 1,200.00

If the index rises by 10% from 240.00 to 264.00, the investor's profit
is $13,200.00, again like the portfolio of 500 stocks. But instead of earning

USING INDEX OPTIONS AND FUTURES IN MARKET RISK POSITIONS

the appreciation in his stocks, he earns it in the futures contract; and instead of collecting dividends he collects interest on his Treasury bills.

	Index + 10%
Initial contract value of futures (241.80 × $500.00)	($120,900.00)
Expiring value of futures (264.00 × $500.00)	$132,000.00
Profit from futures	$ 11,100.00
Interest income from T-bills (7% on $120,000.00 for 3 months)	$ 2,100.00
TOTAL PROFIT	$ 13,200.00

If the index declines 10% from 240.00 to 216.00, the loss is $10,800.00—again identical to that of the portfolio of 500 stocks.

	Index − 10%
Initial contract value of futures (241.80 × $500.00)	($120,900.00)
Expiring value of futures (216.00 × $500.00)	$108,000.00
Loss from futures	($ 12,900.00)
Interest income from T-bills (7% on $120,000.00 for 3 months)	$ 2,100.00
TOTAL LOSS	($ 10,800.00)

The overall pattern of the risk and returns of holding the S&P 500 Index futures contract for three months is shown in Figure 8.2. It is identical in every way to that of Figure 8.1, the pattern of holding the portfolio of 500 stocks.

Even the downside tolerance point is the same—237.60. To calculate this point for the futures investment we divide the profit anticipated when the index is unchanged by the number of contracts in the position times the contract multiplier and subtract the result from the initial index price.

Profit per contract		Profit when unchanged		Number of contracts		Contract multiplier
2.40	=	$1200.00	÷	(1	×	$500.00)

151

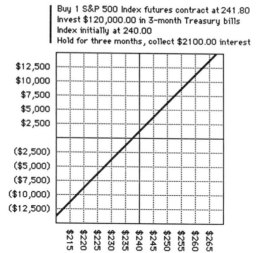

FIGURE 8.2. Buying index futures as an alternative to buying stocks

Down-side tolerance point		Initial index price		Profit per contract
237.60	=	240.00	−	2.40

In the context of actual investment practice, these two alternative methods for achieving the same results have important differences. First, arguing in favor of holding stocks, stockholders have voting rights in each company whose stock comprises the index; these rights are unavailable to holders of futures contracts. Second, arguing in favor of neither alternative, stockholders are subject to the risks and benefits of possible changes in the amount of timing of dividend payouts; since such payouts are implicit in the price of futures contracts, they are effectively locked in when the contract is traded.

Third, arguing in favor of futures, stockholders must contend with the managerial complexities of trading complex portfolios; futures contract holders enjoy the convenience of effectively trading the broad market with a single transaction. Fourth, and also arguing in favor of futures, stockholders must pay commission and market impact costs that are approximately 10 times greater than those paid by futures contract holders. This drastic difference in transaction costs makes index futures contracts an extremely attractive vehicle for investors whose frequent trading in and out of the market would otherwise excessively erode returns.

Finally another crucial practical difference between investing in stocks and investing in futures is pricing. In the example, we've assumed that the futures contract could be traded at the theoretical value calculated by the valuation formula, and under that assumption we've seen that a position in futures can very closely duplicate the risks and returns of owning a portfolio of stocks. But futures contracts are by no means always priced at their formula values. To the extent to which futures are *under*priced, buyers receive an advantage, augmenting the convenience and transaction cost benefits of using futures. On the other hand, *over*-pricings can be so severely disadvantageous that buyers may be better off investing in stocks.

Of all the investors who use index futures contracts as a substitute for stocks to take risk positions in the broad market, those most sensitive to mispricing are index funds. The goal of index funds is to perfectly replicate the performance of a benchmark index. No attention is given to market timing or stock selection; the funds seek not to beat the market, but rather to *be* the market. For an index fund manager holding cash to be committed to the stock market, underpricing in futures contracts may present an extremely attractive alternative to stocks. For just as buying *fairly priced* futures is almost certain to *replicate* the peformance of the index, buying *underpriced* futures is almost certain to *outperform* the index.

Mispricing is a double-edged sword for index funds because their futures positions will have to be rolled forward periodically to replace expiring contracts with longer term ones, but there is no certainty whatsoever that the contracts can be replaced at advantageous, or even fair, prices. But this possibility shouldn't deter a manager from buying underpriced contracts when they are available. Even if long-term contracts are overpriced when it comes time to roll forward, the short-term contracts can be replaced with stocks on expiration day.

Although index futures are an attractive alternative for index funds with money that has yet to be invested in stocks, transaction costs limit the attractiveness of switching out of an already established stock position and into futures. Let's calculate what it would cost to liquidate a stock portfolio equivalent to one futures contract. One contract has an underlying value of $120,000.00.

Underlying contract value		Index price		Contract multiplier
$120,000.00	=	240.00	×	$500.00

At 50.00 per share the contract value of $120,000.00 represents 2400 shares.

Number of shares		Underlying contract value		Price per share
2400	=	$120,000.00	÷	50.00

At $0.05 per share, first to liquidate the stocks and later to repurchase them, the total stock commissions in a stock-to-futures and futures-to-stock round-turn switch would be $240.00.

Total commissions		Number of shares of stock		Round-trip commissions per share
$240.00	=	2400	×	$0.10

Assuming that the stocks could be sold at ⅛ of a point (0.125) per share lower than the last sale quotation, the total market impact cost on the stock side of the switch would be $300.00. There is effectively no market impact cost in buying the stocks back when the futures expire—any impact when they are bought market-on-close will be perfectly offset in a higher cash-settlement value for the expiring futures.

Total market impact		Number of shares of stock		Market impact per share
$300.00	=	2400	×	0.125

Assuming that the futures contract can be bought for 0.05 higher than the last sale quotation, the total market impact cost on the futures side of the switch would be only $25.00. Because the futures are cash-settled against the price of the index at expiration, there would be no market impact cost to liquidate them.

Total market impact		Market impact on futures price		Contract multiplier
$25.00	=	0.05	×	$500.00

Assuming a round-turn futures commission rate of $25.00, the total transaction cost of the stocks-to-futures switch would be $590.00. There-fore an index fund manager holding stocks would only be justified in switching them into futures contracts if the futures were underpriced by more than $590.00 per contract.

Total transaction cost		Commissions			Market impact	
		Stock	Futures		Stock	Futures
$590.00	=	$240.00 +	$25.00	+	$300.00 +	$25.00

To determine the deviation of the futures price from its theoretical value at which the necessary underpricing can be captured we begin by dividing the total transaction cost by the contract multiplier:

Required price deviation		Total transaction cost		Contract multiplier
$1.18	=	$590.00	÷	$500.00

Next we simply subtract the required price deviation from the theoretical value of the futures contract. The result is the futures price below which an index fund manager would be justified in switching out of stocks and into futures contracts.

Futures price that justifies switch		Theoretical value		Required price deviation
240.62	=	241.80	−	1.18

THE LEVERAGE OF BUYING INDEX FUTURES

So far we have constructed a strategy of buying index futures to explicitly mimic every economic detail of a comparable position in a portfolio of stocks. When institutional investors buy portfolios of stocks, they generally commit funds to pay for them in full, so one important element of stock ownership that we've replicated with futures is this initial cash payment. But the contract value of index futures never has to be paid; therefore in examining futures as an alternative to stocks, we've assumed that the money that would have been spent to buy the stocks would be invested in Treasury bills instead. In doing this, we have intentionally ignored one of the most useful properties of index futures: *leverage*.

Let's look again at the investor with $120,000.00 to invest in the market for three months. In the preceding example he bought one three-month S&P 500 Index futures contract at 241.80 and invested $120,000.00 in Treasury bills, replicating the initial negative cash flow that would have resulted from buying a portfolio of stocks. Now let's assume that the investor wishes to take full advantage of the power of leverage. On the basis of the initial margin requirement of $6000.00 per futures contract, the $120,000.00 in Treasury bills would allow the purchase of 20 contracts.

Maximum number of contracts	Value of T-bills		Initial margin requirement per contract
20	= $120,000.00	÷	$6000.00

Figure 8.3 illustrates the pattern of risks and rewards associated with this levered strategy. While superficially the diagonal line appears to be the same line we've seen in the previous figures, closer examination reveals two crucial distinctions. First, the line is shifted down in relation to the zero line, reflecting the *cost* of leverage; and second, the profit and loss figures are both dramatically amplified, reflecting the *power* of leverage.

If the underlying index remains unchanged over the three-month period, the position will show a *loss* of $15,900.00. Earlier, when the investor had bought only a single futures contract, the interest earned on his Treasury bills was sufficient to overcome the loss from premium erosion in the futures, leaving him with a small *profit* of $1200.00. But, now, owning 20 contracts but still earning interest on the same Treasury bills as before, losses in the futures overwhelm the interest income. This should not be taken to imply that the purchase of futures contracts with

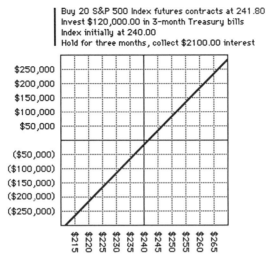

FIGURE 8.3. The leverage of buying index futures

leverage is a losing proposition. On the contrary, this premium erosion is simply the cost of leverage, similar to the interest that is charged by a brokerage house when an investor buys stocks on margin.

	Index Unchanged
Initial contract value of futures (241.80 × $500.00 × 20)	($2,418,000.00)
Expiring value of futures (240.00 × $500.00 × 20)	$2,400,000.00
Loss from futures	($ 18,000.00)
Interest income from T-bills (7% on $120,000.00 for 3 months)	$ 2,100.00
TOTAL LOSS	($ 15,900.00)

Earlier, when the investor bought stocks directly or bought a single futures contract, his down-side tolerance point was 237.60—the point at which he would no longer show a profit. But now, note in Figure 8.3 that the levered position doesn't show a profit unless the index rises from 240.00 to a price high enough that the expiration value of the futures will offset the cost of leverage. This *up-side break-even point* can be precisely calculated by determining the cost of leverage per contract and adding this to the initial index price of 240.00. The result is 241.59, the point in Figure 8.3 at which the risk/return line passes above the center of the chart into the region representing profit;

Cost of leverage per contract		Loss when unchanged		Number of contracts		Contract multiplier
1.59	=	$15,900.00	÷	(20	×	$500.00)

Up-side break-even point		Cost of leverage per contract		Initial index price
241.59	=	1.59	+	240.00

If the cost of leverage is clearly visible when the index is unchanged, the power of leverage is made glaringly obvious when the index rises 10%, from 240.00 to 264.00. Whereas earlier when the investor had owned a single contract his profit was $13,200.00, with 20 contracts his profit is $224,100.00. But even in this scenario leverage is not without cost. Note that although he held 20 times the number of contracts he had held earlier, the investor's profit is only about 17 times greater.

	Index + 10%
Initial contract value of futures (241.80 × $500.00 × 20)	($2,418,000.00)
Expiring value of futures (264.00 × $500.00 × 20)	$2,640,000.00
Profit from futures	$ 222,000.00
Interest income from T-bills (7% on $120,000.00 for 3 months)	$ 2,100.00
TOTAL PROFIT	224,100.00

It is a cliche in investment literature, but nonetheless quite true, that leverage is a double-edged sword. As its power will amplify the investor's return on capital on the up-side, so it will amplify his losses on the downside. If the index declines 10%, from 240.00 to 216.00, the investor loses $255,900.00. When he held a single contract, his loss in the same circumstance was only $10,800.00; by holding 20 contracts, he loses far more than his initial $120,000.00 risk capital.

	Index − 10%
Initial contract value of futures (241.80 × $500.00 × 20)	($2,418,000.00)
Expiring value of futures (216.00 × $500.00 × 20)	$2,160,000.00
Loss from futures	($ 258,000.00)
Interest income from T-bills (7% on $120,000.00 for 3 months)	$ 2,100.00
TOTAL LOSS	($ 255,900.00)

SELLING INDEX FUTURES AS AN ALTERNATIVE TO SHORT-SELLING PORTFOLIOS OF STOCKS

We now return to the idea of using index futures to replicate perfectly a position that an investor might ordinarily execute directly in the stock market. But this time, instead of considering an investor who wishes to buy stocks in anticipation of a rise in the market, we examine the case of an investor who wishes to do just the opposite: to sell stocks short in anticipation of a decline.

It would be convenient if selling stocks short could be thought of as the perfectly symmetrical opposite of buying them, but unfortunately it cannot. A number of structural elements of the securities markets profoundly distort the economics of short-selling in theory and can occasionally make it difficult or impossible to achieve in practice.

First, for one investor to sell stock short, another who already owns the stock has to be willing to lend it to the first investor to sell. From time to time owners of certain stocks, particularly stocks involved in mergers and acquisitions, may be unwilling to lend their shares. At such times a *short squeeze* can occur if the lender suddenly requires the borrower to immediately return the borrowed stock, forcing him to buy it in the open market at prices that may be far from favorable.

Second, assuming stock to borrow can be found, the short-seller must post collateral with the lender to guarantee the loan (apart from the margin he must post with his broker), tying up some or all of the proceeds of the short-sale. This creates a fundamental economic asymmetry between buying and short selling: buying stocks ties up funds that could otherwise be invested to earn interest, and although the proceeds from selling stocks one already owns can be fully reinvested to earn interest *only a portion of the proceeds from short-selling stocks can be reinvested*.

Third is the New York Stock Exchange's *plus-tick rule*, which permits short-sales to be executed only at prices representing a plus-tick from the previous, different price. Instituted after the Great Crash to limit the power of short-sellers to drive prices down, the rule makes the execution of short-sales in a falling market difficult or impossible.

Stock index futures effectively eliminate all three of these barriers to short-selling. Futures do not have to be borrowed in order to be sold short—short-sellers have merely to find a willing buyer. There is no asymmetrical limitation on the ability to reinvest the proceeds of a short-sale—potential reinvestment income is anticipated perfectly in the theoretical value formula and is therefore implicit in any contract sold at a

160

fair price. And there is no plus-tick rule governing the trading of index futures.

Let's adjust our earlier examples to see them from the perspective of an investor wishing to short-sell a $120,000.00 portfolio of S&P 500 stocks for a three-month period, starting with the index at 240.00. For convenience we make the simplifying assumption that he can reinvest all the proceeds from his short-sale, although realistically this is only true for a small number of investors.

Figure 8.4 illustrates the pattern of risks and returns associated with this position. If the index is unchanged after three months, the short-seller has a profit of $900.00 due to income from the reinvestment in Treasury bills of the proceeds of the short-sale, even after making restitution for dividends to the lender of the stocks. If the index rises by 10% from 240.00 to 264.00, the investor experiences a loss of $11,100.00; if the index declines by 10% from 240.00 to 216.00, the short-seller's profit is $12,900.00.

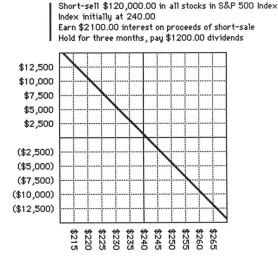

FIGURE 8.4. Short-selling the S&P 500 Index

	Index Unchanged	Index + 10%	Index − 10%
Short-sale of stocks	$120,000.00	$120,000.00	$120,000.00
Repurchase of stocks	$120,000.00	$132,000.00	$108,000.00
Profit (loss) from stocks	0	($ 12,000.00)	$ 12,000.00
Interest income on T-bills (7% on $120,000.00 for 3 months)	$ 2,100.00	$ 2,100.00	$ 2,100.00
Restitution of dividends	($ 1,200.00)	($ 1,200.00)	($ 1,200.00)
TOTAL PROFIT (LOSS)	$ 900.00	($ 11,100.00)	$ 12,900.00

Just as the long stock position had a *down-side* tolerance point, this short stock position has an *up-side* tolerance point. To calculate it we begin by determining the net percentage interest income from the Treasury bills over the holding period, offset by the restitution of dividends:

Holding period net interest yield		Value of Treasury bills		Interest income		Dividends
0.75%	=	$120,000.00	÷	($2100.00	−	$1200.00)

The up-side tolerance point—241.80—is the current index price plus the net percentage interest income:

Up-side tolerance point		Index price		Holding period net interest yield
241.80	=	240.00	+	0.75%

Short-selling one S&P 500 Index futures contract produces exactly the same pattern of risks and returns, as illustrated in Figure 8.5. If the index is unchanged after three months, the investor's profit is $900.00, just as it was in the stock position, but instead of earning interest on Treasury bills he profits from premium erosion in his short futures contract and is not required to make restitution for dividend payments. If the index rises by 10% from 240.00 to 264.00, the investor's total loss is $11,100.00; if the index declines by 10% from 240.00 to 216.00, the investor's total

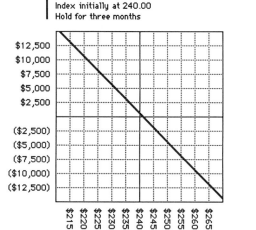

FIGURE 8.5. Selling index futures as an alternative to short-selling stock

profit is $12,900.00, both just as they were in the same circumstances in the stock position.

	Index Unchanged	Index + 10%	Index − 10%
Initial value of short futures	$120,900.00	$120,900.00	$120,900.00
Expiration value of futures	($120,000.00)	($132,000.00)	($108,000.00)
Profit (loss) from futures	$ 900.00	($ 11,100.00)	$ 12,900.00
TOTAL PROFIT (LOSS)	$ 900.00	($ 11,100.00)	$ 12,900.00

The up-side tolerance point of the short futures position is the same as that of the short stock position—241.80. It is no coincidence that it is identical to the initial price of the futures contract as well. The futures were sold at a *premium* to the initial index price of 240.00, so the position

163

will not show a loss at expiration unless the index price rises enough to overcome it.

It is interesting to note that not all short stock or short futures positions will necessarily be structured this way. If restitution of the index's dividend payments through expiration is greater than the interest income from the reinvestment of the proceeds of the short-sale, the investor will show a loss when the index is unchanged. For example, let's double the dividend payments in the previous example, from $1200.00 to $2400.00. Now, with the index unchanged at expiration the short stock position shows a loss of $300.00, rather than the profit of $900.00 realized before. Performance with the index up and down 10% is similarly degraded. This pattern of risks and returns is illustrated in Figure 8.6.

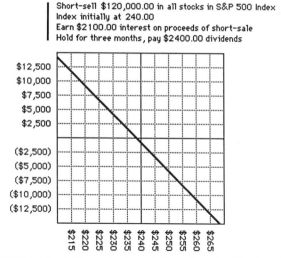

FIGURE 8.6. Selling the S&P 500 Index; double dividends

	Index Unchanged	Index + 10%	Index − 10%
Short-sale of stocks	$120,000.00	$120,000.00	$120,000.00
Repurchase of stocks	($120,000.00)	($132,000.00)	($108,000.00)
Profit (loss) from stocks	0	($ 12,000.00)	$ 12,000.00
Interest income on T-bills (7% on $120,000.00 for 3 months)	$ 2,100.00	$ 2,100.00	$ 2,100.00
Restitution of dividends	($ 2,400.00)	($ 2,400.00)	($ 2,400.00)
TOTAL PROFIT (LOSS)	($ 300.00)	($ 12,300.00)	$ 11,700.00

With this higher dividend assumption, the theoretical value of the futures contract is no longer 241.80, a premium to the index price of 240.00. Now it is 239.40, a discount to the index price, but as before selling one contract replicates the short stock position perfectly (Figure 8.7).

	Index Unchanged	Index + 10%	Index − 10%
Initial value of short futures	$119,700.00	$119,700.00	$119,700.00
Expiration value of futures	($120,000.00)	($132,000.00)	($108,000.00)
Profit (loss) from futures	($ 300.00)	($ 12,300.00)	$ 11,700.00
TOTAL PROFIT (LOSS)	($ 300.00)	($ 12,300.00)	$ 11,700.00

Neither version of the position now has an up-side tolerance point—both now share a *down-side break-even point* of $239.40, again identical to the futures price. It is no longer a question of how high the index can rise before the position fails to show a profit. Now the question is how low the index must fall before the position fails to show a loss:

165

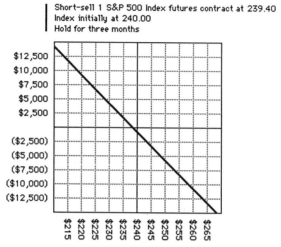

FIGURE 8.7. Selling index futures as an alternative to short-selling stock; double dividends

Holding period interest yield		Value of Treasury bills		Interest income		Dividends
(−0.025%)	=	$120,000.00	÷	($2100.00	−	$2400.00)

Down-side break-even point		Index price		Holding period interest yield
239.40	=	240.00	+	(−0.025%)

LEVERAGE IN SELLING INDEX FUTURES

When we looked at the leverage of buying index futures compared with investing directly in stocks, we saw that leverage works essentially as a process of *financing*. It allows investor to control larger amounts of stock than he could afford to do if he had to pay cash. But leverage has an entirely different meaning in the context of short-selling, because short-selling doesn't require paying cash to begin with. Here leverage is not a process of financing but of *margining*—the posting of a performance bond to guarantee an investor's ability to bear risk.

When institutional investors are permitted to sell short at all, they are generally required to deposit 100% of the value of the short-sale as margin. The cash proceeds from the short-sale are not counted in satisfaction of this requirement; for example, in the earlier example of the investor who sold short a $120,000.00 portfolio of stock, we made the unstated assumption that the investor was able to post $120,000.00 in Treasury bills in a futures account as margin (beyond the $120,000.00 investment in Treasury bills made with the proceeds of the short-sale). Although this requirement is not without practical importance to an investor wishing to short-sell stocks, it is of no economic importance to the pattern of risks and returns in the example. Even if we assume that the investor had found it necessary to borrow the $120,000.00 margin requirement, he could earn interest on it by holding it in the form of Treasury bills, thus offsetting his borrowing costs with interest income.

If the investor in our example were willing and able to allocate $120,000.00 to meet margin requirements, the leverage of index futures would allow him to take a much larger effective risk position than he could take by short-selling stocks. A margin of $120,000.00 allows an investor to sell short a $120,000.00 portfolio of stocks, but we have seen earlier that the same position can be achieved by selling a single S&P 500 Index futures contract at 241.80. An investor who wants to take full advantage of the power of leverage in index futures could sell as many as 20 contracts.

Figure 8.8 illustrates the pattern of risks and returns associated with selling short 20 contracts. If the index were unchanged over the three-month holding period, the investor's profit would be $18,000.00, due entirely to premium erosion in the futures. In the earlier example in which he sold short a single contract his profit was only $900.00. Because the position is now 20 times larger, so is the profit. This reflects the fact that in this context there is no cost of leverage in the sense of a financing charge as there was earlier when the investor *bought* 20 contracts. Here

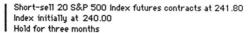

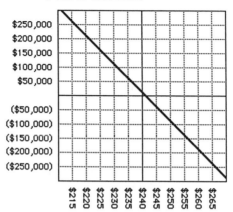

FIGURE 8.8. Leverage in selling index futures

leverage doesn't *finance* the larger position—it simply *margins* it.

If the index declines 10% from 240.00 to 216.00, the investor's profit is $258,000.00, 20 times the profit of $12,900.00 earned earlier with a single contract. Because the position is now simply larger, not fundamentally different, the upside tolerance point remains 241.80. But if the index rises by 10%, from 240.00 to 264.00, the investor's loss is $222,000.00, 20 times the loss of $11,100.00 earned earlier with a single contract and far more than his $120,000.00 risk capital.

	Index Unchanged	Index + 10%	Index − 10%
Initial value of futures	$2,418,000.00	$2,418,000.00	$2,418,000.00
Expiring value of futures	($2,400.000.00)	($2,640,000.00)	($2,160,000.00)
Profit (loss) from futures	$ 18,000.00	($ 222,000.00)	$ 258,000.00
TOTAL PROFIT (LOSS)	$ 18,000.00	($ 222,000.00)	$ 258,000.00

BUYING INDEX CALL OPTIONS AS AN ALTERNATIVE TO BUYING PORTFOLIOS OF STOCKS

So far we have concentrated on index futures—first, on how they can be used to replicate positions that investors might ordinarily take with portfolios of stocks, and second, on how their tremendous leverage can be used to create positions with much greater potential for risk and return than an investor could afford to achieve with stocks. The use of futures contributes convenience, lower transaction costs, the potential for favorable mispricing, and leverage, but it does nothing fundamentally to alter the basic pattern of risks and returns. By using index *options* or *options-on-futures*, on the other hand, investors can create entirely different patterns that may more closely match their true risk/return preferences, while continuing to enjoy most of the benefits of futures.

Let's return to our example: an investor with $120,000.00 to invest for three months in the stock market with the S&P 500 Index at 240.00. A direct investment in the 500 stocks that make up the index, or alternatively an investment in Treasury bills and an S&P 500 Index futures contract, led to an essentially symmetrical risk and return pattern—profit or loss dollar for dollar with the S&P 500 Index, plus income from dividends. Now let's consider the pattern of risk and return with a purchase of three-month S&P 500 Index call options with a strike-price of 240.00. We've selected at-the-money calls so that at expiration any appreciation in the underlying index will be completely reflected in the exercise value of the calls.

To scale a position in calls to the investor's risk capital of $120,000.00 we begin by calculating the underlying value of one contract—the index price times the contract multiplier.

Call's underlying value		Index price		Contract multiplier
$24,000.00	=	240.00	×	$100.00

To determine the number of calls to buy we divide the risk capital of $120,000.00 by the underlying value of $24,000.00:

Contracts required		Risk capital		Call's underlying value
5	=	$120,000.00	÷	$24,000.00

By using the options valuation procedure and assuming an index volatility of 15%, the theoretical value for a three-month, European, 240.00-strike-price call is 7.96. Assuming that the options could be purchased at theoretical value, the investor would have to spend $3980.00 to buy five contracts:

Investment required to buy		Call price		Number of contracts		Contract multiplier
$3980.00	=	7.96	×	5	×	$100.00

The balance of the $120,000.00 risk capital that could be invested in Treasury bills would be $116,020.00:

Remaining capital in T-bills		Total risk capital		Investment required to buy calls
$116,020.00	=	$120,000.00	–	$3980.00

From a strategic point of view options-on-futures can be used interchangeably with options in this strategy and all the strategies we discuss later. For convenience, and to avoid repetition, the examples are generally drawn in terms of options. We leave it to the reader to make the simple adjustments required for options-on-futures.

The only translation consistently required is the number of contracts in a given position. Because the contract multiplier for options-on-futures is $500.00, five times greater than the contract multiplier for options, an investor need use only one-fifth as many options-on-futures contracts; for example, to create a position with an aggregate underlying value of $120,000.00 we would need only one options-on-futures contract:

Call option-on-future's aggregate underlying value		Strike-price		Contract multiplier
$120,000.00	=	240.00	×	$500.00

The investment required to buy one options-on-futures contract would be the same as the investment required to buy five cash-settled options at the same price:

Investment required to buy		Option-on-futures price		Number of contracts		Contract multiplier
$3980.00	=	7.96	×	1	×	$500.00

Figure 8.9 illustrates the pattern of risks and returns associated with

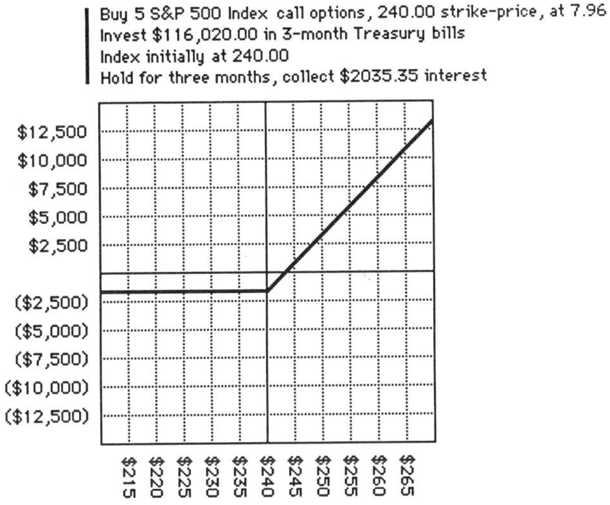

Buy 5 S&P 500 Index call options, 240.00 strike-price, at 7.96
Invest $116,020.00 in 3-month Treasury bills
Index initially at 240.00
Hold for three months, collect $2035.35 interest

FIGURE 8.9. Buying index call options as an alternative to buying stocks

buying call options as an alternative to a portfolio of stocks. It is unlike any pattern we have looked at so far. In the right half of the chart, the region representing index prices higher than the call's strike-price, the risk/return line moves up diagonally point-for-point with changes in the underlying index price. But in the left half of the chart, which represents index prices below the option's strike-price, the risk/return line flattens out and is unchanged in value, regardless of changes in the index price.

Let's examine the processes that shape this unique pattern. After three months, if the underlying index is unchanged at 240.00, the $3980.00 investment in options will expire worthless but interest income from Treasury bills trims the investor's loss to only $1949.65.

	Index Unchanged
Initial cost of calls (7.96 × 5 × $100.00)	($3,980.00)
Exercise value of calls (expire worthless)	0
Loss from calls	($3,980.00)
Interest income on T-bills (7% on $116,020.00 for 3 months)	$2,030.35
TOTAL LOSS	($1,949.65)

Earlier, when we examined the outcomes of investing directly in stocks and again when we replicated these outcomes with futures, we saw that the investor's return with the index unchanged after three months was a profit of $1200.00. But when the investor uses options to take a position in the market, his position will not be profitable unless the underlying index is high enough to give the calls sufficient exercise value to repay their initial cost. To calculate this up-side break-even point we use a procedure similar to the one we developed earlier for examining levered futures positions. We begin by determining the net cost per option in the position. In this case we simply offset the investment required for the five contracts by the interest income earned and divide the result by 5:

Cost per contract		Investment to buy calls		T-bill income	Number of contracts		Contract multiplier
3.90	=	$3980.00	−	$2030.35 ÷	(5	×	$100.00)

Next, we simply add the net cost per contract to the call's strike price:

Up-side break-even point		Net cost per contract		Call's strike-price
243.90	=	3.90	+	240.00

The upside break-even point for the position is 243.90. At this point in Figure 8.9 the risk/reward line crosses above the centerline of the chart and passes into the region representing profit. At this point each call would have an exercise value of $390.00; the aggregate exercise value of the position would be $1950.00, just about the amount required to repay the cost to establish the position, less the offsetting Treasury bill income:

Exercise value of call		Index price		Option's strike-price		Contract multiplier
$390.00	=	(243.90	−	240.00)	×	$100.00

Aggregate exercise value of position		Exercise value of call		Number of calls in position
$1950.00	=	$390.00	×	5

If the stock rallies beyond the up-side break-even point, the position will show a healthy profit; for example, if the index rallies by 10%, from 240.00 to 264.00, each of his options will have an exercise value of $2400.00 for an aggregate exercise value of $12,000.00:

Exercise value of call		Index price	Call's strike-price		Contract multiplier
$2400.00	=	(264.00	−	240.00) ×	$100.00

Aggregate exercise value of position		Exercise value of call		Number of calls in position
$12,000.00	=	$2400.00	×	5

Including the interest income from Treasury bills, the investor's total profit with the index up 10% is $10,050.35, somewhat less than the $13,200.00 profit he saw earlier when he invested directly in stocks.

	Index + 10%
Initial cost of calls ($7.96 × 5 × $100.00)	($ 3,980.00)
Exercise value of calls ($24.00 × 5 × $100.00)	$12,000.00
Profit from calls	$ 8,050.00
Interest income on T-bills (7% on $116,020.00 for 3 months)	$ 2,030.35
TOTAL PROFIT	$10,050.35

When the investor established his position directly in stocks, or replicated it with futures, he earned a profit of $1200.00 even when the index was unchanged; with options he cannot even break even until the index rises to 243.90. With stocks or futures his profit with the index up 10% was $13,200.00; with options, only $10,050.35. But the advantage gained in return for these handicaps is that the buyer of a call option is assured that *his investment cannot do any worse than a known maximum loss* equal to the cost of the options, minus any interest earned on the leftover cash invested in Treasury bills:

Maximum loss in position		Cost of calls		Interest on T-bills
$1949.65	=	$3980.00	−	$2030.35

Although this example has been set up to replicate a position in stocks as closely as possible, when an investor chooses to buy index call options or options-on-futures he is inevitably making a profoundly different kind of investment. He is engaging in a subtle trade-off—in exchange for the assurance of a known maximum loss he sacrifices performance. If the options are fairly priced according to our valuation procedure, then presumably the trade-off is economically equitable; therefore an investor faces not so much an opportunistic choice driven by relative values but rather a managerial choice driven by his attitude toward the pattern of risks and returns.

THE LEVERAGE OF BUYING INDEX CALL OPTIONS

We have examined how index options or options-on-futures can be used as special alternatives to a direct investment in the stock market. Now we'll consider how they can be used for leverage. Let's see what would happen if the investor with $120,000.00 risk capital were to devote it entirely to purchasing three-month 240.00 strike-price S&P 500 Index call options. With a price of 7.96 the investor could afford to buy 150.75 contracts:

Number of contracts		Risk capital		Cost per contract		Contract multiplier
150.75	=	$120,000.00	÷	7.96	×	$100.00

If the investor preferred to work with options-on-futures at the same price, he would buy 30.15 contracts:

Number of contracts		Risk capital		Cost per contract		Contract multiplier
30.15	=	$120,000.00	÷	7.96	×	$500.00

Figure 8.10 illustrates the pattern of risks and returns associated with this position. In shape it is identical to the preceding pattern. The maximum loss is realized at and below the strike-price; above the strike-price the risk/return line rises diagonally. The difference is that in this chart the dollar amounts of profit and loss have been tremendously increased, thus reflecting the power of leverage, and the up-side break-even point has been moved to the right to reflect the cost of leverage.

If the index declines or is unchanged over the three-month holding period, the calls will expire worthless and the investor will lose his entire $120,000.00 investment. Previously, with a purchase of only five contracts, his loss with the index unchanged or down 10% was only $1970.00. This reflected not only the smaller initial cost of the position but the interest income from his Treasury bills he can no longer afford to buy. If the index rises 10% from 240.00 to 264.00, the investor's profit will be $241,800.00. Recall that in the levered futures position the profit was $224,100.00

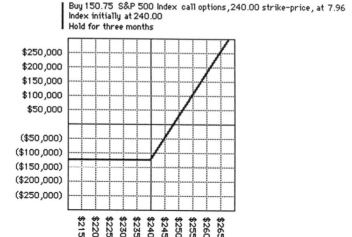

FIGURE 8.10. Leverage in buying index call options

	Index Unchanged	Index + 10%	Index − 10%
Initial cost of calls	($120,000.00)	($120,000.00)	($120,000.00)
Exercise value of calls	0	$361,800.00	0
Profit (loss) from calls	($120,000.00)	$244,536.00	($120,000.00)
TOTAL PROFIT (LOSS)	($120,000.00)	$244,536.00	($120,000.00)

The cost of leverage with options is much higher than it was earlier when the investor used index futures. With a levered position in futures he lost only $15,900.00 with the index unchanged. But for its higher price, leverage with options offers much more than the mere financing afforded by futures. With options the investor has the benefit of an assured maximum loss—no matter how much the index declines, the loss can never be greater than the price paid for the options. Recall that in the levered futures position his loss was $255,900.00 when the index declined by 10%.

Using the procedure we developed earlier, we can calculate the up-side break-even point for the levered options position to be 247.96:

176

Up-side break-even point		Net cost per contract		Call's strike-price
247.96	=	7.96	+	240.00

In the levered futures position the up-side break-even point was somewhat lower at 241.59. But with futures the investor was exposed to unlimited loss on the down-side. With options the investor is assured of a maximum loss of $120,000.00, with the possibility of up-side rewards that could potentially be greater than those of the futures position.

Figure 8.11 overlays the patterns of levered positions in options and futures, respectively. It is an instructive lesson in the subtle risk/reward trade-offs an investor must make when contemplating investments in options. Note that the broken line (representing the risks and rewards of the levered futures position) dominates the solid line (representing the risks and rewards of the levered options position) in the central region of the chart at index prices close to the initial price of 240.00. The solid line dominates at the extreme left and right edges of the chart, the regions

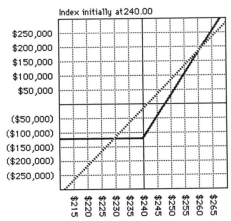

Buy 150.75 S&P 500 Index call options, 240.00 strike-price, at 7.96
Hold for three months

Buy 20 S&P 500 Index futures contracts at $241.80
Invest $120,000.00 in 3-month Treasury bills
Hold for three months, collect $2100.00 interest

Index initially at 240.00

FIGURE 8.11. Comparing the leverage of buying index call options with the leverage of buying index futures

regions representing index prices are greatly changed downward or upward, respectively. Investors may prefer one pattern to the other on the basis of the emphasis they place on highly unlikely, but nevertheless potentially catastrophic, events.

SELLING INDEX PUT OPTIONS AS AN ALTERNATIVE TO BUYING PORTFOLIOS OF STOCKS

We have just seen that buying index call options or options-on-futures can be a unique managerial alternative to buying portfolios of stocks. Another alternative using index options or options-on-futures—and one that produces yet another entirely different pattern of risks and returns—would be to short-sell index put options.

Using our options valuation procedure and all the assumptions that produced a call value of 7.96, a three-month, European, 240.00-strike-price put option would be valued at 6.27. Let's consider what would happen if instead of buying five calls the investor in our earlier example sold short five puts. The short-sale would result in proceeds of $3135.00, which, along with the investor's $120,000.00 risk capital, would be invested in Treasury bills:

Proceeds of put short-sale		Put price		Number of puts		Contract multiplier
$3135.00	=	6.27	×	5	×	$100.00

Figure 8.12 illustrates the pattern of risks and returns associated with this strategy. If the index is unchanged at expiration, the investor's profit is $5289.86—$3135.00 put premium collected as the options expire worthless, plus $2,154.86 interest on Treasury bills.

	Index Unchanged
Initial proceeds from sale of puts	
(6.27 × 5 × $100.00)	$3,135.00
Exercise value of puts	0
Profit from puts	$3,135.00
Interest income on T-bills (7% on $123,135.00	
for 3 months)	$2,154.86
TOTAL PROFIT	$5,289.86

In the preceding example, when the investor bought five calls, he experienced a loss of $1949.65 when the index was unchanged at expiration. We interpreted this as the fair price for the assurance of a *known max-*

179

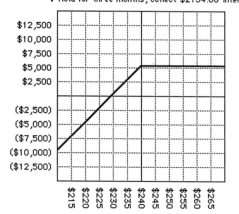

Sell 5 S&P 500 Index put options, 240.00 strike-price, at $6.27
Invest $123,135.00 in 3-month Treasury bills
Index initially at 240.00
Hold for three months, collect $2154.86 interest

FIGURE 8.12. Selling index put options as an alternative to buying stocks

imum loss but *potentially unlimited profit*. Conversely, when the investor now short-sells puts instead with the index unchanged, he experiences a profit of $5289.86 and this is the fair price he receives for the assurance of a *known maximum gain* but a *potentially enormous loss*. No matter how far the underlying index may rise by expiration, the puts he sold short will expire worthless, and the most he can hope to collect on them is the initial price, $3135.00. No matter what happens to the index the Treasury bills will still yield just $2154.86.

If the index declines by 10% from 240.00 to 216.00, each of his puts will have an exercise value of $2400.00 for an aggregate exercise value of $12,000.00:

Exercise value of put		Put's strike-price		Index price		Contract multiplier
$2400.00	=	240.00	−	216.00	×	$100.00

Aggregate exercise value of position		Exercise value of put		Number of puts in position
$12,000.00	=	$2400.00	×	5

Offset by the initial proceeds of the short-sale and income from his Treasury bills, the investor's loss with the index down 10% is $6710.14.

	Index – 10%
Initial proceeds from sale of puts (6.27 × 5 × $100.00)	$ 3,135.00
Exercise value of puts (24.00 × 5 × $100.00)	($12,000.00)
Loss from puts	($ 8,865.00)
Interest income on T-bills (7% on $123,135.00 for 3 months)	$ 2,154.86
TOTAL LOSS	($ 6,710.14)

Similar to the way we calculated the up-side break-even point when the investor bought five calls, we can calculate the down-side tolerance point when he short-sells puts—229.42. Above this index price the premium initially received from the short-sale and the interest income from his Treasury bills are sufficient to repay the exercise value of the short puts. Below this point the exercise value of the puts becomes great enough to cause a net loss:

Proceeds per contract		Put sale proceeds		T-bill income		Number of contracts		Contract multiplier
$10.58	=	$3135.00	+	$2154.86	÷	(5	×	$100.00)

Down-side tolerance point		Put's strike-price		Net proceeds per contract
229.42	=	240.00	−	$10.58

By short-selling put options the investor subjects himself to losses on the down-side beneath the tolerance point limited only by the fact that the underlying index can't be priced lower than zero. But this is less risk than he would have taken by buying a portfolio of stocks for which short-selling five puts is an explicit alternative. To demonstrate, consider that if the index declines to zero the investor would bear a loss of $120,000.00 in the depreciation of his portfolio of stocks; if we assume that he receives the expected $1200.00 in dividends despite the calamitous decline, his net loss would be $118,800.00.

	Index at Zero
Cost of stocks	($120,000.00)
Sale of stocks	0
Loss from stocks	($120,000.00)
Dividends	$ 1,200.00
TOTAL LOSS	($118,800.00)

If he had sold five puts instead, his losses would not be quite as severe. True, the puts would have an aggregate exercise value in all five contracts of $120,000.00, which the seller would have to pay to the buyer in cash. But Treasury bill interest and the initial proceeds from selling the puts would trim the total loss to $114,710.14, $4089.82 less than the alternative investment directly in stocks.

	Index at Zero
Initial proceeds from sale of puts (6.27 × 5 × $100.00)	$ 3,135.00
Exercise value of puts (240.00 × 5 × $100.00)	($120,000.00)
Loss from puts	($116,865.00)
Interest income on T-bills (7% on $123,135.00 for 3 months)	$ 2,154.86
TOTAL LOSS	($114,710.14)

LEVERAGE IN SELLING INDEX PUT OPTIONS

The claim that selling puts is less risky in a market disaster than owning a portfolio of stocks is true only if the position is *covered*. A short put position is covered if its *aggregate underlying value* is no greater than the amount of cash that would have been required to buy the portfolio—in this case $120,000.00.

Aggregate underlying value		Index price		Contract multiplier		Number of puts sold
$120,00.00	=	240.00	×	$100.00	×	5

Now let's see what could happen if the investor used the full power of margin to create an uncovered, or *naked*, position in short puts. The margin requirement for each put would be the greater of the results of the two alternative formulas we discussed earlier, in this case $1827.00 per contract.

5% of index price (240.00)		12.00	2% of index price (240.00)		4.80
Market price of option	+	6.27	Market price of option	+	6.27
Out-of-the-money amount	−	0			0
		18.27			11.07
Contract multiplier	×	$100.00	Contract multiplier	×	$100.00
Total margin requirement		$1832.00	Total margin requirement		$1107.00

Because the proceeds of the put sale can be applied toward the requirement, the investor would have to allocate only $1200.00 per contract out of the $120,000.00 risk capital:

Net requirement		Total requirement		Put price		Contract multiplier
$1200.00	=	$1812.00	−	(6.27	×	$100.00)

A useful shortcut is to remember that for at-the-money and in-the-money options, because there can be no out-of-the-money deduction, the net requirement will always be 5% of the index price, times the contract multiplier:

183

Net requirement		5% of index price		Contract multiplier
$1200.00	=	12.00	×	$100.00

At $1200.00 per contract a deposit of $120,000.00 in Treasury bills will margin 100 contracts:

Maximum contracts to margin		Total margin deposit		Net requirement per contract
100	=	$120,000.00	÷	$1200.00

By selling 100 contracts the investors will have initial proceeds of $62,700.00, which can be reinvested in Treasury bills:

Total proceeds		Number of puts sold		Put price		Contract multiplier
$62,700.00	=	100	×	6.27	×	$100.00

Figure 8.13 illustrates the pattern of risks and returns associated with this position. With the index unchanged at expiration, the investor earns

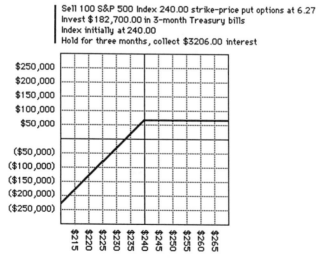

FIGURE 8.13. Leverage in selling index put options

a profit of $65,897.25—the initial proceeds of $62,700.00 plus Treasury-bill interest of $3197.25. When he sold only five puts, his profit was only $5289.86.

	Index Unchanged	Index + 10%	Index – 10%
Initial proceeds from puts	$62,700.00	$62,700.00	$ 62,700.00
Exercise value of puts	0	0	($241,800.00)
Profit (loss) from puts	$62,700.00	$62,700.00	($177,300.00)
Interest income on T-bills (7% on $182,700.00 for 3 months)	$ 3,197.25	$ 3,197.25	$ 3,197.25
TOTAL PROFIT (LOSS)	$65,897.25	$65,897.25	($174,102.75)

Just as when he sold only five puts, the profit he earns when the index is unchanged at expiration is the most he can ever hope to make in the levered position. No matter how high the index rises, he will earn no more than $62,700.00 from the expiration of the puts, and the Treasury bills will yield no more than $3197.25. The price the investor pays for enlarging his profit potential from $5289.86 to $65,897.25, of course, is the greater likelihood of loss. When he sold five puts his down-side tolerance point was 229.42; now with 100 puts it rises to 233.41:

Proceeds per contract		Put sale proceeds	T-bill income	Number of contracts		Contract multiplier
$6.59	=	$62,700.00 +	$3197.25 ÷	(100	×	$100.00)

Down-side tolerance point		Put's strike-price		Net proceeds per contract
233.41	=	240.00	–	$6.59

Not only is loss more likely—now there is the possibility for loss beyond the investor's initial risk capital. If the index has declined 10% at expiration from 240.00 to 214.00, each of his short puts requires him to pay an exercise value of $2400.00—all 100 together will have an aggregate exercise value of $240,000.00. Offset by the initial proceeds and interest

185

income, the investor's net loss is $174,102.75, more than he lost with five short puts when the index fell to zero and far more than his $120,000.00 risk capital.

In the worst case, in which the index falls to zero, we have seen that the investor loses $118,800.00 with purchase of stocks and $114,710.14 if he sells five puts. But when he sells 100 puts he must pay an aggregate exercise value of $2,400,000.00 if the index falls to zero. Offset by proceeds from the sale and interest income, his net loss would be $2,334,102.75.

	Index at Zero
Initial proceeds from sale of puts	
(6.27 × 100 × $100.00)	$ 62,700.00
Exercise value of puts (240.00 × 100 × $100.00)	($2,400,000.00)
Loss from puts	($2,337,300.00)
Interest income on T-bills (7% on	
$182,700.00 for 3 months)	$ 3,197.25
TOTAL LOSS	($2,334,102.75)

BUYING INDEX PUT OPTIONS AS AN ALTERNATIVE TO SHORT-SELLING PORTFOLIOS OF STOCKS

We have already seen that investments in stocks cannot be accurately replicated by buying call options—buying options inevitably produces a unique, nonlinear pattern of returns. Now we will focus on buying *put* options as an alternative to *short-selling* portfolios of stocks, and unfortunately we will find that our replication problems become even more difficult. Recall from our earlier discussions that, although short positions in stocks must be *margined*, they do not have to be *financed*. In fact, they generate a positive cash flow that can be invested in Treasury bills while the stocks are held short. Put options, on the other hand, although they are geared to return a profit when the index declines, require an initial cash investment when they are purchased, just as call options do. To come as close as possible to constructing a position in put options to replicate short-selling a portfolio of stocks we must borrow the funds required to buy the puts.

As he did with calls, the investor will buy five contracts, to establish a position with an aggregate underlying value of $120,000.00. At a theoretical value of 6.27 the position will have an aggregate cost of $3135.00, financed by borrowing (we assume that the rate for borrowing is 7%):

Investment required to buy		Put price		Number of contracts		Contract multiplier
$3135.00	=	6.27	×	5	×	$100.00

Figure 8.14 illustrates the pattern of risks and returns associated with this position. It is the characteristic shape of the options positions we have looked at already, but it is flipped in the chart to reflect that this one will be profitable when the underlying index declines and will register a fixed loss of $3189.86 when the index rises or remains unchanged.

If the index declines by 10% from 240.00 to 216.00, each option will have an exercise value of $2400.00, for an aggregate exercise value of $12,000.00. Including the cost of financing the initial cost of the position, the investor will show a profit of $8785.14. With stocks or futures his profit was $12,900.00.

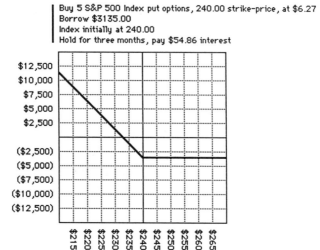

Buy 5 S&P 500 Index put options, 240.00 strike-price, at $6.27
Borrow $3135.00
Index initially at 240.00
Hold for three months, pay $54.86 interest

FIGURE 8.14. Buying index put options as an alternative to short-selling stocks

	Index Unchanged	Index + 10%	Index − 10%
Initial cost of puts	($3,135.00)	($3,135.00)	($ 3,135.00)
Exercise value of puts	0	0	$12,000.00
Profit (loss) from puts	($3,135.00)	($3,135.00)	$ 8,865.00
Financing ($3135.00 at 7% for 3 months)	($ 54.86)	($ 54.86)	($ 54.86)
TOTAL PROFIT (LOSS)	($3,189.86)	($3,189.86)	$ 8,785.14

Earlier, when the investor sold short a $120,000.00 portfolio of stocks and again when he sold a single S&P 500 Index futures contract, he earned a profit of $900.00 when the index was unchanged. When he buys puts, he will not break even until the index declines sufficiently to allow the exercise value of the puts to repay their initial cost, plus the cost of financing their purchase. Just as we calculated the up-side break-even point required for the investor's call position to be profitable, so (with some simple modifications) we can calculate the *down-side break-even point* for this put position—233.62:

Cost per contract		Investment in puts		Financing cost		Number of contracts		Contract multiplier
6.38	=	$3160.0	+	$54.86	÷	(5	×	$100.00)

Up-side break-even point		Put's strike-price		Net cost per contract
233.62	=	240.00	−	6.38

THE LEVERAGE OF BUYING INDEX PUT OPTIONS

Once again the peculiarities of short-selling add an element of complexity to our otherwise straightforward deliberations. In the short strategies we have examined so far there has been in each case a natural rationale to appropriately scale the size of the options or futures position. For futures as an alternative to stocks we sold one contract to replicate a $120,000.00 short position in stocks because the underlying value of one contract in the example happened to be $120,000.00; in the preceding put position five contracts were purchased with borrowed funds to create a position with an aggregate underlying value of $120,000.00; and in the levered futures position the investor established the largest permissible futures position using the same $120,000.00 margin requirement he would have had to post anyway to hold short the portfolio of stocks. But now, if the investor is once again permitted to borrow, there is no natural limit to the number of puts he might wish to buy.

Admitting that the figure is somewhat arbitrary, let's say that he will buy 150.75 contracts, the same number of calls he bought in an earlier example. At least this way the put position will be scaled to a level of risk with which we are already familiar. At 6.27 per contract the total position would require the investor to borrow $94,520.25. Over three months the cost to finance this borrowing at 7% would be $1654.10:

Total cost of puts		Put price		Number of puts		Contract multiplier
$94,520.25	=	6.27	×	150.75	×	$100.00

Figure 8.15 illustrates the pattern of risks and returns associated with this position. Note that it is precisely the same pattern that resulted from the previous example in which the investor bought only five contracts, but that all the profit and loss numbers are multiplied by 30. Because all that has changed is the size of the position, the down-side break-even point is 233.62 in both examples.

FIGURE 8.15. Leverage in buying index put options

	Index Unchanged	Index + 10%	Index − 10%
Initial cost of puts	($94,520.25)	($94,520.25)	($ 94,520.25)
Exercise value of puts	0	0	$361,800.00
Profit (loss) from puts	($94,520.25)	($94,520.25)	$267,279.75
Financing ($94,520.25 at 7%)	($ 1,654.10)	($ 1,654.10)	($ 1,654.10)
TOTAL PROFIT (LOSS)	($96,174.35)	($96,174.35)	$265,625.65

SELLING INDEX CALL OPTIONS AS AN ALTERNATIVE TO SHORT-SELLING PORTFOLIOS OF STOCKS

Earlier we saw how selling index put options could be an alternative to buying calls for an investor who anticipated a rising market. Now we examine the idea of selling call options as an alternative to buying puts for an investor who anticipates a falling market. Let's consider what would happen if, instead of buying five puts, the investor in our earlier example sold short five calls at 7.96. Five calls is a covered position because its aggregate *underlying value* is no greater than the risk capital that would have gone into buying stocks instead of selling calls—in this case $120,000.00:

Aggregate underlying value		Index price		Number of puts sold		Contract multiplier
$120,000.00	=	240.00	×	5	×	$100.00

The short-sale of five calls would result in proceeds of $3980.00, which would be invested in Treasury bills during the holding period:

Proceeds of call short-sale		Call price		Number of contracts		Contract multiplier
$3980.00	=	7.96	×	5	×	$100.00

Figure 8.16 illustrates the pattern of risks and returns associated with this strategy. If the index is unchanged or down at expiration, the investor's profit is $4049.65—$3980.00 in put premium collected as the options expire worthless, plus $69.65 interest from Treasury bills. If the index rises by 10% from 240.00 to 264.00, each of his options will have an exercise value of $2400.00, for an aggregate exercise value of $12,000.00. Offset by the initial proceeds of the short-sale and income from his Treasury bills, the investor's loss is $7950.35. Recall that when the investor sold a portfolio of stocks short his loss was $11,100.00.

FIGURE 8.16. Selling index call options as an alternative to short-selling stocks

	Index Unchanged	Index + 10%	Index − 10%
Initial proceeds from calls	$3,800.00	$ 3,800.00	$3,800.00
Exercise value of calls	0	($12,000.00)	0
Profit (loss) from calls	$3,800.00	($ 8,020.00)	$3,800.00
Interest income on T-bills (7% on $3980.00 for 3 months)	$ 69.65	$ 69.65	$ 69.65
TOTAL PROFIT (LOSS)	$4,049.65	($ 7,950.35)	$4,049.65

In the earlier examples, when he simply sold short a portfolio of stocks, his profit was only $900.00 in the same circumstances, and when he bought five puts he experienced a loss of $3189.86—but this loss was his known maximum. Now, when the investor short-sells calls instead, with the index unchanged he experiences a profit is $4049.65—and this is his *maximum gain*. No matter how far the underlying index may fall by expiration, the calls he sold short will still expire worthless and the most he can hope to collect on them is what he initially sold them for, $3980.00; no matter what happens to the index, the Treasury bills will still yield just $69.65.

Just as we calculated the down-side tolerance point for a short-sale of five puts, we can calculate the *up-side* tolerance point for a short-sale of five calls—248.09. Below this index price the premium initially received from the short-sale and the interest income from his Treasury bills is sufficient to repay the exercise value of the short calls. Above this point the exercise value of the calls becomes great enough to cause a net loss. The 248.09 is the index price in Figure 8.16 at which the risk return line crosses down through the center of the chart into the region representing losses:

Proceeds per contract		Proceeds from calls		T-bill income		Number of contracts		Contract multiplier
8.09	=	$3980.00	+	$69.65	÷	(5	×	$100.00)

Up-side tolerance point		Call's strike-price		Net proceeds per contract
248.09	=	$240.00	+	$8.09

When we compared the risks in a market catastrophe of covered short puts versus a portfolio of stocks, we discovered that the short puts were less risky. Comparing covered short calls with a short portfolio of stocks, the same thing is true. Theoretically there is no limit to how far the underlying index might rise over a given holding period, but as an extreme example let's see what would happen if the index doubled from 240.00 to 480.00. The portfolio of stocks would show a loss of $120,000.00, offset by $2100.00 in interest income—a net loss of $117,900.00.

	Index + 100%
Proceeds from short-sale of stocks	$120,000.00
Repurchase of stocks	($240,000.00)
Loss from stocks	($120,000.00)
Interest income on T-bills (7% on $120,000.00 for 3 months)	$ 2,100.00
TOTAL LOSS	($117,900.00)

The position with five short calls, on the other hand, fares somewhat better. The investor must pay an aggregate exercise value of $120,000.00, but this is offset by the initial proceeds from the calls and interest income—the net loss is $116,089.65, an improvement of $1810.35.

	Index + 100%
Initial proceeds from sale of calls	
(7.96 × 5 × $100.00)	$ 3,980.00
Exercise value of calls (240.00 × 5 × $100.00)	($120,000.00)
Loss from calls	($116,020.00)
Interest income on T-bills	
(7% on $3980.00 for 3 months)	$ 69.65
TOTAL LOSS	($116,089.65)

LEVERAGE IN SELLING INDEX CALL OPTIONS

If the investor in the preceding example were willing to lower his up-side tolerance point in exchange for higher profits with the index un-changed or down, he could sell a larger number of calls. When we dis-cussed leverage in selling index futures, we said that ordinarily an investor would post $120,000.00 in Treasury bills to margin a $120,000.00 short stock position.

Recalling the shortcut for calculating the net margin requirement for selling at the money index options, we can determine that if the investor wished to commit all of this $120,000.00 to margining short calls he could sell 100 calls:

Net requirement		5% of index price		Contract multiplier
$1200.00	=	12.00	×	$100.00

Maximum contracts to margin		Total margin deposit		Net requirement per contract
100	=	$120,000.00	÷	$1200.00

At 7.96 the proceeds from selling 100 contracts would be $79,600.00, which would be reinvested in Treasury bills:

Proceeds of call short-sale		Call price		Number of contracts		Contract multiplier
$79,600.00	=	7.96	×	100	×	$100.00

Figure 8.17 illustrates the pattern of risks and returns associated with this strategy. With the index unchanged or down, the investor's profit would be the initial proceeds from the sale plus interest from the Treas-ury bills, a total of $80,993.00. As with any short options position, this will be the investor's maximum profit. But if the index rises, he is ex-posed to unlimited losses. If the index rises 10% from 240.00 to 264.00, each call will have an exercise value of $2400.00—the position of 100 will have an aggregate exercise value of $240,000.00. Offset by the initial proceeds from sale of the calls and the interest on the Treasury bills, the investor's total loss is $159,607.00, far more than the $120,000.00 margin deposit.

196

Sell 100 S&P 500 Index call options, 240.00 strike-price, at 7.96
Invest $79,600.00 in Treasury bills
Index initially at 240.00
Hold for three months, collect $1393.00 interest

FIGURE 8.17. Leverage in selling index call options

	Index unchanged	Index + 10%	Index − 10%
Initial proceeds from calls	$79,600.00	$ 79,600.00	$79,600.00
Exercise value of calls	0	($240,000.00)	0
Profit (loss) from calls	$79,600.00	($160,400.00)	$79,600.00
Interest income on T-bills (7% on $79,600.00 for 3 months)	$ 1,393.00	$ 1,393.00	$ 1,393.00
TOTAL PROFIT (LOSS)	$80,993.00	($159,607.00)	$80,993.00

Of course, this is by no means as bad as it can get. Unlike the case with short puts, in which losses are limited by the fact that the under-lying index cannot trade below zero, losses in short calls are almost limitless. Revisiting the extreme case in which the index doubles from 240.00 to 480.00, we find that the aggregate exercise value the call seller would have to pay totals $2,400,000.00. Offset by the initial proceeds from sale of the calls and the interest on the Treasury bills, the investor's total loss is $2,319,007.00.

	Index + 100%
Initial proceeds from sale of calls (7.96 × 100 × $100.00)	$ 79,600.00
Exercise value of calls (240.00 × 100 × $100.00)	($2,400,000.00)
Loss from calls	($2,320,400.00)
Interest income on T-bills (7% on $79,600.00 for 3 months)	$ 1,393.00
TOTAL LOSS	($2,319,007.00)

TRADING APPLICATIONS OF INDEX OPTIONS AND FUTURES

So far we have concentrated on using index options and futures for strategic positioning in the market. But they can be just as useful on a tactical basis, in day-to-day trading situations. For active traders their tremendous liquidity and low transaction costs make them natural vehicles for intra-day speculations, and for investors with longer time horizons they can be used to smooth out the inevitable bumps in the daily implementation of any strategy.

Consider the case of a $100 million mutual fund that wishes to be 100% invested in the stock market at all times. If one day a flood of deposits from investors totaling $20 million flows in, the fund can no longer be said to be fully invested. Now its assets total $120 million but only $100 million is invested. The fund has been put into a relatively bearish investment posture, without its manager having made an intentional asset allocation decision.

The manager might elect to simply buy more stocks with the newly deposited money. But doing that in a hurry could be very costly, both in market impact and in the risk of hasty decisions. Instead, he could buy index futures with an underlying value equivalent to the newly deposited $20 million. Any move in the broad market will be perfectly reflected in the futures contracts, so the fund is effectively 100% invested again.

While he waits for the right moments to buy the right stocks, the manager can patiently hold his futures contracts, earning interest on the $20 million that hasn't been spent. As he gradually buys the stocks he wants to own, he sells an equivalent value in futures contracts. Finally, when the entire $20 million is invested in stocks, the manager will have sold off all his futures.

In practice, the manager may be wise not to replace in full his futures position with stocks. By always retaining some portion of his total portfolio in futures, he maintains the capability to trade easily in and out of the market as daily cash inflows and outflows cause his total portfolio value to fluctuate.

Pension managers often face the frustration of anticipating future cash flows from their plan sponsors while wishing to act on a critical market decision before the funds arrive; for example, consider the case of a pension manager who, on September 15, anticipates a major rally in the stock market but who knows that new contributions from the plan sponsor won't be received until December 15. In the past he would have had no alternative but to wait, living with the potential frustration of seeing his forecast come true, only too soon to take advantage of it. But with index options or futures the manager can establish a levered market position in September in anticipation of funds to be received in December. The tremendous leverage of index options and futures allows him to take market positions margined by as little as 5% of the value of the commitment and can take the desired position he wants without tying up a prohibitive amount of assets.

If his forecast is correct, the anticipated market move will be reflected perfectly in profits in his options or futures contracts. In December he can add these profits to the funds he will receive and establish the stock positions he would have established in September if he'd had the cash to do so.

9. ARBITRAGE WITH INDEX OPTIONS AND FUTURES

Webster's *Third New International Dictionary* defines *arbitrage* as "simultaneous purchase and sale of the same or equivalent security, commodity contract, insurance or foreign exchange on the same or different markets in order to profit from price discrepancies." In today's world of computerized market reporting and instantaneous telecommunications, such a transaction is a rare opportunity indeed. Nowadays, when investors speak of arbitrage they are generally referring to what has traditionally been called *risk arbitrage*: speculating on the stocks of companies involved in mergers and acquisitions. Most contemporary literature on true arbitrage focuses on its use as a conceptual tool for the relative valuation of equivalent securities. In fact, we've already used this approach to create our valuation formula for index futures and our valuation procedures for index options and options-on-futures. Our TANSTAAFL rule could be accurately restated as *TANSTAARAO—There Ain't No Such Thing As A Riskless Arbitrage Opportunity*.

Index options, futures, options-on-futures, and their underlying indexes, present some of the few remaining opportunities in today's efficient markets to earn arbitrage profits, in the dictionary sense of the word. In our strategic examples and our valuation procedures we've already acquired some fluency in thinking of index instruments as interchangeable alternatives. So the next natural step is to develop strategies that exploit those times when these interchangeable alternatives become temporarily mispriced in relation to each other. Happily, these times are not as rare as one might think.

ARBITRAGE BETWEEN INDEX FUTURES AND PORTFOLIOS OF STOCKS

By arbitraging index futures against portfolios of stocks making up their underlying indexes, it is possible—and, in fact, quite simple—for an investor to create an investment position that will behave just like a short-term money market instrument. Like such an instrument, it will be essentially riskless, it will pay an interest rate, and it will have a defined maturity. The difference is that, from time to time, this "synthetic money market instrument" can pay a much higher rate than actual money market instruments.

The strategy is implemented by purchasing a portfolio of stocks designed specifically to track the index underlying an index futures contract. Ideally, this portfolio would contain all the index stocks, held in exactly the proportions in which they are represented in the index. Against this portfolio the investor would sell index futures contracts. Since any change in the value of the stocks will be perfectly mirrored in the futures, the position is virtually riskless with respect to market direction. The profit in the position comes from the dividends earned in the stock portfolio, and the capture of the premium in the futures contracts.

As an example, let's use the Major Market Index. Let's assume the index is at 340.00, with a dividend yield of 4%. If the riskless interest rate is 7%, according to our valuation formula the fair price of a three-month futures contract would be 342.55.

With the index at 340.00, the underlying value of a futures contract would be $85,000.00:

Index price		Contract multiplier		Underlying value of contract
340.00	×	$250.00	=	$85,000.00

Like a classic dictionary arbitrage, the investor would establish the position by selling the index in one market and buying simultaneously in the other. Specifically, he would sell one futures contract on the Chicago Board of Trade and simultaneously buy an $85,000.00 portfolio of the 20 stocks that make up the index on the New York Stock Exchange.

Because the Major Market Index is price-weighted, to construct the portfolio to perfectly track it the investor would buy an equal number of shares of each stock. To determine exactly how many shares to buy per futures contract sold, we divide the futures contract multiplier by the divisor of the index. The divisor undergoes periodic revision, but can be obtained readily from the American Stock Exchange or most brokerage houses. For example, if the divisor were 5, the investor would buy 50 shares of each stock in the index.

Number of shares of each stock to buy, per futures contract		Contract multiplier		Index divisor
50	=	$250.00	÷	5

Next, all the investor has to do is wait three months for the synthetic money market instrument to mature. After three months, when the futures expire, the position will show a positive result—the "yield" of the synthetic money market instrument—regardless of whether the underlying index is unchanged, up, or down.

If the index is unchanged at expiration, $850.00 dividend income and $637.50 premium erosion in the futures contract add up to a profit of $1487.50. The same result is obtained when the market makes a substantial move, because the futures contract and the portfolio of stocks perfectly hedge each other. For instance, if the index rises by 10% over the three months, from 340.00 to 374.00, profits in the portfolio of stocks are offset by losses in the futures contract, and the investor still earns exactly $1487.50. If the index declines 10%, from 340.00 to 306.00, losses in the portfolio of stocks are offset by profits in the short futures contract; again, the net profit is $1487.50.

	Index Unchanged	Index +10%	Index −10%
Costs of stocks	($85,000.00)	($85,000.00)	($85,000.00)
Sale of stocks	$85,000.00	$93,500.00	$76,500.00
Profit (loss) from stocks	0	$ 8,500.00	($ 8,500.00)
Initial contract value of futures	$85,637.50	$85,637.50	$85,637.50
Value of expiring futures	($85,000.00)	($93,500.00)	($76,500.00)
Profit (loss) from futures	$ 637.50	($ 7,862.50)	$ 9,137.50
Dividend income	$ 850.00	$ 850.00	$ 850.00
TOTAL PROFIT (LOSS)	$ 1,487.50	$ 1,487.50	$ 1,487.50

203

For a three-month holding period, the profit of $1487.50 on an $85,000.00 investment represents a yield of 7% annually for the synthetic money market instrument, exactly the riskless rate we assumed when we calculated the theoretical value of the futures contract. Figure 9.1 illustrates the pattern of risks and returns associated with this strategy—a perfectly straight, flat line. This reflects the fact that the synthetic money market instrument returns $1487.50 at expiration regardless of the price of the underlying index.

Although we have said that premium erosion in the futures contract is a component of this strategy's profitability, it would produce exactly the same results if the futures contract were priced at a discount to the index—*as long as this is calculated by the valuation formula as the futures' theoretical value.* For example, according to the valuation formula, if we were to double our dividend yield assumption from 4% to 8%, the theoretical value would fall from 342.55 to 339.15. Plugging these figures into the strategy shows that although profit from premium erosion is turned into loss from discount erosion, the increased dividend income compensates perfectly—the synthetic money market instrument still returns $1487.50 whether the index is up, down, or unchanged.

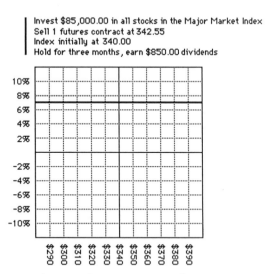

FIGURE 9.1. The "synthetic money-market instrument" strategy

	Index Unchanged	Index + 10%	Index − 10%
Cost of stocks	($85,000.00)	($85,000.00)	($85,000.00)
Sale of stocks	$85,000.00	$93,500.00	$76,500.00
Profit (loss) from stocks	0	$ 8,500.00	($ 8,500.00)
Initial contract value of futures	$84,787.50	$84,787.50	$84,787.50
Value of expiring futures	($85,000.00)	($93,500.00)	($76,500.00)
Profit (loss) from futures	($ 212.50)	($ 8,712.50)	$ 8,287.50
Dividend income	$ 1,700.00	$ 1,700.00	$ 1,700.00
TOTAL PROFIT (LOSS)	$ 1,487.50	$ 1,487.50	$ 1,487.50

This strategy could be implemented just as well by arbitraging futures contracts on the S&P 500 Index or the New York Stock Exchange Composite Index against portfolios of stocks consisting of their respective components. But it should be noted that it cannot be implemented using the Value Line Composite Index. As we discussed earlier in the section on the various indexes, because of the Value Line's construction, no portfolio of stocks will perfectly track it.

For investors looking not for arbitrage opportunities but simply for a high-yield alternative to Treasury bills or a money-market account, this synthetic money market instrument can be an extremely attractive investment opportunity, although in practice it is not entirely riskless. First, there is the risk that the stocks in the index will not pay the dividends anticipated when the position is set up. If all dividends were entirely suspended, the full expected yield from the strategy would not be realized, but no loss of principal would result. Second, there is some risk that the required multiple simultaneous transactions in the portfolio of stocks will not be made on a timely basis. Most brokerage firms now offer specialized services geared toward such *program trading*, so in practice there is little chance that this risk factor could have a substantial effect.

At this point, the reader could not be blamed for asking if all this weren't an awful lot of trouble to go to just to earn the riskless interest rate—why not just buy Treasury bills? The answer is that an investor wouldn't bother to set up this position unless he could sell the futures contract at a price *higher than its fair value*, resulting in a synthetic money market instrument that would outperform any alternatives of comparable risk. As an example, consider the same position if the futures contract could have been sold at 345.10 rather than 342.55 as we assumed before.

If the index were unchanged at expiration, the investor would have a profit of $2125.00—a yield of 10%. As Figure 9.2 illustrates, the results are the same as before, regardless of the price of the index at expiration.

	Index Unchanged	Index + 10%	Index – 10%
Cost of stocks	($85,000.00)	($85,000.00)	($85,000.00)
Sale of stocks	$85,000.00	$93,500.00	$76,500.00
Profit (loss) from stocks	0	$ 8,500.00	($ 8,500.00)
Initial contract value of futures	$86,275.00	$86.275.00	$86,275.00
Value of expiring futures	($85,000.00)	($93,500.00)	($76,500.00)
Profit (loss) from futures	$ 1,275.00	($ 7,225.00)	$ 9,775.00
Dividend income	$ 850.00	$ 850.00	$ 850.00
TOTAL PROFIT (LOSS)	$ 2,125.00	$ 2,125.00	$ 2,125.00

If an investor could borrow the $85,000.00 required to establish the position at any rate of interest lower than the 10% yield of the synthetic money market instrument, he could capture any differential as a pure

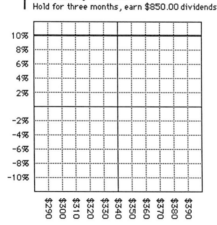

FIGURE 9.2. The "synthetic money-market instrument" strategy when futures are overpriced

206

arbitrage. As an example, let's say the investor in our example had borrowed the $85,000.00 at 8.5%.

Profit from synthetic money market instrument:	2,125.00
Interest expense (8.5% on $85,000.00 for 3 months):	($1,806.25)
NET PROFIT	$ 318.75

The interest expense for his borrowing would cut the profits considerably, from $2125.00 to $318.75. But since the funds required to establish the position were entirely borrowed, the investor had to commit no capital of his own to earn this profit—so even a profit of only $318.75 represents an infinite return on capital. It is hard to imagine why any astute investor with access to borrowing at 8.5% wouldn't wish to trade this position as many times as the marketplace would allow.

To determine the futures price that would justify borrowing to trade the synthetic money market instrument strategy, the investor need only recalculate the futures contract's theoretical value using his effective borrowing rate in place of the riskless rate normally used in the calculation. Recall that we calculated the normal theoretical value for the three-month futures contract at 342.55, assuming an underlying index price of 340.00, a riskless rate of 7%, and a dividend yield of 4%:

Futures value		Index price		Interest at riskless rate		Dividends
342.55	=	340.00	+	$5.95	−	$3.40

Replacing the riskless rate of 7% with the investor's borrowing rate of 8.5% produces a theoretical value of 343.825, the price above which it becomes profitable to borrow at 8.5% to finance the synthetic money market instrument:

Futures value		Index price		Interest at borrowing rate		Dividends
343.825	=	340.00	+	$7.225	−	$3.40

When index futures contracts are trading *below* their theoretical values, the synthetic money market instrument strategy can be implemented in reverse—by buying an index futures contract and short-selling a portfolio of stocks—with exactly the same results. But in practice the various

207

peculiarities and difficulties associated with short-selling that we've already encountered make this version of the strategy somewhat impractical for most market participants. To understand how this might work under ideal circumstances, let's rework the previous example in reverse, where the investor can buy a futures contract well below its theoretical value of 342.55—let's say at 340.55.

The investor will invest the proceeds of the short-sale in Treasury bills, earning interest to offset the costs of restitution of dividends and premium erosion in the futures contract. Because he will earn more interest than he will pay in restitution of dividends and because he will have relatively little erosion in his futures contract because he bought it at below theoretical value, this position will result in a profit of $500.00.

	Index Unchanged	Index + 10%	Index − 10%
Sale of stocks	$85,000.00	$85,000.00	$85,000.00
Repurchase of stocks	($85,000.00)	($93,500.00)	($76,500.00)
Profit (loss) from stocks	0	($ 8,500.00)	$ 8,500.00
Initial contract value of futures	($85,137.50)	($85,137.50)	($85,137.50)
Value of expiring futures	$85,000.00	$93,500.00	$76,500.00
Profit (loss) from futures	($ 137.50)	$ 8,362.50	($ 8,637.50)
Interest income on T-bills (7% on $85,000.00 for 3 months)	$ 1,487.50	$ 1,487.50	$ 1,487.50
Restitution of dividends	($ 850.00)	($ 850.00)	($ 850.00)
TOTAL PROFIT	$ 500.00	$ 500.00	$ 500.00

As Figure 9.3 illustrates, the pattern of risks and returns associated with the reverse synthetic money market instrument strategy is another flat line, indicating that this strategy, too, returns the same result, regardless of the index price at expiration. Note that the profit of $500.00 is earned on a cash investment of zero. All an investor would have to do to establish this position is post securities as margin for the short stock and the long futures contract. As difficult as short-selling can sometimes be, the notion of a riskless return on an investment of zero is so attractive that many market participants are strongly motivated to overcome the difficulties. The thorniest difficulty to overcome is most investors' inability to reinvest the entire proceeds of short-sales. This lowers the amount of interest income they can expect to receive to offset the restitution of

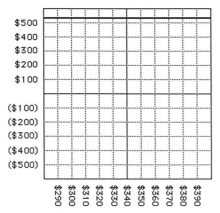

Sell short $85,000.00 in all stocks in the Major Market Index
Buy 1 futures contract at 340.55
Invest $85,000.00 in Treasury bills
Index initially at 340.00
Hold for three months, collect $1487.50 interest, pay $850.00 dividends

FIGURE 9.3. The reverse "synthetic money-market instrument" strategy

dividends; for example, let's reconsider the preceding example, assuming that the investor could reinvest only half the proceeds of the short-sale. By working with this assumption the position results in a *loss* of $243.75.

	Index Unchanged	Index + 10%	Index − 10%
Sale of stocks	$85,000.00	$85,000.00	$85,000.00
Repurchase of stocks	($85,000.00)	($93,500.00)	($76,500.00)
Profit (loss) from stocks	0	($ 8,500.00)	$ 8,500.00
Initial contract value of futures	($85,137.50)	($85,137.50)	($85,137.50)
Value of expiring futures	$85,000.00	$93,500.00	$76,500.00
Profit (loss) from futures	($ 137.50)	$ 8,362.50	($ 8,637.50)
Interest income on T-bills (7% on $42,500.00 for 3 months)	$ 743.75	$ 743.75	$ 743.75
Restitution of dividends	($ 850.00)	($ 850.00)	($ 850.00)
TOTAL LOSS	($ 243.75)	($ 243.75)	($ 243.75)

The investor can determine when the futures price is sufficiently low to justify the reverse synthetic money market instrument strategy by

209

recalculating its theoretical value using the effective short-sale reinvestment rate instead of the Treasury bill rate. If the investor can reinvest only half the proceeds of the short-sale, the riskless interest rate is effectively halved, from 7% to 3.5%. When we recalculate the theoretical value of the futures contract, using a 3.5% interest rate, we get 339.57, the futures price below which it will be profitable to implement the reverse synthetic money market instrument.

Futures value		Index price		Interest at half riskless rate		Dividends
$339.57	=	$340.00	+	$2.97	−	$3.40

The investor who can borrow at 8.5% and reinvest half the proceeds of short-sales now has two "trigger points" to tell him whether to implement the strategy and, if so, in which direction. When the futures trade *above* 343.825, the investor can profit from the synthetic money market instrument, and when they trade below 339.57 he can profit from the reverse synthetic money market instrument.

If an investor were willing to introduce the risk that the stock side of the synthetic money market instrument arbitrage might not perfectly track the index underlying the futures contracts in the position, he could attempt to increase its yield. To see how this might work consider the case of an investor who is confident that he can create a portfolio of stocks that will always move twice as much as the Major Market Index. In the language of Modern Portfolio Theory such a portfolio is said to have a *beta* of 2.00. Let's assume that this portfolio has the same dividend yield as the index, 4%.

If such a portfolio could be created, the investor could sell twice as many futures contracts against it as he ordinarily would, and still be perfectly hedged. This means he could capture twice as much premium and thereby enhance the returns of the strategy. Now, whether the index is unchanged, higher, or lower at expiration—assuming that the 2.00 beta portfolio of stocks is unchanged—his profit is $2125.00, a yield of 10%, even though he sold the futures at their theoretical value of 342.55.

	Index Unchanged	Index + 10%	Index − 10%
Cost of stock	($ 85,000.00)	($ 85,000.00)	($ 85,000.00)
Repurchase of stock	$ 85,000.00	$102,000.00	$ 68,000.00
Profit (loss) from stock	0	$ 17,000.00	$ 17,000.00
Initial contract value of futures	$171,275.00	$171,275.00	$171,275.00
Value of expiring futures	($170,000.00)	($187,000.00)	($153,000.00)
Profit (loss) from futures	$ 1,275.00	($ 15,725.00)	$ 18,275.00
Dividend income	$ 850.00	$ 850.00	$ 850.00
TOTAL PROFIT	$ 2,125.00	$ 2,125.00	$ 2,125.00

Figure 9.4 illustrates this strategy's pattern of risks and returns. The line will be completely flat as long as the 2.00 beta portfolio behaves as predicted. But an investor who employs this approach is taking a risk because he is truly hedging a portfolio of apples with futures on oranges. If the Major Market Index and the 2.00 beta portfolio are both substantially unchanged during the holding period, the risk will be some amount of unpredictable drift between the two sides of the hedge, which could just as easily work to the investor's advantage as to his disadvantage. But, if the broad market rallies strongly and the 2.00 beta portfolio doesn't

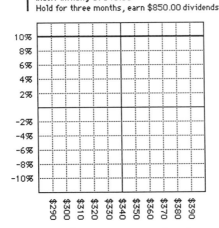

FIGURE 9.4. The "synthetic money-market instrument" strategy with a high-beta portfolio.

211

in fact move twice as much as the index, the investor could realize substantial losses.

To understand this risk assume that the index rallies 10%, but the stock portfolio, instead of rallying 20% as predicted, rallies only 15%. In this event the position would produce a *loss* of $2125.00 rather than an anticipated profit of the same amount.

	Index +10%
Cost of stocks	($ 85,000.00)
Sale of stocks, beta 1.50	$ 97,750.00
Profit from stocks	$ 12,750.00
Contract value of futures (342.55 × $250.00 × 2)	$171,275.00
Value of expiring futures, index up 10% (374.00 × $250.00 × 2)	($187,000.00)
Loss from futures	($ 15,725.00)
Dividend income	$ 850.00
TOTAL LOSS	($ 2,125.00)

As Figure 9.5 illustrates, this particular failure of the portfolio to behave as predicted is a windfall in the event of a broad market decline. To see how this might work reverse the market scenario to one in which the index declines 10% and the stocks decline 15% instead of the expected 20%. In this event the investor's profit is $6375.00—a yield of 30% on the "enhanced synthetic money market instrument."

	Index − 10%
Cost of stocks	($ 85,000.00)
Sale of stocks, beta 1.50	$ 72,250.00
Loss from stocks	($ 12,750.00)
Contract value of futures (342.55 × $250.00 × 2)	$171,275.00
Value of expiring futures, index down 10% (306.00 × $250.00 × 2)	($153,000.00)
Profit from futures	$ 18,275.00
Dividend income	$ 850.00
TOTAL PROFIT	$ 6,375.00

Of course there is the possibility that the 2.00 beta portfolio will decline *more* than predicted—say, a beta of 2.50 rather than the anticipated

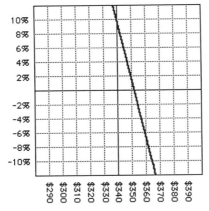

Invest $85,000.00 in stock portfolio with 2.00 beta relative to MMI
Sell 2 futures contracts at 342.55
Index initially at 340.00
Hold for three months, earn $850.00 dividends
2.00 beta portfolio performs at 1.50 beta

FIGURE 9.5. The "synthetic money-market instrument" strategy with a high-beta portfolio, when the portfolio exhibits a lower beta than anticipated

2.00—turning the down-side gain of $6375.00 into a loss of $2125.00. By the same token this performance on the up-side scenario would turn that earlier loss of $2125.00 into a gain of $6375.00. This possibility is illustrated in Figure 9.6, an exact mirror image of Figure 9.5.

	Index Unchanged	Index +10%	Index −10%
Cost of stocks	($ 85,000.00)	($ 85,000.00)	($ 85,000.00)
Sale of stocks, beta 2.50	$ 85,000.00	$106,250.00	$ 63,750.00
Profit (loss) from stocks	0	$ 21,250.00	($ 21,250.00)
Initial contract value of futures	$171,275.00	$171,275.00	$171,275.00
Value of expiring futures	$170,000.00	$187,000.00	$153,000.00
Profit (loss) from futures	($ 1,275.00)	($ 15,725.00)	($ 18,275.00)
Restitution of dividends	($ 850.00)	($ 850.00)	($ 850.00)
TOTAL PROFIT (LOSS)	$ 1,275.00	$ 6,375.00	($ 2,125.00)

Earlier we noted that, although it appeared that the investor was profiting from premium erosion in the short futures contract, the synthetic

213

Invest $85,000.00 in stock portfolio with 2.00 beta relative to MMI
Sell 2 futures contracts at 342.55
Index initially at 340.00
Hold for three months, earn $850.00 dividends
2.00 beta portfolio performs at 2.50 beta

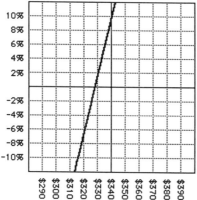

FIGURE 9.6. The "synthetic money-market instrument" strategy with a high-beta portfolio, when the portfolio exhibits a higher beta than anticipated

money market instrument strategy would work just as well if he sold the contract at a discount, provided that was its theoretical value. The only factor that can cause the theoretical value of a futures contract to be at a discount to the index price is an index dividend yield in excess of the riskless interest rate—and if this were the case increased dividend payments would offset losses from discount erosion. But, now, when we are contemplating the notion of selling twice as many futures contracts against the same dollar value of stocks, the increased dividend payments will reimburse only half the losses. As a result, this enhanced version of the synthetic money market strategy only succeeds when the theoretical value of the futures is at a premium to the index.

Earlier we examined the case in which, with a dividend yield of 8% and a riskless interest rate of 7%, the theoretical value of the three-month futures would be 339.15, a discount to the index price of 340.00. Plugging these figures into the 2.00 beta strategy produces quite inferior results—a return of $1275.00, a 6% yield, instead of the anticipated $2125.00, a 10% yield.

	Index Unchanged	Index + 10%	Index − 10%
Cost of stocks	($ 85,000.00)	($ 85,000.00)	($ 85,000.00)
Sale of stocks, beta 2.00	$ 85,000.00	$102,000.00	$ 68,000.00
Profit (loss) from stocks	0	$ 17,000.00	($ 17,000.00)
Initial contract value of futures	$169,575.00	$169,575.00	$169,575.00
Value of expiring futures	($170,000.00)	($187,000.00)	($153,000.00)
Profit (loss) from futures	($ 425.00)	($ 17,425.00)	$ 16,575.00
Dividend income	$ 1,700.00	$ 1,700.00	$ 1,700.00
TOTAL PROFIT	$ 1,275.00	$ 1,275.00	$ 1,275.00

In practice, commission and market impact costs limit the opportunities to implement the synthetic money market instrument strategy. Commissions have to be paid round-turn for both the stocks and the futures, but market impact costs only have to be paid going in. The futures are cash-settled against the closing price of the index at expiration and the stocks can be sold market-on-close; therefore any impact of dumping the stocks will be perfectly offset in the settlement price of the futures.

The position requires the purchase of 50 shares each of the 20 stocks in the index; the portfolio would then contain a total of 1000 shares. At $0.05 per share going in and again coming out, or $0.10 round trip, the total commission cost to trade the stocks would be $100.00.

Total commission		Round-turn commission per share		Number of shares in portfolio
$100.00	=	$0.10	×	1000

The round-trip commission rate for futures comparable to $0.05 per share for stocks would be about $25.00.

For the stocks let's assume that the market impact costs going in would be ⅛ of a point, or $0.125, per share of stock for a total of $125.00.

Total market impact cost		Market impact cost per share		Number of shares in portfolio
$125.00	=	0.125	×	1000

For futures let's assume that market impact costs going in would be $0.05 per contract, or $12.50:

Total market impact cost		Market impact cost per contract		Contract multiplier
$12.50	=	0.05	×	$250.00

The sum of all these transaction costs is $275.00:

Total transaction cost		Commissions		Market impact	
		Stock	Futures	Stock	Futures
$275.00	= $100.00 +	$25.00	+ $125.00 +	$25.00

Over three months the total transaction cost of $275.00 represents an annualized 1.29% on the $85,000.00 investment. For the arbitrage to be profitable an investor would have to wait to implement the strategy until its yield were rich enough to absorb this cost.

Very little can be done about the commissions, but by altering the implementation of the strategy to eliminate market impact total transaction costs can be cut significantly. The difference is in the methodology for establishing the initial position. Instead of buying stocks and selling a futures contract, the investor buys one futures contract and sells another with a more distant maturity. To see how trading this *futures spread* allows an investor to set up the synthetic money market instrument without market impact cost, construct a scenario in which the investor in our preceding example buys one three-month futures contract and sells one six-month contract. With the index at 340.00, if the fair price for the three-month contract is 342.55 (a premium of 2.55 to the index), the fair price for the six-month contract must be 345.10 (a premium of 5.10, or twice 2.55, to the index). The investor would place an order with his broker to sell the spread for a net credit of 2.55.

Net credit to investor		Sell price, 6-month futures		Buy price, 3-month futures
2.55	=	345.10	−	342.55

When this order is executed, the investor will have paid no market impact cost—he entered his order at a limit of 2.55 and would not receive execution at any price worse than that.

The investor would hold the spread in his futures account, margined with Treasury bills, until the expiration of the three-month futures contract. On the day the three-month futures contract expires, he would place market-on-close orders on the New York Stock Exchange to buy the 20 stocks to replace the expiring futures contract. Again, he is paying no market impact cost because any price rise he causes in the stocks by buying them at the market will be perfectly offset in the cash settlement of his expiring futures contract. He is equally indifferent to any price changes in the overall market that may have occurred over the first three months, and for just the same reason: any change in the index will be perfectly offset in the cash settlement of his expiring futures contract.

Now the investor has established the synthetic money market instrument strategy—long stocks against short futures. From this point implementation of the strategy does not differ from the way it was first described. An examination of this strategy as 2 three-month holding periods with the index unchanged, up 10% and down 10% in each period, shows that nine outcomes are possible and each returns $1487.50.

At 3-Month Expiration	Index Unchanged	Index Unchanged	Index Unchanged
Initial value, 3-month contract	($85,637.50)	($ 85,637.50)	($85,637.50)
Expiring value, 3-month contract	$85,000.00	$ 85,000.00	$85,000.00
Profit (loss), 3-month contract	$ 637.50	$ 637.50	$ 637.50

At 6-Month Expiration	Index Unchanged	Index + 10%	Index − 10%
Initial value, 6-month contract	$86,275.00	$ 86,275.00	$86,275.00
Expiring value, 6-month contract	($85,000.00)	($ 93,500.00)	($76,500.00)
Profit (loss), 6-month contract	$ 1,275.00	$ 7,225.00	($ 9,775.00)
Cost of stocks in 3 months	($85,000.00)	($ 85,000.00)	($85,000.00)
Sale of stocks in 6 months	$85,000.00	$ 93,500.00	$76,500.00
Profit (loss) from stocks	0	$ 8,500.00	($ 8,500.00)
Dividend income	$ 850.00	$ 850.00	$ 850.00
TOTAL PROFIT	$ 1,487.50	$ 1,487.50	$ 1,487.50

At 3-Month Expiration	Index +10%	Index +10%	Index +10%
Initial value, 3-month contract	($85,637.50)	($ 85,637.50)	($85,637.50)
Expiring value, 3-month contract	$93,500.00	$ 93,500.00	$93,500.00
Profit (loss), 3-month contract	$ 7,862.50	$ 7,862.50	$ 7,862.50

At 6-Month Expiration	Index Unchanged	Index +10%	Index −10%
Initial value, 6-month contract	$86,275.00	$ 86,275.00	$86,275.00
Expiring value, 6-month contract	($93,500.00)	($102,850.00)	($84,150.00)
Profit (loss), 6-month contract	($ 7,225.00)	($ 16,575.00)	$ 2,125.00
Cost of stocks in 3 months	($93,500.00)	($ 93,500.00)	($93,500.00)
Sale of stocks in 6 months	$93,500.00	$102,850.00	$84,150.00
Profit (loss) from stocks	0	$ 9,350.00	($ 9,350.00)
Dividend income	$ 850.00	$ 850.00	$ 850.00
TOTAL PROFIT	$ 1,487.50	$ 1,487.50	$ 1,487.50

At 3-Month Expiration	Index − 10%	Index − 10%	Index − 10%
Initial value, 3-month contract	($85,637.50)	($ 85,637.50)	($85,637.50)
Expiring value, 3-month contract	$76,500.00	$ 76,500.00	$76,500.00
Profit (loss), 3-month contract	($ 9,137.50)	($ 9,137.50)	($ 9,137.50)

At 6-Month Expiration	Index Unchanged	Index + 10%	Index − 10%
Initial value, 6-month contract	$86,275.00	$86,275.00	$86,275.00
Expiring value, 6-month contract	($76,500.00)	($84,150.00)	($68,850.00)
Profit (loss), 6-month contract	$ 9,775.00	$ 2,125.00	$17,425.00
Cost of stocks in 3 months	($76,500.00)	($76,500.00)	($76,500.00)
Sale of stocks in 6 months	$76,500.00	$84,150.00	$68,850.00
Profit (loss) from stocks	0	$ 7,650.00	($ 7,650.00)
Dividend income	$ 850.00	$ 850.00	$ 850.00
TOTAL PROFIT	$ 1,487.50	$ 1,487.50	$ 1,487.50

The $1487.50 profit, when the spread is sold at 2.55, is identical to the profit realized when the single contract was sold at 342.55, a 2.55 premium to the index—a 7% yield on a three-month investment of $85,000.00. If the spread had been sold for 5.10, the yield would have been 10%, identical to the profit realized when the single futures contract was sold for 345.10, a 5.10 premium to the index. Although the investor has had to bear an extra $25.00 for a second futures commission, all market impact costs have been eliminated at a saving of $150.00. This changes the total transaction cost from $275.00 to $150.00, or, as an annualized percentage of capital, from 1.29 to 0.7%.

It might be argued that with this technique the holding period of the synthetic money market instrument has been implicitly stretched from three months to six. Strictly speaking, this is true, but it must be noted that almost no capital had to be committed until the last three months, when the stocks were purchased to replace the expiring three-month futures contract.

Transaction costs can be reduced even further if the investor elects to hold the synthetic money market instrument longer than the three months initially planned. This can be accomplished by "rolling over" the short

219

futures contract in the position: either buying it back or letting it expire, but either way replacing it with another contract of longer maturity, and continuing to hold the portfolio of stocks for another three months. This rollover adds another $25.00 futures commission to the transaction costs and brings the total up to $200.00, but it also adds three months to the holding period over which the cost can be amortized. As a result transaction costs as an annualized percentage of capital fall from 0.71 to 0.47%. Rolling over a second time three months later would raise the total transaction costs to $225.00 but lower the annualized percentage of 0.35%. A third rollover, extending the life of the synthetic money market instrument to a full year, raises total transaction costs to $250.00 but lowers the annualized percentage to 0.29%.

Another practical burden that encumbers investors who seek to exploit the synthetic money market instrument strategy is the margin requirement imposed on the futures side of the position. Initial margin is the requirement that investors who hold futures contracts post cash or Treasury securities as a performance bond against their positions. To see how this requirement might work against investors, consider the investor in our earlier examples with $85,000.00 capital invested in the Major Market Index's component stocks. Let's assume that this is all the capital he has at his disposal. To sell a futures contract to complete the synthetic money market instrument the investor would have to post the initial margin for hedgers of $1200.00, but because all his capital is tied up in stocks he would have to sell $1200.00 worth of stocks to raise the cash necessary to meet the margin requirement. After this sale, he would own only $83,800.00 worth of stocks, so that now the futures contract, with an underlying value of $85,000.00, is more of a hedge than he needs.

One solution to this problem would be for the investor to borrow against the stocks, buy Treasury bills with the proceeds, and deposit the bills in his brokerage account in satisfaction of the margin requirement. Since in practice the interest rate for borrowing is likely to exceed the yield on Treasury bills, this solution is not without cost. Unfortunately, certain investors are prohibited from borrowing against their stocks even if they were willing to bear this cost.

Another solution to this problem would be to deposit the stocks themselves with the futures brokers to meet the margin requirement. This way the investor is not required to sell any stocks, so the futures contract remains an appropriately sized hedge, but it assumes that the broker will agree to this unconventional arrangement and that the investor is unrestricted as to who may have custody of his stocks.

Yet another problem is variation margin, the requirement that investors who trade futures contracts settle their profits and losses in cash each day, on a mark-to-the-market basis, whether or not the positions are closed out. If the futures side of the synthetic money market instrument moves against the investor and cash in the futures account is insufficient to cover the variation margin requirement, an equity call is issued and the investor must respond by depositing cash. Conversely, if the futures component moves in the investor's favor and variation margin produces a cash excess in the account, he may opt to withdraw and reinvest it.

If we assume the worst case—that the investor has no cash in his futures account and the futures component of his hedge position moves against him, he would have to raise cash to cover his losses, requiring him either to sell some of his stocks or borrow against them. As we've already seen in the context of the initial margin requirement, either of these ways of satisfying the variation margin requirement would degrade performance of the strategy. Of course, conversely, if the futures component moves in favor of the investor, the ability to reinvest the unexpected positive cash flow can enhance performance.

To understand how these effects operate let's return to our first example of the synthetic money market instrument strategy in which the investor bought an $85,000.00 portfolio of the 20 Major Market Index stocks and sold a futures contract at 342.55. Without consideration of the effects of variation margin, his profit was $1487.50, a yield of 7%, regardless of movements of the index during the holding period.

In the case in which the index moves up 10% by expiration, the futures side of the position showed a loss of $7862.50, necessitating a deposit of cash into the futures account to satisfy the variation margin requirement. In practice, the amount of cash required would fluctuate daily with the price of the futures contract. For simplicity let's assume that the full loss in the futures component of the hedge occurred on the very first day of the three-month holding period and never fluctuated from that level. In the circumstances the investor would have had to deposit $7862.50 for three months.

If he borrowed $7862.50 at 7%, he would pay $137.59 in interest over the three-month holding period. This financing cost would reduce the investor's profit from $1487.50 to $1361.19 and the yield from 7% to 6.3%.

In the case in which the index declines 10% by expiration, the effect of variation margin operates precisely the reverse. The variation margin provided by the profit in the futures component of the position gives the investor the use of $9137.50 for three months. At 7% interest, the investor could have earned $159.91. This interest income raises his profit from $1487.50 to $1647.41 and his annualized yield from 7% to 7.7%.

As an intuitive way of characterizing these effects, we could say that
the effect of variation margin makes futures positions appear larger than
they would otherwise be. This is because when the futures component
of a position moves against an investor, the effect makes the move even
worse by requiring the investor to commit cash to finance the variation
margin. When the futures component moves in favor of an investor, the
effect makes the move even more favorable by allowing the investor to
reinvest the variation margin.

If the variation margin effect makes futures positions effectively larger,
it can be neutralized in the example we've been using by reducing the
number of futures contracts sold short. The shorting of fewer contracts
means that the variation margin effects will be offset by adjustments in
the profits on the downside, or losses on the upside, in the futures component of the position.

The simple formula for determining the precise number of futures contracts in the position depends on the holding period of the position—in
this example, three months—and on the interest rate expected to prevail
during the holding period—in this example 7%. According to this formula, instead of shorting one futures contract, the investor would short
only 0.9828 contracts:

Adjusted futures position	Inverse of	One plus	Interest rate	Holding period in year
0.9828 (rounded) =	1 ÷	(1 +	7%) ×	0.25

In the case in which the index moves up 10% the reduction in short
futures contracts reduces the *loss* in the futures component of the position. When considered with the cost of financing the variation margin,
this adjustment effectively returns the same $1487.50 profit originally
anticipated when the synthetic money market instrument was set up. In
the case in which the index is unchanged or declines 10% the reduction
in short futures contracts reduces the *profit* in the futures component of
the position. When considered with the interest income from the reinvestment of variation margin, the return is, once again, the anticipated
$1487.50.

	Index Unchanged	Index +10%	Index −10%
Cost of stocks	($85,000.00)	($85,000.00)	($85,000.00)
Sale of stocks	$85,000.00	$93,500.00	$76,500.00
Profit (loss) from stocks	0	$ 8,500.00	($ 8,500.00)
Initial contract value of futures	$84,164.62	$84,164.62	$84,164.62
Value of expiring futures	($83,538.08)	($91,891.89)	($75,184.27)
Profit (loss) from futures	$ 626.54	($ 7,727.27)	$ 8,980.34
Interest income (7% on $626.54)	$ 10.96		
Interest income (7% on $8980.34)			$ 157.16
Financing cost ($7727.27 at 7%)		($ 135.23)	
Dividend income	$ 850.00	$ 850.00	$ 850.00
TOTAL PROFIT	$ 1,487.50	$ 1,487.50	$ 1,487.50

In the examples it has been granted for the sake of simplicity that the full eventual profit or loss in the futures component of the position was realized immediately upon establishment of the position and underwent no subsequent fluctuations during the holding period. This allowed a single, static adjusted position to be maintained throughout the holding period. In practice, the only way to implement the neutralizing adjustment strategy with exactitude anywhere near the degree possible in the simplified example would be to view the three-month holding period as a connected series of daily periods and to use the formula to recalculate the appropriate adjusted futures position every day. To determine how the passage of time affects the initial adjusted futures position of 0.9828 contracts, let's use the formula to recalculate the position when one-third of the three-month period has elapsed:

Adjusted futures position		Inverse of		One plus		Interest rate		Holding period in year
0.9885 (rounded) =		1	÷	(1	+	7%)	×	0.1667

The adjusted position rises from 0.9828 contracts to 0.9885 contracts. It will continue to rise at a rate of 0.0002 contracts per day until the end of the holding period. As another month passes it will rise to 0.9942 contracts:

Adjusted futures position	Inverse of	One plus		Interest rate		Holding period in year
0.9942 (rounded) =	1	÷	(1	+	7%)	×	0.0833

Finally, with only one day remaining in the holding period, the adjusted position will have risen to 0.9998 contracts:

Adjusted futures position	Inverse of	One plus		Interest rate		Holding period in year
0.9998 (rounded) =	1	÷	(1	+	7%)	×	0.0027

An additional consideration in the periodic readjustment of the futures position is the changes in the interest rate. For any given holding period the higher the interest rate, the smaller the adjusted position; for example, we calculate the adjusted position for a three-month holding period when the interest rate is 10%—0.9756 contracts, compared with 0.9828 at 7%. Raising the interest rate to 20% and recalculating reduces the adjusted position from 0.9756 contracts to 0.9524 contracts:

Adjusted futures position	Inverse of	One plus		Interest rate		Holding period in year
0.9756 (rounded) =	1	÷	(1	+	10%)	×	0.25

Adjusted futures position	Inverse of	One plus		Interest rate		Holding period in year
0.9524 (rounded) =	1	÷	(1	+	20%)	×	0.25

These examples make it clear that if recalculations are not made with respect to changes in the interest rate the adjustment of the futures position will be inaccurate and the neutralizing technique may be less than perfectly effective.

Transaction costs are not a constraint to the practical application of the neutralizing adjustment technique. Because the adjustments gradually move the futures position toward the same number of contracts that would have been sold without the neutralizing technique, the total transaction costs will not be any greater.

In practice, however, there are two difficulties in executing these daily adjustments with sufficient precision to perfectly neutralize the effects of variation margin. First, the position must be large enough so that the daily adjustments can be made in whole contracts. At the rate of 0.0002 contract per day for every contract held the investor would have to start out with almost 5000 contracts to be able to adjust by selling a single whole contract every day. Second, there can be no assurance that the adjustments can be made at fair prices. If the investor is forced to sell severely underpriced contracts, his performance will suffer accordingly.

ARBITRAGE BETWEEN INDEX OPTIONS AND PORTFOLIOS OF STOCK

When the synthetic money market instrument strategy is implemented with futures, the investor is, in effect, making a binding agreement to sell in three months the stock portfolio he is buying today. The strategy can be implemented with index options or options-on-futures instead of futures contracts, but the investor must engineer his options to create the same binding agreement to sell. In other words, the investor must fashion out of options a "synthetic futures contract."

As we discussed earlier, an option contract is binding only on its seller—to the buyer exercising it is a right, not an obligation. And for the seller the obligation will be invoked only at expiration if the option is in-the-money. So to create a short "synthetic futures contract" for use in the synthetic money market instrument strategy an investor must simultaneously *buy a put* (which he will exercise if the index is *below* the strike-price at expiration, thus *receiving* in cash the difference between the strike-price and the index price) and *sell a call* (which will be exercised by its buyer if the index is *above* the strike-price at expiration, thus obligating the investor to *pay* in cash the difference between the strike-price and the index price).

To see this process in action let's rework our earlier example of the synthetic money market instrument strategy using options in this combination. If we assume that the volatility of the MMI is 15%, the options valuation procedure produces a theoretical value for the American, three-month, 340.00-strike-price calls of 11.29, and for the puts a value of 9.10.

When the investor establishes the stock portfolio side of the position, he will have to rescale it to account for the fact that although the futures contracts have a contract multiplier of $250.00 the options have a contract multiplier of only $100.00. So instead of buying 50 shares of each stock in the index, for a total investment of $85,000.00, he would buy only 20 shares of each stock for a total investment of $34,000.00:

Number of shares of each stock to buy, per futures contract		Contract multiplier		Index divisor
20	=	$100.00	÷	5

The investor would set up the options side of the position by simultaneously buying one put option at 9.10 (for an investment of $910.00) and short-selling one call option at 11.29 (for proceeds of $1129.00). Taken together, the options side of the position generates net proceeds of $219.00, which he would invest in Treasury bills:

Cost to buy put		Put price		Contract multiplier
$910.00	=	9.10	×	$100.00

Proceeds from sale of call		Call price		Contract multiplier
$1129.00	=	11.29	×	$100.00

Net proceeds from options position		Proceeds from sale of call		Cost to buy put
$219.00	=	$1129.00	−	$910.00

If the market is unchanged at expiration, both the put and the call expire worthless. The investor's profit consists of the initial proceeds from the options side of the position, the dividends received on the portfolio of stocks, and interest on the Treasury bills—a total of $562.83.

	Index Unchanged
Cost of stocks	($34,000.00)
Sale of stocks	$34,000.00
Profit from stocks	0
Initial cost of put option (9.10 × $100.00)	($ 910.00)
Initial proceeds from call option (11.29 × $100.0)	$ 1,129.00
Exercise value of put option (expires worthless)	0
Exercise value of call option (expires worthless)	0
Profit from options	$ 219.00
Interest on Treasury bills (219.00 at 7% for 3 months)	$ 3.83
Dividend income	$ 340.00
TOTAL PROFIT	$ 562.83

The $562.83 profit is less than the $1487.50 the investor earned when he implemented the synthetic money market instrument strategy with futures, primarily because he has down-scaled the position by investing only $34,000.00 instead of $85,000.00. But his yield has slipped, too, from

7 to 6.6%. We discuss the complex issue shortly that gives rise to this effect.

If the index declines 10% by expiration, from 340.00 to 306.00, the loss in the stock portfolio side of the position is compensated by the exercise value in the put option. The investor's profit is still $562.83, a 6.6% yield for the synthetic money market instrument.

	Index − 10%
Cost of stocks	($34,000.00)
Sale of stocks	$30,600.00
Loss from stocks	($ 3,400.00)
Initial cost of put option (9.10 × $100.00)	($ 910.00)
Initial proceeds from call option (11.29 × $100.00)	$ 1,129.00
Exercise value of put option (34.00 × $100)	$ 3,400.00
Exercise value of call option (expires worthless)	0
Profit from options	$ 3,619.00
Interest on Treasury bills ($219.00 and 7% for 3 months)	$ 3.83
Dividend income	$ 340.00
TOTAL PROFIT	$ 562.83

If the index rises by 10% by expiration from 340.00 to 374.00, the profits in the stock portfolio side of the position are absorbed by the losses in the call option sold short. The investor's profit is still $562.83, a 6.6% yield.

	Index + 10%
Cost of stocks	($34,000.00)
Sale of stocks	$37,400.00
Profit from stocks	$ 3,400.00
Initial cost of put option (9.10 × $100.00)	($ 910.00)
Initial proceeds from call option (11.29 × $100.00)	$ 1,129.00
Exercise value of put option (expires worthless)	0
Exercise value of call option (34.00 × $100)	($ 3,400.00)
Loss from options	($ 3,181.00)
Interest on Treasury bills ($219.00 at 7% for 3 months)	$ 3.83
Dividend income	$ 340.00
TOTAL PROFIT	$ 562.83

Figure 9.7 illustrates the pattern of risks and returns associated with this strategy—the same flat line that always represents the synthetic money market instrument.

Just as the investor in our earlier example received an enhanced yield on his synthetic money market instrument when he was able to sell the futures contract above its theoretical value, he can increase his yield if he can trade his options position for greater net proceeds than the $219.00 the valuation procedure calculated; for example, let's assume that he could buy the put option not for 9.10 but for 8.00 and could sell the call option not for 11.29 but for 12.00. He would invest the net proceeds of $400.00 in Treasury bills:

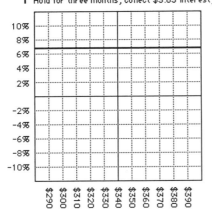

Invest $34,000.00 in all stocks in the Major Market Index
Buy 1 340.00 strike-price put option at 9.10
Sell 1 340.00 strike-price call option at 11.29
Invest $219.00 in Treasury bills
Index initially at 340.00
Hold for three months, collect $3.83 interest, $340.00 dividends

FIGURE 9.7. The "synthetic money-market instrument" with index options

Cost to buy put		Put price		Contract multiplier
− $800.00	=	8.00	×	$100.00

Proceeds from sale of call		Call price		Contract multiplier
$1200.00	=	12.00	×	$100.00

Net proceeds from options position		Proceeds from sale of call		Cost to buy put
$400.00	=	$1200.00	−	$800.00

If the market is unchanged at expiration, his profits are now $747.00, an annualized yield of 8.8%. The investor's profit will be $747.00 regardless of the index price at expiration, as illustrated in Figure 9.8—yet another entirely flat pattern of risks and returns.

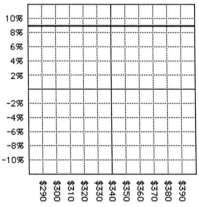

Invest $34,000.00 in all stocks in the Major Market Index
Buy 1 340.00 strike-price put option at 8.00
Sell 1 340.00 strike-price call option at 12.00
Invest $400.00 in Treasury bills
Index initially at 340.00
Hold for three months, collect $7.00 interest, $340.00 dividends

FIGURE 9.8. The "synthetic money-market instrument" with mispriced index options

	Index Unchanged	Index +10%	Index −10%
Cost of stocks	($34,000.00)	($34,000.00)	($34,000.00)
Sale of stocks	$34,000.00	$37,400.00	$30,600.00
Profit (loss) from stocks	0	$ 3,400.00	($ 3,400.00)
Initial cost of put	($ 800.00)	($ 800.00)	($ 800.00)
Initial proceeds from call	$ 1,200.00	$ 1,200.00	$ 1,200.00
Exercise value of put	0	0	$ 3,400.00
Exercise value of call	0	($ 3,400.00)	0
Profit (loss) from options	$ 400.00	($ 3,000.00)	$ 3,800.00
Interest income on T-bills (7% on $400.00 for 3 months)	$ 7.00	$ 7.00	$ 7.00
Dividend income	$ 340.00	$ 340.00	$ 340.00
TOTAL PROFIT	$ 747.00	$ 747.00	$ 747.00

As we considered earlier with futures, the investor would earn sub-stantial arbitrage profits if he could borrow the funds to trade the synthetic money market instrument at any rate below its 8.8% yield. The following formula allows the investor to calculate the initial options proceeds required to justify financing the strategy at a given borrowing rate; for example, assuming that the investor can borrow at 10%, he would require proceeds of $476.63 from the options side of the position for the arbitrage to be profitable:

$$\begin{matrix} \text{Options} \\ \text{proceeds} \end{matrix} = \begin{matrix} \text{Fraction} \\ \text{of} \\ \text{year} \end{matrix} \times \frac{\text{Borrowing rate Cost of stocks Annual dividends}}{\text{One plus Treasury bill rate}}$$

$$\$476.63 = 0.25 \times \frac{(10\% \times \$34,000.00) - \$1360.0}{1.07}$$

If the options were priced so that the net initial proceeds from the options side of the position were *less* than the $219.00 calculated by the valuation model, the investor could profit from the "reverse synthetic money market instrument" strategy, just as he did in an earlier example in which the futures were priced below theoretical value; for example, if the put he would ordinarily buy were priced at 9.50 instead of 9.10, he could sell it, and if the call he would ordinarily sell were priced at 10.50 instead of 11.29 he could buy it. His net initial cost of establishing the options side of the position would be $100.00.

Proceeds from sale of put		Put price		Contract multiplier
$950.00	=	9.50	×	$100.00

Cost to buy call		Call price		Contract multiplier
$1050.00	=	10.50	×	$100.00

Net cost of options position		Cost to buy call		Proceeds from sale of put
$100.00	=	$1050.00	−	$950.00

On the stock side of the position he would sell short a $34,000.00 portfolio of the 20 MMI stocks and reinvest the proceeds (less the $100.00 cost of the options position) in Treasury bills. If the market is unchanged at expiration, his profit is $153.25. It will be the same regardless of the index price at expiration; Figure 9.9 illustrates this now-familiar pattern of returns—a flat line.

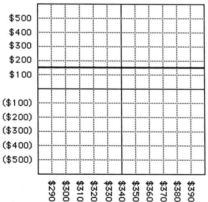

Sell short $34,000.00 in all stocks in the Major Market Index
Buy 1 340.00 strike-price call option at 10.50
Sell 1 340.00 strike-price put option at 9.50
Invest $33,900.00 in Treasury bills
Index initially at 340.00
Hold for three months, collect $593.25 interest, pay $340.00 dividends

FIGURE 9.9. The reverse "synthetic money-market instrument" with mispriced index options

	Index Unchanged	Index + 10%	Index − 10%
Proceeds from short sale of stocks	$34,000.00	$34,000.00	$34,000.00
Cost to repurchase stocks	($34,000.00)	($37,400.00)	($30,600.00)
Profit (loss) from stocks	0	($ 3,400.00)	$ 3,400.00
Initial proceeds from put	$ 950.00	$ 950.00	$ 950.00
Initial cost of call	($ 1,050.00)	($ 1,050.00)	($ 1,050.00)
Exercise value of put	0	0	$34,400.00
Exercise value of call	0	($ 3,400.00)	0
Profit (loss) from options	($ 100.00)	($ 3,300.00)	$ 3,500.00
Interest income on T-bills (7% on $33,900.00 for 3 months)	$ 593.25	$ 593.25	$ 593.25
Restitution of dividends	$ 340.00	$ 340.00	$ 340.00
TOTAL PROFIT	$ 153.25	$ 153.25	$ 153.25

As before, when we examined the reverse synthetic money market instrument strategy with futures, the profit of $153.25 may seem small, but it is earned on a cash investment of zero, and so could be said to represent an infinite return on capital. Using a variation of the formula considered earlier, the investor could calculate how much he could pay for the options component of the position and still earn a profit, given the effective rate at which he could reinvest the proceeds of the short sale; for example, if he can reinvest only three-quarters of the proceeds in Treasury bills, the Treasury bill rate is effectively only three-quarters of 7%, or 5.25%. According to the formula, in these circumstances he can earn arbitrage profits by implementing the reverse synthetic money market instrument strategy only if he can buy the options component of the position for less than $100.95.

Options cost	Fraction of year		Effective T-bill rate: $\dfrac{\text{Stock proceeds} \quad \text{Annual dividends}}{\text{One plus effective Treasury bill rate}}$
$100.95 =	0.25	×	$\dfrac{(5.25\% \times \$34,000.00) - \$1360.0}{1.0525}$

In the choice between options and futures to implement the synthetic money market instrument strategy, the most important consideration may be yield—an investor is probably better off using the instruments that will maximize his return. Nonetheless, a number of subtle differences lie between futures and options that may influence an investor's decision in favor of futures even if options offers a slightly higher return.

The only argument in favor of using options is that it circumvents the problems of initial and variation margin for futures contracts that we discussed earlier. Whereas the synthetic money market instrument strategy with futures required that the investor post initial margin funds beyond what he'd already committed to the portfolio of stocks, the equivalent options position can be margined by a Market Index Option Escrow Receipt backed by the stock portfolio itself.

The first point in favor of use of futures is the fact that transaction costs associated with use of options in the strategy are slightly higher. Earlier we examined the sources of transaction costs when futures are used; now let's perform the same examination with options.

The position we've been using as an example requires buying 20 shares each of the 20 stocks in the MMI; therefore the portfolio would contain a total of 400 shares. At $0.05 per share going in and again coming out, or $0.10 round trip, the total commission cost to trade the stocks would be $40.00:

Total commission		Round-trip commission per share		Number of shares in portfolio
$40.00	=	$0.10	×	400

The commission rate for options comparable to $0.05 per share for stocks would be about $3.00 per contract, going in and again at expiration, for both the put and the call—a total of $12.00.

For the stocks let's assume that the market impact costs going in would be ⅛ of a point, or 0.125, per share of stock, for a total of $125.00. As for futures, because of the cash-settlement mechanism, market impact costs only have to be considered going in, not again at expiration:

Total market impact cost		Market impact cost per share		Number of shares in portfolio
$48.00	=	0.125	×	400

For the options let's assume that market impact costs going in would be ⅛ of a point, or 0.125, per contract, for both the put and the call:

Total call market impact cost		Market impact cost for call		Contract multiplier
$12.50	=	0.125	×	$100.00

Total put market impact cost		Market impact cost for put		Contract multiplier
$12.50	=	0.125	×	$100.00

Total options market impact cost		Total call market impact cost		Total put market impact cost
$25.00	=	$12.50	+	$12.50

The sum of all these transaction costs is $125.00:

Total transaction cost		Commissions		Market impact	
		Stock	Futures	Stock	Futures
$125.00	=	$40.00 +	$12.00 +	$48.00 +	$25.00

Over three months the total transaction cost of $125.00 represents an annualized 1.47% on the $34,000.00 investment, compared with 1.29% when the strategy was implemented with futures.

The techniques we discussed earlier in connection with futures implementation are equally effective with options, but never lower their transaction costs below those of futures. The technique of setting up the strategy through a spread position between expiration months adds another $12.00 in round-trip options commissions but saves the $48.00 market impact costs in the stocks, thus creating a net savings of $36.00. This lowers the total transaction cost to $89.00, or 1%, but it is still higher than 0.71% when this technique was applied with futures.

Extending the maturity of the strategy another three months adds $12.00 in commissions but doubles the holding period. This raises the total transaction cost to $101.00 but lowers the annualized costs to 0.59%, still higher than 0.47% when this technique was applied with futures. A second extension lowers the annualized cost to 0.44%, still higher than 0.35% with futures. A third extension lowers the annualized cost to 0.37%, still higher than 0.29% with futures.

Another argument in favor of futures is execution risk. It can be difficult to execute the synthetic money market instrument strategy because it requires simultaneous trades on two separate exchanges in multiple assets—several hundred of them if an investor chooses to use an index like the New York Stock Exchange Composite or the S&P 500. The use of options exacerbates execution risk because it requires that the investor trade two options—a put and a call—rather than a single futures contract. Many investors set up their synthetic money market instrument trades through specialized brokers who guarantee the execution at an agreed implied yield. But ultimately their performance can be damaged by execution risk too: because the brokers perceive greater risk in using options, they will offer the investors less attractive guarantees than for the comparable trade with futures.

The final risk factor arguing in favor of futures—and one that no broker's guarantee can mitigate—is the risk of exercise prior to expiration of short options in the position. With the exception of the S&P 500 options listed on the Chicago Board Options Exchange and the Institutional Index options on the American Stock Exchange, index options and options-on-futures are subject to exercise at any time. With cash-settled options the possibility of premature assignment of an exercised short options position exposes the synthetic money market instrument strategy to unpredictable, unquantifiable, and potentially catastrophic risk.

Yet, ironically, it is this very risk that causes the synthetic money market instrument strategy executed with options to yield only 6.6% in the earlier example, as opposed to 7% with futures. The valuation procedure calculated options values that led to only a 6.6% yield because, from a certain perspective, premature exercise is not a risk but an advantage. To see why this might be so, let's see how the investor in our example would fare if he chose to exercise the put in his position exactly midway through the three-month holding period. Let's say that the exercise occurs when the index price is 320.00, placing the put 20.00 in-the-money (obviously the investor would never exercise it unless it were in-the-money because it would have no exercise value).

First, the investor would receive in cash the $20.00 by which the strike-price is above the index price, times the contract multiplier, for a total of $2000.00:

Exercise value of put		Strike-price		Index price		Contract multiplier
$2000.00	=	(340.00	−	320.00)	×	$100.00

Next, he would instantaneously liquidate his portfolio of stocks, receiving $32,000. Note that this is $2000.00 less than the $34,000.00 he initially paid for it, which offsets the $2000.00 received in the assignment of the exercise.

Next, he sells the small amount of Treasury bills he had purchased, recouping his principal of $219.00 and 1.05 month's interest of $1.91.

Finally, he buys in his short-call option for whatever price the market is asking, let's say that he pays ⅛ of a point.

	Index at 320.00
Cost of stocks	($34,000.00)
Sale of stocks	$32,000.00
Loss from stocks	($ 2,000.00)
Initial cost of put option (9.10 × $100.00)	($ 910.00)
Initial proceeds from call option (11.29 × $100.00)	$ 1,129.00
Exercise value of put option (20.00 × $100.00)	$ 2,000.00
Repurchase of call option (⅛ × $100.00)	($ 12.50)
Profit from options	$ 2,206.50
Interest on Treasury bills ($219.00 at 7% for 1½ months)	$ 1.91
Dividend income	$ 170.00
TOTAL PROFIT	$ 378.41

The investor's net profit is $378.41, somewhat less than the $562.83 he had anticipated. But, because his holding period was cut in half, his annual yield increased to 8.9%, which is substantially higher than the 6.6% anticipated.

The possibility of enhanced returns through premature exercise is what justifies anticipated returns slightly lower than when the strategy is implemented with futures. But this possibility is contingent on the investor being able to liquidate the stock portfolio and the call at the same moment that he exercises the put. This may be realistic when the investor is in perfect control of the exercise decision, but it is very unrealistic when he finds that his short call has been exercised against him. Holders of options notify the exchange through their brokers of their intention to exercise in the afternoon at the close of trading, but sellers getting assigned generally do not find out about it until just before the opening of trading on the following day—and by that time it may be too late to act.

The risk is that by unexpectedly losing his call position, the investor suddenly finds himself unhedged—one of the three legs of his synthetic money market instrument is gone. He is faced with the choice of liquidating the remaining components of the position or selling new options to replace the exercised ones. Unwinding the unhedged balance of the position is preferable, because by doing so the investor will lock in an enhanced yield. But there is no assurance that this can be done at prices that will be to the investor's liking, especially if the market happens to make an adverse move while he is attempting to trade. Selling new options is not a realistic solution, because they will probably be exercised prematurely, too, creating the problem all over again the next morning.

For an investor who trades the reverse synthetic money market instrument strategy, premature exercise offers all the same risks and has none of the potential advantages. Although in the preceeding example shortening the holding period increased the strategy's yield, traded in reverse it would sharply decrease it. Let's return to the earlier example in which the investor sold the put at 9.50 and bought the call at 10.50, expecting to earn $153.25. If the investor is assigned on the short put midway through the three-month holding period, when the index has declined to 320.00, he would have to pay out the $2000.00 exercise value of the put. Next, he would buy in the portfolio of stocks for $32,000.00, realizing an offsetting profit of $2000.00. Then he would sell his Treasury bills, realizing $296.62 interest. Finally he would sell his call—let's say he receives ⅛ of a point for it.

	Index at 320.00
Proceeds from short-sale of stocks	$34,000.00
Repurchase of stocks	($32,000.00)
Profit from stocks	$ 2,000.00
Initial proceeds from put option (9.50 × $100.00)	$ 950.00
Initial cost of call option (10.50 × $100.00)	($ 1,050.00)
Exercise value of put option (20.00 × $100.00)	($ 2,000.00)
Proceeds from sale of call option (⅛ × $100.00)	$ 12.50
Profit from options	($ 2,087.50)
Interest on Treasury bills ($33,900.00 at 7% for 1½ months)	$ 296.62
Dividend income	($ 170.00)
TOTAL PROFIT	$ 35.12

The resulting profit of $35.12 is only 23% of the anticipated $153.25, earned in 50% of the anticipated holding period—the yield is effectively cut in half. But even this unpleasant scenario is optimistic under the circumstances. There is no certainty that the investor could really buy back the stocks on the morning he receives his assignment notice at prices prevailing the afternoon before when the put was exercised.

If the investor used options-on-futures to set up the synthetic money market instrument, premature exercise would present no risks. When the holder of an options-on-futures contract exercises it, the seller assumes a position in the underlying futures contract with a cost basis equal to the strike-price—the seller of a *call* assumes a *short* futures position and the seller of a *put* assumes a *long* futures position. Premature exercise of one of the options-on-futures in the position does not necessitate liquidating the other two legs because the resulting futures position takes over the work of the exercised option.

There is one unusual circumstance in which premature exercise of options-on-futures will produce windfall profits. Consider the case of an investor who buys a portfolio of stocks designed to closely track the NYSE Composite Index, buys a put option-on-futures, and sells a call option-on-futures. Let's say that the index rises dramatically midway through the holding period and that the short call is exercised, causing the investor to assume a short futures position in its place. If the index stays anywhere above the strike-price through expiration, the position will perform normally and the exercise will not have interfered with its anticipated yield. But if the market declines below the strike-price by expiration, whereas his short call option-on-futures would simply expire worthless, the short futures contract will continue to appreciate point for point—any amount by which the index price closes below the strike-price at expiration will be an unanticipated additional profit.

For an option seller to be able to anticipate when he is likely to be assigned on a short position it is worthwhile to consider what might motivate the buyer of an option to exercise it prematurely. Let's consider the case of an investor who owns a 300.00 strike-price call option on the MMI with one week until expiration with the index priced at 340.00.

One simple factor that might motivate him to exercise his call is liquidity. Deep in-the-money options like this one don't trade frequently, so they tend to be quoted with wide spreads between the bid and offer prices. In our exploration of options valuation we developed the rule for an American call that its value could never be less than the index price minus the strike-price, or in this case 40.00. This is because no alert investor would ever sell it for less when he could easily realize this minimum value simply by exercising. Hence, with the index at 340.00, if the best bid for the 300.00 strike-price call is less than 40.00, the investor, who would otherwise have sold it, may choose to exercise it prematurely as an alternative means of liquidation. Of course, the owner of a put option might prematurely exercise for exactly the same reason.

Another factor motivating possible premature exercise is the payment of dividends in the underlying index. To understand why this might be so let's assume that the investor in the example owns his call option as an explicit alternative to owning a portfolio of stocks making up the index. We'll also assume that the index is to pay a 0.50 dividend the next day, but no more dividends through expiration one week later. In this circumstance the investor holding the call option can choose between, on the one hand, continuing to hold it though expiration and, on the other hand, exercising it and replacing it with a portfolio of the stocks. If he chooses the former, he knows that the underlying index will be marked down by 0.50 on the ex-dividend day, diminishing his option's exercise value by $50.00:

Diminished exercise value of call		Dividend payment		Contract multiplier
$50.00	=	0.50	×	$100.00

If the investor chooses instead to exercise the call and replace it with a portfolio of stocks until expiration, he can avoid losing this exercise value: although the stock portfolio will get marked down on the ex-dividend date, he will be compensated by receipt of the dividend in cash. The cost of a portfolio to replace the call would be $34,000.00—the aggregate strike-price of the call—minus the $4000.00 proceeds from the exercise, for a net replacement cost of $30,000.00

Value of replacement portfolio		Strike-price		Contract multiplier
$34,000.00	=	340.00	×	$100.00

Exercise value of call		Index price	Strike-price		Contract multiplier
$4000.00	=	340.00	− 300.00	×	$100.00

Net cost to replace		Value of replacement portfolio		Exercise value of call
$30,000.00	=	$34,000.00	−	$4000.00

The net cost of purchasing the portfolio of stocks will tie up cash that could otherwise be invested in Treasury bills or incur an outright financing cost if the purchase is fully financed. At the Treasury bill rate of 7% financing $30,000.00 for one week would cost the investor $40.38.

Because the $40.38 financing cost of replacing the option with a portfolio of stocks is less than the $50.00 reduction in exercise value, a case could be made that the call should be exercised prematurely.

However, an investor should never decide to exercise prematurely on the sole basis of this logic because there is an additional benefit of continuing to hold the call through expiration that we have not examined so far—the benefit of limited risk. By holding the call the most the investor can lose is the $4000.00 he could have received by exercising; but if he replaces it with a stock portfolio, he stands to lose the entire $30,000.00 net cost. Quantifying the benefits of this risk limitation is not as easy as the previous calculation, but fortunately the options valuation procedure holds a simple answer. If we eliminate the steps in the procedure that check for violations of the minimum price rules applicable to American options, the procedure will compute the value of a European option, an option that cannot be exercised early. If this European value is less than the current exercise value of the call, the procedure is telling us that the call is worth more dead than alive—it should be prematurely exercised and replaced with a portfolio of stock.

It is important to note that the holder of a call need never have to consider exercising on the basis of this reasoning at any time other than just before an ex-dividend day. If his purpose is only to prevent the reduction of exercise value due to an ex-dividend markdown of the index, he might as well wait until the last minute to exercise to delay paying the financing cost on the replacement stock position for as long as possible. Therefore as a general rule we can expect to see more premature exercises of index calls just before large ex-dividend days.

Similar, but inverse, considerations may motivate the premature exercise of a put option. For a put an upcoming ex-dividend date makes the put *more* desirable to hold. When the index price is marked down the following day, the put's exercise value will *increase* by $50.00. And because the replacement stock is sold short, rather than paying a financing charge the investor can *earn* interest on it. Of course, the risk limitation benefit of the put versus a portfolio of stocks still argues against exercising.

As with a call, the way to determine whether a put should be exercised prematurely is to calculate its European value. This value is less than the put's current exercise value, the put should be exercised and replaced with a portfolio of short stock.

ARBITRAGE BETWEEN INDEX OPTIONS AND INDEX FUTURES

We've seen that index futures can be arbitraged against portfolios of stocks. Index options can be also when they are fashioned into synthetic futures contracts. So it stands to reason that index options can be arbitraged against index futures.

For this section we use the New York Stock Exchange Composite Index because it underlies all three types of index instrument—options, futures, and options-on-futures. Let's say that the index price is 140.00, the volatility is 15%, the annual dividend yield is 4%, and the interest rate is 7%. In these circumstances the futures valuation formula would value the three-month futures contracts at 141.05; the options valuation procedure would value the three-month, 140.00-strike-price calls at 4.70, and the puts at 3.78.

First let's see what would happen if an investor brought one futures contract at 141.05 and sold against it one synthetic futures contract, by simultaneously buying five puts at 3.78 and selling short five calls at 4.70. The investor must trade five synthetic futures contracts against one actual futures contract because their contract multipliers are $100.00 and $500.00, respectively. The options side of the trade will produce initial net proceeds of $460.00, with which the investor would purchase Treasury bills:

Cost to buy put		Put price		Contract multiplier		Number of contracts
$1890.00	=	3.78	×	$100.00	×	5

Proceeds from sale of call		Call price		Contract multiplier		Number of contracts
$2350.00	=	4.70	×	$100.00	×	5

Net proceeds from options position		Proceeds from sale of call		Cost to buy put
$460.00	=	$2350.00	−	$1890.00

Figure 9.10 illustrates the pattern of risks and returns associated with

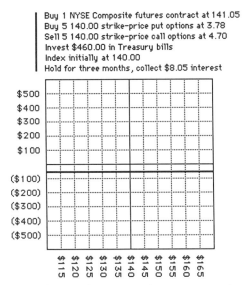

Buy 1 NYSE Composite futures contract at 141.05
Buy 5 140.00 strike-price put options at 3.78
Sell 5 140.00 strike-price call options at 4.70
Invest $460.00 in Treasury bills
Index initially at 140.00
Hold for three months, collect $8.05 interest

FIGURE 9.10. Arbitrage between index options and index futures

this strategy—another straight, flat line. Whether the index is unchanged, up or down at expiration, the position generates a *loss* of $56.95.

	Index Unchanged	Index +10%	Index −10%
Initial contract value of futures	($70,525.00)	($70,525.00)	($70,525.00)
Expiration value of futures	$70,000.00	$77,000.00	$63,000.00
Profit (loss) from futures	($ 525.00)	$ 6,475.00	($ 7,525.00)
Initial cost of puts	($ 1,890.00)	($ 1,890.00)	($ 1,890.00)
Initial proceeds from calls	$ 2,350.00	$ 2,350.00	$ 2,350.00
Exercise value of puts	0	0	$ 7,000.00
Exercise value of calls	0	($ 7,000.00)	0
Profit (loss) from options	$ 460.00	($ 6,540.00)	$ 7,460.00
Interest income on T-bills (7% on $460.00 for 3 months)	$ 8.05	$ 8.05	$ 8.05
TOTAL LOSS	($ 56.95)	($ 56.95)	($ 56.95)

At first glance we might expect that a riskless position like this, traded at theoretical value and requiring no initial cash investment, should precisely break even. But because of the possible advantages of premature exercise that we examined earlier, the theoretical values justify this small loss when the position is held all the way into expiration. But just as before the possibility of premature exercise holds risk as well as opportunity.

If the investor believed that the valuation procedure's assessment of the value of the premature exercise component was erroneous, he could earn a profit by executing the arbitrage in reverse—selling the futures contract, selling the puts, and buying the calls. This way the options component would generate an initial cost of $460.00 that would have to be financed, but the reverse arbitrage would still turn the previous loss of $56.95 into a profit of $56.95. This profit would be earned regardless of the index price at expiration, as illustrated in Figure 9.11.

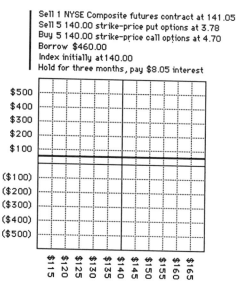

FIGURE 9.11. Reverse arbitrage between index options and index futures

	Index Unchanged	Index +10%	Index −10%
Initial contract value of futures	$70,525.00	$70,525.00	$70,525.00
Expiration value of futures	($70,000.00)	($77,000.00)	($63,000.00)
Profit (loss) from futures	$ 525.00	($ 6,475.00)	$ 7,525.00
Initial cost of puts	$ 1,890.00	$ 1,890.00	$ 1,890.00
Initial proceeds from calls	($ 2,350.00)	($ 2,350.00)	($ 2,350.00)
Exercise value of puts	0	0	($ 7,000.00)
Exercise value of calls	0	$ 7,000.00	0
Profit (loss) from options	($ 460.00)	$ 6,540.00	$ 7,460.00
Financing cost ($460.00 at 7%)	($ 8.05)	($ 8.05)	($ 8.05)
TOTAL PROFIT	$ 56.95	$ 56.95	$ 56.95

A profit could be earned on the arbitrage—without betting against the procedure's valuation of the premature exercise factor—if the index instruments involved were sufficiently mispriced; for example, let's return to our initial example in which the investor buys a futures contract, buys puts, and sells calls. But this time we'll change the prices in the investor's favor: 140.50 for the futures, 3.50 for the puts, and 4.85 for the calls. The options component of the position would generate initial proceeds of $675.00, instead of the $460.00 seen before.

Cost to buy put		Put price		Contract multiplier		Number of contracts
1750.00	=	3.50	×	$100.00	×	5

Proceeds from sale of call		Call price		Contract multiplier		Number of contracts
2425.00	=	4.85	×	$100.00	×	5

Net proceeds from options position		Proceeds from sale of call		Cost to buy put
$675.00	=	$2425.00	−	$1750.00

At these prices the position would generate a profit of $436.81, regardless of the index price at expiration, as illustrated in Figure 9.12.

245

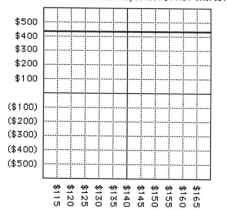

```
Buy 1 NYSE Composite futures contract at 140.50
Buy 5 140.00 strike-price put options at 3.50
Sell 5 140.00 strike-price call options at 4.85
Invest $675.00 in Treasury bills
Index initially at 140.00
Hold for three months, collect $11.81 interest
```

FIGURE 9.12. Arbitrage between mispriced index options and index futures

	Index Unchanged	Index +10%	Index −10%
Initial contract value of futures	($70,250.00)	($70,250.00)	($70,250.00)
Expiration value of futures	$70,000.00	$77,000.00	$63,000.00
Profit (loss) from futures	($ 525.00)	$ 6,475.00	($ 7,525.00)
Initial cost of puts	($ 1,750.00)	($ 1,750.00)	($ 1,750.00)
Initial proceeds from calls	$ 2,425.00	$ 2,425.00	$ 2,425.00
Exercise value of puts	0	0	$ 7,000.00
Exercise value of calls	0	($ 7,000.00)	0
Profit (loss) from options	$ 675.00	($ 6,325.00)	$ 7,675.00
Interest income on T-bills (7% on $675.00 for 3 months)	$ 11.81	$ 11.81	$ 11.81
TOTAL PROFIT	$ 436.81	$ 436.81	$ 436.81

A simple formula that an investor can use determines the profitability of this arbitrage, given any set of prices for the index instruments:

246

Arbitrage profit		Call price		Put price		One + periodic rate
$436.81	=	{[($4.85	−	$3.50)	×	1.0175]
		Futures price		Index price		Contract multiplier
	−	($140.50	−	$140.00)}	×	$500.00

A simple transformation of the formula makes it appropriate for calculating the potential profits of the reverse arbitrage:

Arbitrage profit		Futures price		Index price
$56.95	=	{$141.05	−	$140.00
		Call price	Put price	One + periodic rate	Contract multiplier
	−	[($4.65 | − | $3.73)	×	1.0175]}	×	$500.00

ARBITRAGE BETWEEN CASH-SETTLED INDEX OPTIONS AND OPTIONS-ON-FUTURES

In our exploration of the valuation of index options and options-on-futures, we discovered that while their *expiration values* are identical, the *current values* of these two types of options are somewhat different; for example, although the NYSE Composite cash-settled call in our earlier example was valued at 4.70 with the index at 140.00, the otherwise identical call option-on-futures would be valued at 4.72. Let's see if we can earn arbitrage profits by simultaneously buying the lower valued cash-settled call and selling the higher valued call option-on-futures.

We could imagine an extreme condition that might lead to the call options-on-futures being priced even higher over the cash-settled calls than they are now. For instance, if the futures contract underlying the call were priced at 145.00 instead of the theoretical value of 141.05, the call options-on-futures could not be priced less than 5.00, because the minimum value of an American call option-on-futures cannot be less than the futures price minus the strike-price. But we won't invoke this extreme condition for this example—we'll assume that an investor is satisfied trying to capture just the 0.02 difference between the theoretical values of 4.70 and 4.72 (this minute difference is probably an artifact of the valuation procedure, but it is nonetheless instructive as an example).

The investor would sell one call option-on-futures at 4.72 and simultaneously buy five cash-settled calls at 4.70 each. As earlier, the investor must buy five cash-settled calls against one call option-on-futures because their contract multipliers are $100.00 and $500.00, respectively. Establishing the position, the investor receives proceeds of $2360.00 from the sale of the call option-on-futures but he must pay $2350.00 for the cash-settled calls. He can invest the $10.00 net proceeds in Treasury bills.

Proceeds from sale of call option-on-futures		Call price		Contract multiplier		Number of contracts
$2360.00	=	4.72	×	$500.00	×	1

Cost to buy cash-settled calls		Call price		Contract multiplier		Number of contracts
$2350.00	=	4.70	×	$100.00	×	5

Net initial proceeds from arbitrage		Proceeds from sale of call option-on futures		Cost to buy cash-settled call
$10.00	=	$2360.00	−	$2350.00

At expiration, if the index is unchanged or lower, both options will expire worthless and the investor's profit will be the initial proceeds of $10.00 plus interest on the Treasury bills, a total of $10.18 earned on a cash investment of zero. If the index rises 10% by expiration, from 140.00 to 154.00, the exercise value of the long cash-settled calls will be equal to the exercise value of the short call options-on-futures—the two will cancel out and the investor's profit remains $10.18. Figure 9.13 illustrates the pattern of risks and returns associated with this strategy—another flat line.

	Index Unchanged	Index + 10%	Index − 10%
Initial proceeds from call o-o-f	$2,360.00	$2,360.00	$2,360.00
Expiration value of call o-o-f	0	($7,000.00)	0
Profit (loss) from call o-o-f	$2,360.00	($4,640.00)	$2,360.00
Initial cost of cash calls	($2,350.00)	($2,350.00)	($2,350.00)
Expiration value of cash calls	0	$7,000.00	0
Profit (loss) from cash calls	($2,350.00)	$4,650.00	($2,350.00)
Interest income on T-bills (7% on $10.00 for 3 months)	$ 0.18	$ 0.18	$ 0.18
TOTAL PROFIT	$ 10.18	$ 10.18	$ 10.18

For this arbitrage, premature exercise holds out the possibility of important benefits. If the price relationship between the options comes into

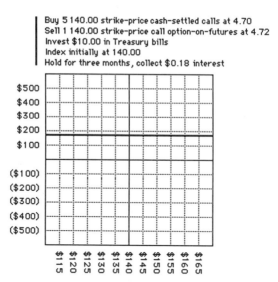

Buy 5 140.00 strike-price cash-settled calls at 4.70
Sell 1 140.00 strike-price call option-on-futures at 4.72
Invest $10.00 in Treasury bills
Index initially at 140.00
Hold for three months, collect $0.18 interest

FIGURE 9.13. Arbitrage between American cash-settled calls and American call options-on-futures

line before expiration and the investor wishes to unwind the position early, it may be to his advantage to do this by exercising his long cash-settled calls simply as an alternative to selling them. On the other hand, if he is assigned on his short call option-on-futures, it will be replaced by a short futures contract. If the index rises after the assignment, gains in the cash-settled calls will perfectly offset losses in the short futures contract. But if the index declines through the strike-price after the assignment, the investor will earn windfall profits. Whereas his short call option-on-futures would have merely expired worthless, the short futures contract that replaces it will continue to appreciate point for point with any index decline.

The theoretical values of the otherwise identical *puts* are 3.78 and 3.69 for cash-settled and futures-settled, respectively. These prices might have led the investor to put on the arbitrage in *reverse*—selling the cash-settled puts and buying the put option-on-futures. But for this strategy, premature exercise represents nothing but risk. If the investor is assigned on his short cash-settled puts, he will suddenly find himself holding the long put option-on-futures completely unhedged. If he is unable to liquidate it at favorable prices, he may experience a loss. On the other hand, if he chooses to exercise his long put option-on-futures, it will be replaced with a short futures contract. If the index is above the strike-price after the exercise, the investor's short cash-settled puts will expire worthless but his short futures contract will continue to go against him point for point above the strike-price with any rally.

Since premature exercise is a benefit to the investor who trades the arbitrage and a risk to the investor who trades the *reverse* arbitrage, there is a case to be made that the valuation procedure should be revised to take this into account. Such a revision would create somewhat higher theoretical values for cash-settled options than for options-on-futures, forcing investors who trade the arbitrage to compensate those who trade the reverse for the risk they bear.

An intriguing variation on the arbitrage, and one that introduces new questions about the consequences of premature exercise, uses options on the S&P 500 Index. The cash-settled options on this index are European, so they cannot be prematurely exercised, whereas the options-on-futures are American, so they can be exercised at any time. With the S&P 500 at 240.00, the theoretical value of a three-month, 240.00-strike-price, European, cash-settled put is 6.27, and the value of an otherwise identical American put option-on-futures is 6.32. Let's see what might happen if an investor bought five European cash-settled puts at 6.27 and sold one American put option-on-futures at 6.32. Here again, the investor must buy five cash-settled puts against one put option-on-futures because their contract multipliers are $100.00 and $500.00, respectively. Establishing the position, the investor receives proceeds of $3160.00 from the sale of the put option-on-futures but must pay $3135.00 for the cash-settled puts. The $25.00 net proceeds can be invested in Treasury bills to earn $0.44 interest:

Proceeds from sale of put option-on-futures		Put price		Contract multiplier		Number of contracts
$3160.00	=	6.32	×	$500.00	×	1

Cost to buy cash-settled put		Put price		Contract multiplier		Number of contracts
$3135.00	=	6.27	×	$100.00	×	5

Net initial proceeds from arbitrage		Proceeds from sale of put option-on futures		Cost to buy cash-settled put
$25.00	=	$3160.00	−	$3135.00

At expiration, regardless of the price of the index, the investor's profit will be the initial proceeds of $25.00 plus interest on the Treasury bills—a total of $25.44. Figure 9.14 illustrates this pattern of risks and returns, yet another flat line.

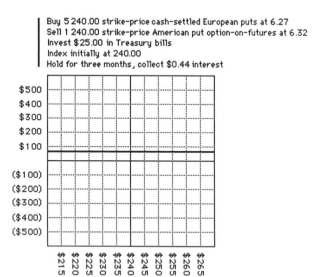

FIGURE 9.14. Arbitrage between European cash-settled calls and American call options-on-futures

	Index Unchanged	Index + 10%	Index − 10%
Initial proceeds from put o-o-f	$3,160.00	$ 3,160.00	$3,160.00
Expiration value of put o-o-f	0	($12,000.00)	0
Profit (loss) from put o-o-f	$3,160.00	($ 8,840.00)	$3,160.00
Initial cost of cash puts	($3,135.00)	($ 3,135.00)	($3,135.00)
Expiration value of cash puts	0	$12,000.00	0
Profit (loss) from cash puts	($3,315.00)	8,865.00	($3,135.00)
Interest income on T-bills			
(7% on $25.00 for 3 months)	$ 0.44	$ 0.44	$ 0.44
TOTAL PROFIT	$ 25.44	$ 25.44	$ 25.44

Because the long cash-settled put is European, the investor cannot exercise it prematurely under any circumstance. But if the index were to decline and the investor were assigned on the short American put option-on-futures, it would be replaced by a long futures contract. If the index then remained below the strike-price at expiration, the expiration value of the long futures contract and the exercise value of the long cash-settled puts would cancel each other out, and the investor would end up earning no more or less than the anticipated $25.44 profit. If, on the other hand, the index rose above the strike-price by expiration, the investor would earn windfall profits—his long cash-settled puts would expire worthless but the long futures contract would appreciate point for point as the index rose.

Unlike the previous arbitrage strategy, doing this arbitrage in *reverse* presents none of the risk from premature exercise we discussed earlier. Because the short cash-settled option cannot be prematurely exercised, the investor will never be left holding the put option-on-futures unhedged. On the other hand, exercising the long put option-on-futures, thus converting it into a short futures contract, could expose the investor to risk. If the index moves up through the strike-price, the cash-settled puts will expire worthless, while the short futures contract will go against the investor point for point. However, exercising the long option-on-futures is *strictly voluntary*; unless it is a conscious choice, the investor need never be exposed to this risk.

Because neither the arbitrage nor the reverse arbitrage suffers from the risk of premature exercise, any time cash-settled European options and otherwise identical American options-on-futures are trading at divergent prices there is a realistic opportunity to earn arbitrage profits on a cash investment of zero.

253

10. HEDGING WITH INDEX OPTIONS AND FUTURES

The literature of the options and futures markets portrays a marketplace populated by three types of economic entities—speculators, who use the convenience and leverage of options and futures to take deliberately risky positions; hedgers, who use the liquidity of the options and futures markets to reduce risks they bear in the underlying market; and arbitrageurs, who exploit mispricings and keep the markets efficient. So far we have examined strategies for speculators and arbitrageurs. Now we will concentrate on strategies for hedgers.

Because index options and futures make hedging easy and economical, there has been a groundswell of interest in risk-control strategies since these instruments were first introduced. Specialized investment advisory firms have gone into business offering such "engineered investment products" as "portfolio insurance" and "overwriting," and in just a few years have placed billions of dollars under management. Whereas not long ago institutional investors had to prove their prudence in using options and futures, now those who have been slow to adopt the new risk-control strategies are having to justify why they are *not* using them.

USING INDEX FUTURES TO ELIMINATE THE MARKET COMPONENT OF PORTFOLIO RISK

The goal of many investment strategies is to select portfolios that will outperform the broad market. When the market rises, such portfolios will rise more; when the market declines, such portfolios will decline less. It used to be that, if a portfolio manager were bearish on the broad market, the only way he could protect his portfolio was to liquidate all or part of it. Now, with index futures, a manager can easily eliminate any amount of the market component of risk in his portfolio without disturbing the assets in it. At the extreme, index futures can entirely immunize portfolios of selected stocks from the effects of the broad market. In such an immunized portfolio results can be positive even during periods when the broad market is sharply lower, and even if the portfolio slightly underperforms.

To see how this technique works let's consider the case of an investor who owns a portfolio of specially selected stocks valued at $1,200,000.00 with a dividend yield of 4%. Let's say that, because of superior stock selection, the portfolio's returns move up and down with the market but consistently outperform it by 6% every year. In the language of Modern Portfolio Theory, it would be said that the portfolio has a *beta* of 1.00 and an *alpha* of 6%.

Figure 10.1 illustrates the pattern of risks and returns for this portfolio over a three-month period over a range of prices for the broad market, represented by the S&P 500 Index. A simple formula can tell us how this portfolio will perform relative to a given move in the broad market. For example, if the market returns 5% over three months, the return to the portfolio will be 6.5% (to orient the formula for a three-month holding period, we'll express the annual alpha of 6% as a quarterly alpha of 1.5%):

Portfolio return		Broad market return		Portfolio beta		Portfolio alpha
6.5%	=	(5%	×	1.00)	+	1.5%

Let's say the investor believes there is a chance that there will be a broad market decline over the coming three months but his research indicates that his selected stocks are still worth holding for the long term. His scenario is that the price of the S&P 500 Index will decline by 15%, offset by receipt of 1% in dividends, for a net return of −14%. If the decline materializes and he takes no defensive action, we can calculate the consequences for his portfolio using the formula.

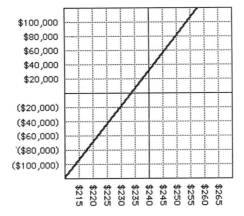

$1,200,000.00 in portfolio of selected stocks
Annual yield = 4%
Annual alpha = 6%
Beta = 1.00
Index initially at 240.00
Hold for three months, earn $12,000.00 dividends

FIGURE 10.1. Holding an active portfolio unhedged

Portfolio return		Broad market return		Portfolio beta		Portfolio alpha
− 12.5%	=	(− 14%	×	1.00)	+	1.5%

The decline would take the price of the portfolio down 13.5%, for a loss of $162,000.00. But receipt of dividend income of $12,000.00 lowers the investor's net loss over the three-month period to $150,000.00, or 12.5% of portfolio value, just as the formula predicted.

	Index − 15%
Value of stocks at beginning of period	($1,200,000.00)
Value of stocks at end of period	$1,038,000.00
Loss from stocks	($ 162,000.00)
Dividends received	$ 12,000.00
TOTAL LOSS	($ 150,000.00)
PERCENTAGE LOSS	(12.5%)

257

As a more defensive alternative, let's say that he chooses to liquidate half his portfolio, parking the proceeds safely in Treasury bills yielding 7% until the anticipated decline has run its course. The benefit of this move is that by converting half his portfolio to cash equivalents he halves his exposure to the broad market, cutting the portfolio's beta from 1.00 to 0.50. The catch is that, now that half the carefully selected stocks are gone, he has cut his alpha in half, from a quarterly 1.5 to 0.75%. We can use the formula to predict how the portfolio will weather the decline, but we'll have to adjust it to account for the fact that by converting half his 4%-yield portfolio to 7% Treasury bills he has increased the portfolio's yield. We transform the 7% annual rate to a 1.75% quarterly rate and then halve it to 0.875% to reflect the fact that only half the value of the portfolio is invested at this yield:

Portfolio return	Broad market return	Portfolio beta	Portfolio alpha	Yield improvement
−5.375% =	(−14%	× 0.50)	+ 0.75%	+ 0.875%

Again the stocks decline 13.5%, but this time only half the portfolio is invested in them, so the loss is half what it was in the previous example—$81,000.00. Dividend income is halved to $6,000.00, but the Treasury bills purchased with the proceeds from selling half the stocks will yield $10,500.00. The investor's net loss over the three-month period is lowered from $150,000.00 to $64,500.00, or from 12.5% of his portfolio value to 5.375%, just as the formula predicted.

	Index −15%
Value of stocks at beginning of period	($ 600,000.00)
Value of stocks at end of period	$ 519,000.00
Loss from stocks	($ 81,000.00)
Dividends received	6,000.00
Interest income ($600,000.00 at 7% for 3 months)	$ 10,500.00
TOTAL LOSS	($ 64,500.00)
PERCENTAGE LOSS	(5.375%)

Ideally, the investor would prefer some means whereby he could maintain the best elements of this defensive strategy—cutting his beta in half and earning extra interest income—but simultaneously avoid the negative element—cutting his alpha in half. Happily, index futures allow him to do just that.

Let's say that the S&P 500 Index is at 240.00. As we saw earlier, if its yield is 4%, and the Treasury bill rate is 7%, the three-month futures would have a theoretical value of 241.80. Each contract represents an underlying value of $120,000.00, so to simulate selling half of his $1,200,000.00 portfolio, the investor would sell five contracts:

Underlying value		Index price		Contract multiplier
$120,000.00	=	240.00	×	$500.00

Number of contracts to sell		Value of portfolio	Percentage to be hedged	Underlying value
5	=	($1,200,000.00 ×	50%)	÷ $120,000.00

If the sale of index futures accomplishes the goal of halving the beta, improving yield, and preserving alpha, the portfolio's performance in a decline, as predicted by the formula, will be a loss of 4.625%—an improvement over the 5.375% loss experienced in the previous example.

Portfolio return		Broad market return	Portfolio beta	Portfolio alpha	Yield improvement
−4.625%	=	(−14% ×	0.50)	+ 1.5%	+ 0.875%

The stocks decline 13.5%, and the portfolio is fully invested, so the loss in stocks is back to what it was in the first example—$162,000.00—and dividend income is back to $12,000.00. The Treasury bills are gone, so there is no interest income. But there is profit in the futures contracts of $94,000.00, compensating for the loss in the stocks and the absence of extra interest income. The investor's net loss over the three-month period is lowered from $64,500.00 to $55,500.00, or from 5.375% of his portfolio value to 4.625%, just as the formula predicted.

	Index – 15%
Value of stocks at beginning of period	($1,200,000.00)
Value of stocks at end of period	$1,038,000.00
Loss from stocks	($ 162,000.00)
Initial market value of futures (241.80 × $500.00 × 5)	$ 604,500.00
Expiration value of futures (204.00 × $500.00 × 5)	($ 510,000.00)
Profit from futures	$ 94,500.00
Dividends received	$ 12,000.00
TOTAL LOSS	($ 55,500.00)
PERCENTAGE LOSS	(4.625%)

That selling index futures contracts against stocks should be a substitute for Treasury bills should be no surprise—in the discussion of index futures arbitrage we called this strategy the synthetic money market instrument. The key difference here between buying real Treasury bills and synthesizing them with index futures is that the futures allow the investor to retain his alpha. The patterns of risks and returns associated with these two approaches to hedging the portfolio is illustrated in Figure 10.2. They are both straight lines, sloped not quite so steeply as the previous pattern. For both the price of down-side protection is a reduction in upside potential. But the line associated with the futures strategy dominates the line associated with the Treasury bill strategy because of the retained alpha.

Using index futures to hedge portfolios is uniquely convenient and appropriate in many institutional contexts, especially in those in which an investor hires multiple managers to independently manage separate components of his total portfolio. In such an environment, the decision to reduce stock holdings to half across an entire portfolio would require that each manager be instructed to liquidate dozens, or perhaps hundreds, of individual stocks. The communications burden of so instructing them is onerous to begin with, but it pales beside the losses the managers may well run up in brokerage commission and market impact costs as they liquidate. By selling index futures, the entire portfolio can be hedged directly by the investor with a single trade—the multiple managers not only don't have to be disturbed, they don't even have to know about it.

In an extreme an investor may wish to sell enough futures to entirely eliminate market risk, to turn his portfolio into an "enhanced synthetic money-market instrument." Regardless of what the broad market returns, the portfolio would return the Treasury bill rate plus alpha. In the

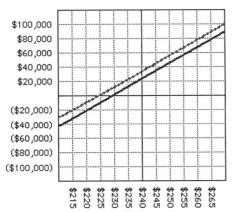

$1,200,000.00 portfolio of selected stocks
Annual yield = 4%
Annual alpha = 6%
Beta = 1.00
Index initially at 240.00

Sell $6,000,000.00 of stocks
Buy $6,000,000.00 Treasury bills
Hold for three months, earn $6000.00 dividends, $10,500.00 interest

Sell 5 S&P 500 Index futures contracts at 241.80
Hold for three months, earn $12,000.00 dividends

FIGURE 10.2. Hedging an active portfolio by (a) selling half the portfolio or (b) selling index futures.

example we've been working with, this would be 3.25% quarterly, or 13% annually.

Portfolio return		Broad market return		Portfolio beta		Portfolio alpha		Yield improvement
3.25%	=	(− 14%	×	0)	+	1.5%	+	1.75%

To do this the investor would simply sell 10 S&P 500 Index futures contracts instead of five. Now, when the market declines, price appreciation and premium erosion in the futures contracts totaling $189,000.00 will entirely offset losses in the stocks, converting the portfolio's return for the quarter to a profit of $39,000.00, the predicted 3.25%.

	Index − 15%
Value of stocks at beginning of period	($1,200,000.00)
Value of stocks at end of period	$1,038,000.00
Loss from stocks	($ 162,000.00)
Initial market value of futures (241.80 × $500.00 × 10)	1,209,000.00
Expiration value of futures, market down 15% (204.00 × $500.00 × 10)	($1,020,000.00)
Profit from futures	$ 189,500.00
Dividends received	$ 12,000.00
TOTAL PROFIT	$ 39,000.00
PERCENTAGE PROFIT	3.25%

Of course, in the event of a rise in the market, losses in the index futures would offset any gains in the stocks. Figure 10.3 illustrates the pattern of risks and returns associated with this strategy—the flat line

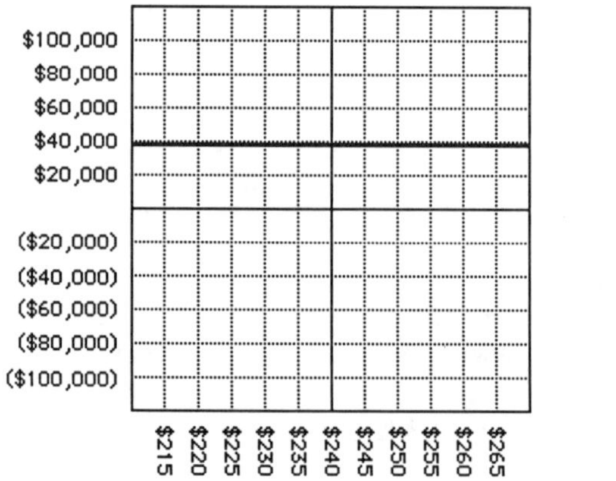

$1,200,000.00 portfolio of selected stocks
Annual yield = 4%
Annual alpha = 6%
Beta = 1.00
Index initially at 240.00

Sell 10 S&P 500 Index futures contracts at 241.80
Hold for three months, earn $12,000.00 dividends

FIGURE 10.3. Converting the active portfolio into a "synthetic money-market instrument"

characteristics of the fully hedged strategies, shifted slightly upward in the chart to reflect the retained alpha.

Now let's complicate the situation by changing one of our key assumptions. Let's say the stocks in the portfolio have a beta of 1.20, rather than 1.00. This means they will return 120% of any return of the broad market. If the market returns 10%, the stock portfolio will return 12%; if the market returns −10%, they will return −12%. We can see by inserting this higher beta into our formula that the portfolio is now at substantially greater risk in the event of a decline. Now the unhedged portfolio stands to lose 15.3% in the decline in our examples, rather than 12.5% as before.

Portfolio return		Broad market return		Portfolio beta		Portfolio alpha
− 15.3%	=	(− 14%	×	1.20)	+	1.5%

The decline would take the price of his portfolio down 16.3% for a loss of $195,600.00. But receipt of dividend income of $12,000.00 lowers the investor's net loss over the three-month period to $183,600.00, or 15.3% of his portfolio value, just as the formula predicted.

	Index − 15%
Value of stocks at beginning of period	($1,200,000.00)
Value of stocks at end of period	$1,004,400.00
Loss from stocks	($ 195,600.00)
Dividends received	$ 12,000.00
TOTAL LOSS	($ 183,600.00)
PERCENTAGE LOSS	(15.3%)

Figure 10.4 illustrates the pattern of risks and returns associated with this higher risk portfolio. It is still a straight line, but it is more steeply sloped than with the 1.00 beta portfolio. The higher beta has the effect of making the portfolio *effectively larger*, exposing it to greater upside gains and greater down-side losses. So to achieve a given risk reduction we will have to sell more index futures contracts. All we have to do is multiply the number of contracts it would ordinarily take to hedge a given dollar value in stocks by beta; for example, to hedge the entire value of the portfolio would require 12 contracts.

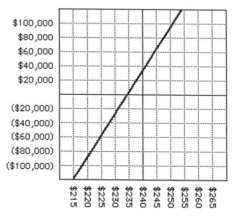

$1,200,000.00 in portfolio of selected stocks
Annual yield = 4%
Annual alpha = 6%
Beta = 1.20
Index initially at 240.00
Hold for three months, earn $12,000.00 dividends

FIGURE 10.4. Holding a high-beta active portfolio unhedged

Number of contracts to sell	Value of portfolio	Percentage to be hedged	Underlying value	Beta
12	= $1,200,000.00 ×	100%	÷ $120,000.00 ×	1.20

With the sale of 12 contracts the portfolio will again be fully hedged, but its return will be somewhat higher than in the earlier example. Now, because he sold more futures contracts and will earn more from premium erosion, it is as though he will earn interest on Treasury bills worth 120% of the portfolio value. We can express this easily by multiplying the 1.75% Treasury bill rate by the beta of 1.20, resulting in a yield improvement rate of 2.10%. According to the formula, this will raise the expected quarterly return of the portfolio to 3.6%, or 14.4% annually.

Portfolio return		Broad market return		Portfolio beta		Portfolio alpha		Yield improvement
3.60%	=	(???	×	0)	+	1.5%	+	2.10%

If the broad market declines, price appreciation and premium erosion in the futures contracts totaling $226,800.00 will entirely offset losses in the stocks, converting the portfolio's return for the quarter to profit of $43,200.00, the predicted 3.6%.

	Index − 15%
Value of stocks at beginning of period	($1,200,000.00)
Value of stocks at end of period	$1,004,400.00
Loss from stocks	($ 195,600.00)
Initial market value of futures (241.80 × $500.00 × 12)	$1,450,800.00
Expiration value of futures (204.00 × $500.00 × 12)	($1,224,000.00)
Profit from futures	$ 226,800.00
Dividends received	$ 12,000.00
TOTAL PROFIT	$ 43,200.00
PERCENTAGE PROFIT	3.6%

Figure 10.5 illustrates once again the flat risk/return line of this fully hedged strategy, shifted somewhat upward in the chart, above the earlier example, reflecting the greater premium erosion associated with the sale of more futures contracts. It is important to note that this pattern will dominate the alternate strategy of simply selling all the stocks and buying Treasury bills. The alternative will simply return the Treasury bill rate of 7% per year, not the enhanced money-market instrument rate of 14.4%.

Conversely, if an investor wished to hedge a portfolio with a *lower* beta, he would sell *fewer* futures contracts; for example, if the beta of this portfolio were 0.70, he would sell seven contracts:

Number of contracts to sell	Value of portfolio	Percentage to be hedged	Underlying value	Beta
7	= $1,200,000.00 ×	100%	÷ $120,000.00 ×	0.70

The effect of selling fewer futures contracts would be to *lower* the expected return of the fully hedged portfolio, just as selling more futures contracts raised it. Fewer futures would earn less premium erosion, effectively lowering the yield improvement factor. To calculate the magnitude of the difference multiply the quarterly Treasury bill rate of 1.75% by the beta, 0.70. This results in a yield improvement rate of 1.225%.

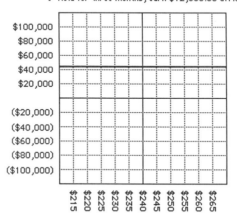

$1,200,000.00 in portfolio of selected stocks
Annual yield = 4%
Annual alpha = 6%
Beta = 1.20
Index initially at 240.00

Sell 12 S&P 500 Index futures contracts at 241.80
Hold for three months, earn $12,000.00 dividends

FIGURE 10.5. Converting the high-beta active portfolio into a "synthetic money-market instrument"

The formula gives an expected return for this fully hedged pc rtfolio of 2.725% quarterly, or 10.9% annually—still better than the return from Treasury bills:

Portfolio return		Broad market return		Portfolio beta		Portfolio alpha		Yield improvement
2.725%	=	(???	×	0)	+	1.5%	+	1.225%

It is important to note that, in practice, beta and alpha can never be more than estimates. Failure of the portfolio to exhibit the estimated beta and alpha can lead to unexpected, and possibly disappointing, results in these kinds of hedging operations. But with this caveat in mind it is clear that if an investor believes his portfolio has a positive alpha it is generally to his advantage to retain it by selling index futures contracts as an alternative to selling the stocks themselves. Of course, if an investor believes the alpha of his portfolio is negative, he should consider liquidating his stocks and replacing them by *buying* index futures.

USING INDEX OPTIONS AND FUTURES TO BUY "PORTFOLIO INSURANCE"

In the hedging strategy we have just examined, the process of risk reduction causes comparable reduction in up-side potential. The TAN-STAAFL rule notwithstanding, many investors would prefer a different pattern. They would be willing to pay a fee in exchange for asymmetrical risks and returns—risk on the down-side limited to a specified floor, but nevertheless full participation in up-side gains (less the fee, of course). Essentially, such investors prefer what has come to be called *portfolio insurance*. Figure 10.6 illustrates an idealized pattern of this type; the risks and returns of an "insured" portfolio are contrasted with those of an entirely unhedged portfolio.

Although insurance companies do not sell portfolio insurance policies as such, it is possible for an investor to strategically duplicate the pattern of returns that would obtain if such policies could be purchased. All an investor seeking insurance has to do is buy index put options, for they are virtually exchange-traded portfolio insurance policies. As an example, let's say an investor holds a $1,200,000.00 stock portfolio that perfectly matches the S&P 500 Index in every way. To ensure that the portfolio

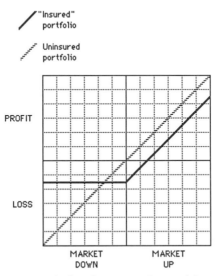

FIGURE 10.6. An idealized pattern of "portfolio insurance"

will experience no loss at the end of a three-month period—other than the cost of the insurance—the investor would buy 50 three-month, cash-settled, European, 240.00-strike-price puts on the S&P 500 Index.

Number of puts to buy		Initial value of portfolio		Index price		Contract multiplier
50	=	$1,200,000.00	÷	(240.00	×	$100.00)

If the index price is 240.00, its volatility, 15%, its yield, 4%, and the riskless interest rate 7%, the theoretical value of such a put would be 6.27. The total cost to buy 50 puts would be $31,350.00:

Total cost of puts		Number of puts		Put price		Contract multiplier
$31,350.00	=	50	×	6.27	×	$100.00

Unfortunately the investor is in no position to write a check for $31,350.00—we've assumed that he is completely invested in stocks. Hypothetically, he could borrow $31,350.00 to buy the puts; if he can get it at 7%, the cost of financing for three months would be $548.62. In practice, many institutional investors would be unable to borrow the money.

As an alternative to borrowing, the investor would have to liquidate a portion of his portfolio to raise cash to pay for the puts. But if he does that he'll no longer need all 50 puts because his portfolio will be somewhat smaller. To determine the precise number of puts required and the leftover amount to remain invested in stocks we would begin by calculating the put price as a percentage of the index price—about 2.6%:

Percentage put price		Put price		Index price
2.612% (rounded)	=	6.27	÷	240.00

Next, we divide the number of puts the investor would have ordinarily bought by 1 plus the percentage put price. The result is the appropriate number of puts to buy to hedge the partially liquidated portfolio—48.73:

Adjusted number of puts to buy		Initial number of puts to buy		One plus percentage put price
48.73 (rounded)	=	50	÷	1.02612 (rounded)

The total cost of buying 48.73 puts—$30,551.83—can be calculated by multiplying 48.73 by the put price of 6.27 times the contract multiplier of $100.00:

Total cost to buy puts		Number of puts		Put price		Contract multiplier
$30,551.83	=	48.73	×	6.27	×	$100.00

The remaining value of the stock portfolio—$1,169,448.17—can be calculated by subtracting the $30,551.83 cost of the puts from the initial portfolio value of $1,200,000.00:

Remaining value of portfolio		Initial value of portfolio		Total cost to buy puts
$1,169,448.17	=	$1,200,000.00	–	$30,551.83

Now we'll examine the results of three strategies under various market scenarios: first, leaving the $1,200,000.00 portfolio entirely uninsured; second, borrowing to buy 50 puts; and third, liquidating a portion of the portfolio to buy 48.73 puts.

If the index declines 10%, from 240.00 to 216.00, the uninsured portfolio declines 10% as well, offset by dividend income. Its total loss is $108,000.00. In the portfolio insured with 50 puts, the expiration value of the puts completely hedges out losses in the stocks, but the portfolio nonetheless shows a relatively small loss of $19,898.62, the cost of the puts and their financing, offset by dividend income. The portfolio insured with 48.73 put shows a slightly smaller loss of $18,857.35, the cost of the puts and the slightly reduced interest income on the partially liquidated stock portfolio.

INDEX − 10%

	Uninsured Portfolio	Insured with 50 Puts 240.00 Strike-Price Borrow $31,350.00	Insured with 48.73 Puts 240.00 Strike-Price Liquidate $30,551.83
Loss in stocks	($120,000.00)	($120,000.00)	($116,944.82)
Expiration value of puts		$120,000.00	$116,944.82
Cost of puts		($ 31,350.00)	($ 30,551.83)
Financing cost		($ 548.62)	
Dividend income	$ 12,000.00	$ 12,000.00	$ 11,694.48
TOTAL PROFIT (LOSS)	($108,000.00)	($ 19,898.62)	($ 18,857.35)

The *benefits* of insurance are obvious when the index declines, just as the benefits of fire insurance are best appreciated right after one's house has burned down. But the *costs* of insurance are obvious when the index is unchanged. In this scenario, the uninsured portfolio shows a small profit of $12,000.00 from dividend income. But the two insured portfolios both show exactly the same small losses they showed when the index declined, $19,898.62 and $18,857.35 respectively.

INDEX UNCHANGED

	Uninsured Portfolio	Insured with 50 Puts 240.00 Strike-Price Borrow $31,350.00	Insured with 48.73 Puts 240.00 Strike-Price Liquidate $30,551.83
Loss in stocks	0	0	0
Expiration value of puts		0	0
Cost of puts		($ 31,350.00)	($ 30,551.83)
Financing cost		($ 548.62)	
Dividend income	$ 12,000.00	$12,000.00	$ 11,694.48
TOTAL PROFIT (LOSS)	$ 12,000.00	($ 19,898.62)	($ 18,857.35)

The cost of insurance is apparent again when the market rises 10%, from 240.00 to 264.00. The uninsured portfolio shows a profit of

$132,000.00 from price appreciation and dividends. The insured portfolios relatively underperform but nonetheless capture most of the gains, returning $100,101.38 and $98,087.47, or 75.8 and 74.3% of the unhedged return, respectively.

INDEX +10%

	Uninsured Portfolio	Insured with 50 Puts 240.00 Strike-Price Borrow $31,350.00	Insured with 48.37 Puts 240.00 Strike-Price Liquidate $30,551.83
Gain in stocks	$120,000.00	$120,000.00	$116,944.82
Expiration value of puts		0	0
Cost of puts		($ 31,350.00)	($ 30,551.83)
Financing cost		($ 548.62)	
Dividend income	$ 12,000.00	$ 12,000.00	$ 11,694.48
TOTAL PROFIT (LOSS)	$132,000.00	$100,101.38	$ 98,087.47

It is interesting to note that the 48.37-put portfolio outperforms the 50-put portfolio when the index is down or unchanged, but the 50-put portfolio outperforms when the index is up. This is because the cost of insurance in the 50-put portfolio is entirely *fixed*—it can never be more than the cost of the puts plus their financing. The *fixed* component of the insurance cost in the 48.73-put portfolio is somewhat lower, because fewer puts are purchased and there is no financing cost. But there is a *variable* component to the cost of insurance in the 48.73-put portfolio as well, though it is only apparent on the up-side. Because a portion of the stock portfolio was liquidated to buy the puts, there will be an impairment of performance on the up-side that will become increasingly apparent the more the index rises.

Figure 10.7 illustrates the patterns of risk and returns associated with all three portfolios. The uninsured portfolio is a single straight line shifted slightly up from the center of the chart to reflect the receipt of dividends. On the down-side the portfolio insured with 50 puts flattens out at a point representing the fixed cost of insurance. On the up-side the line rises parallel to the unhedged portfolio, but it is always dominated by it. On the downside the portfolio insured with 48.73 puts is also flat, but at a slightly higher level than the portfolio insured with 50 puts. On the upside 48.73-put portfolio's line is not quite parallel to those of the other

271

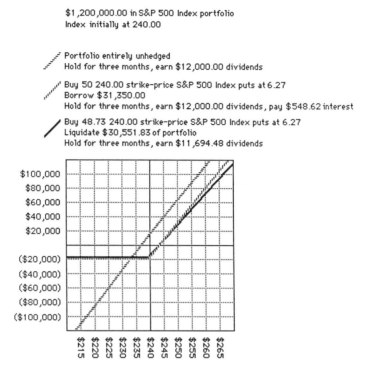

$1,200,000.00 in S&P 500 Index portfolio
Index initially at 240.00

Portfolio entirely unhedged
Hold for three months, earn $12,000.00 dividends

Buy 50 240.00 strike-price S&P 500 Index puts at 6.27
Borrow $31,350.00
Hold for three months, earn $12,000.00 dividends, pay $548.62 interest

Buy 48.73 240.00 strike-price S&P 500 Index puts at 6.27
Liquidate $30,551.83 of portfolio
Hold for three months, earn $11,694.48 dividends

FIGURE 10.7. Portfolio insurance with listed index options

portfolios, reflecting the increasing drag on performance caused by its partial liquidation of the stock portfolio.

Although index put options are effective portfolio insurance policies, they are far from ideal in many respects. First, position limits make it impossible to buy enough puts to insure portfolios of the size held by many institutions. If maximum positions were taken in all put options listed, assuming that liquidity would even permit such a thing, the largest portfolio that could be insured would be in the neighborhood of only $1 billion.

Second, puts can trade at prices significantly higher than the theoretical values calculated for them by the valuation procedure, raising the cost of insurance beyond its true worth. It's true that they can trade lower as well, but it would be preferable if an investor's cost of insurance were not hostage to these random fluctuations.

Third, most index puts are designed with American exercise terms. As we discussed earlier in connection with options valuation, American options will always have higher values than otherwise similar European options because they convey valuable additional rights. These rights may not be useful to buyers of portfolio insurance, who generally hold puts till expiration regardless of the demonstrable optimality of premature exercise.

Fourth, because exchange-listed puts settle against the value of a specific index at expiration, they will perfectly protect only a portfolio that tracks that index. To this extent they could be said to insure only the market component of risk.

Fifth, listed index puts are not *dividend protected*—their strike prices are not adjusted to reflect the constant markdowns of the index price resulting from dividend payments. Because unprotected puts benefit from the resulting downward bias of the index price, they are higher priced than otherwise identical protected puts.

Sixth, index puts are listed only with standardized strike-prices. Buyers of portfolio insurance may have reason to prefer puts further away from the current index price than may be available, or to prefer puts with strike-prices drawn at particular fractional index prices.

For example, consider what would happen if the investor in the example wanted portfolio insurance with a 25% "deductible." Such insurance would reimburse the investor only for losses beyond 25%, much as a $200.00 deductible in an automobile insurance policy reimburses only for losses beyond $200.00. Twenty-five percent is such a large deductible that it could be said to be nothing more than catastrophe insurance, but after substantial market rises there may well be reason to want such protection. With the index at 240.00 the investor would have to buy puts with a strike-price of 180.00—but puts are not available at strike-prices anywhere so distant from the current index price.

Another reason an investor might prefer strike-prices not available on exchanges is to structure insurance to be *self-reimbursing*. In the examples, the insurance protected against losses in the stock portfolio but did not protect against the cost of the insurance itself. It is possible to buy puts whose payoffs when the market is down or unchanged will reimburse the investor for their own initial cost, but such puts have strike-prices generally unavailable on exchanges.

As an example, consider the 259.566524-strike-price, European puts, a peculiar species unlikely ever to be available on an options exchange. According to the valuation procedure, their theoretical value is 19.23, a slight discount to their current exercise value. Of course if these were American puts, they could never be valued lower than their current exercise value. Buying 50 of them would require $96,150.00; if the investor could borrow at 7% to buy them, financing would cost $1682.62:

Total cost of puts		Number of puts		Put price		Contract multiplier
$96,150.00	=	50	×	19.23	×	$100.00

Alternatively, if the investor could not borrow and chose instead to liquidate a portion of his stock portfolio to pay for the puts, he'd want a different option—the 258.735501-strike-price, European puts. According to the valuation procedure, their theoretical value is 18.55, also a slight discount to their current exercise value. We'll return to the procedure we employed earlier to calculate the appropriate number of puts to insure the remaining value of the portfolio. We begin by calculating the percentage put price, about 7.7%:

Percentage put price		Put price		Index price
7.729% (rounded)	=	18.55	÷	240.00

Next, we divide the number of puts the investor would have ordinarily bought by 1 plus the percentage put price. The result is the appropriate number of puts to buy to hedge the partially liquidated portfolio—46.41:

Adjusted number of puts to buy		Initial number of puts to buy		One plus percentage put price
46.41 (rounded)	=	50	÷	1.0773 (rounded)

The total cost of buying 46.41 puts is $86,090.55:

Total cost to buy puts		Number of puts		Put price		Contract multiplier
$86,090.55	=	46.41	×	18.55	×	$100.00

The remaining value of the stock portfolio is $1,113,909.45:

Remaining value of portfolio		Initial value of portfolio		Total cost to buy puts
$1,113,909.45	=	$1,200,000.00	−	$86,090.55

Now when the index is unchanged all three portfolios return exactly the same result—a profit of $12,000.00.

INDEX UNCHANGED

	Uninsured Portfolio	Insured with 50 Puts 259.566 Strike-Price Borrow $96,150.00	Insured with 46.58 Puts 258.735 Strike-Price Liquidate $86,090.55
Loss in stocks	0	0	0
Expiration value of puts		$ 97,832.62	$ 86,951.46
Cost of puts		($ 96,150.00)	($ 86,090.55)
Financing cost		($ 1,682.62)	
Dividend income	$ 12,000.00	$ 12,000.00	$ 11,139.09
TOTAL PROFIT (LOSS)	$ 12,000.00	$ 12,000.00	$ 12,000.00

On the down-side the puts in the insured portfolios will perfectly hedge any depreciation in the value of the stocks—both continue to return exactly $12,000.00. Recall that in the preceding example the two insured portfolios returned losses of $19,898.62 and $18,857.35, respectively, when the index was unchanged or down. These puts with the unusual strike-prices are not only self-reimbursing, and they not only preserve capital, they even insure a positive return equivalent to dividend income.

Because the TANSTAAFL rule has not been repealed, it stands to reason that self-reimbursing insurance should be more expensive, and so it is. On the up-side the insured portfolios will underperform the uninsured portfolio much more markedly. If the index rises 10%, from 240.00 to 264.00, recall that the uninsured portfolio returns a profit of $132,000.00. The insured portfolios, on the other hand, return $34,167.38 and $36,439.48, or 25.8% and 27.6% of the uninsured return, respectively.

INDEX +10%

	Uninsured Portfolio	Insured with 50 Puts 259.566 Strike-Price Borrow $96,150.00	Insured with 46.58 Puts 258.735 Strike-Price Liquidate $86,090.55
Gain in stocks	$120,000.00	$120,000.00	$111,390.94
Expiration value of puts		0	0
Cost of puts		($ 96,150.00)	($ 86,090.55)
Financing cost		($ 1,682.62)	
Dividend income	$ 12,000.00	$ 12,000.00	$ 11,139.09
TOTAL PROFIT (LOSS)	$132,000.00	$ 34,167.38	$ 36,439.48

Figure 10.8 illustrates the patterns of risks and returns associated with these three portfolios. Schematically, they are identical to those in the previous figure, but the values of the insured portfolios have been shifted. Now their flat down-side lines are in the upper half of the chart, signifying profit. But on the right side of the chart, representing the up-side, their lines are much slower to take off and follow the line of the uninsured portfolio into profit.

Since we have examined both types of insurance—regular and self-reimbursing—using theoretical values for put prices, it could be said both have been "fairly priced" given the different types of protection they provide. In choosing between them, or any other of the many ways insurance can be structured, the issue is not which is the "better deal," but rather which one matches an investor's risk/return preferences. Unfortunately, as these examples have demonstrated, exchange-listed index puts are not customizable to the extent necessary to serve every investor's needs.

The final deficiency of index puts is the unavailability of long-term contracts. Currently the longest term contracts listed have a maturity of nine months, but generally the most liquid contracts are those expiring in one or two months. Even if the nine-month puts were sufficiently liquid, many buyers of portfolio insurance would prefer maturities extending for several years. The reason for this preference is that, *per unit of time*, long-term puts are cheaper than short-term puts. It could be said that insurance, like anything else, is cheaper when it's purchased wholesale.

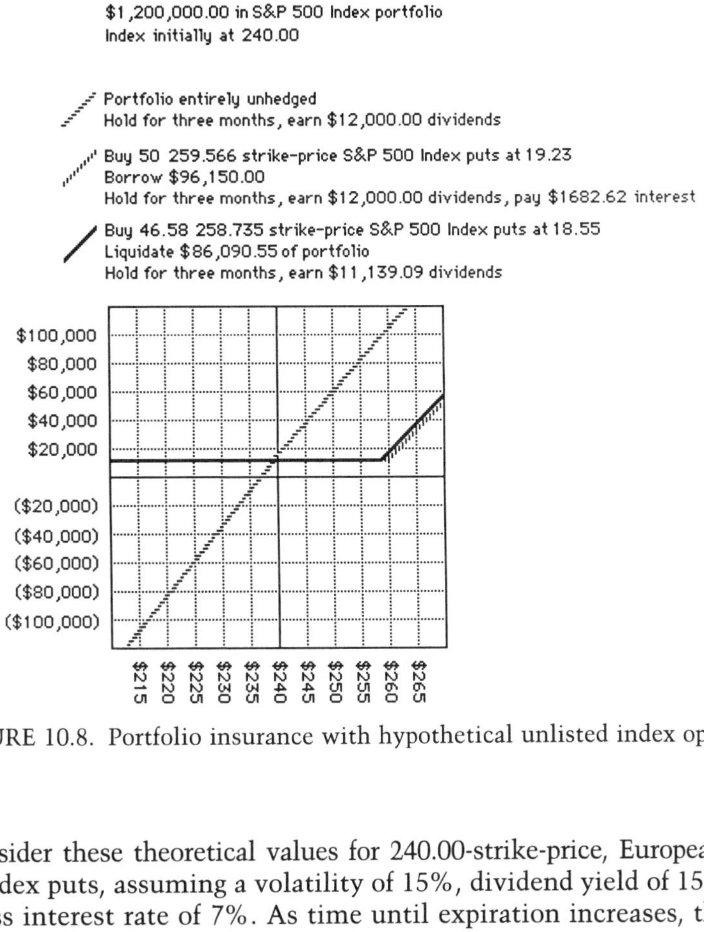
$1,200,000.00 in S&P 500 Index portfolio
Index initially at 240.00
Portfolio entirely unhedged
Hold for three months, earn $12,000.00 dividends
Buy 50 259.566 strike-price S&P 500 Index puts at 19.23
Borrow $96,150.00
Hold for three months, earn $12,000.00 dividends, pay $1682.62 interest
Buy 46.58 258.735 strike-price S&P 500 Index puts at 18.55
Liquidate $86,090.55 of portfolio
Hold for three months, earn $11,139.09 dividends
$100,000
$80,000
$60,000
$40,000
$20,000
($20,000)
($40,000)
($60,000)
($80,000)
($100,000)
$215
$220
$225
$230
$235
$240
$245
$250
$255
$260
$265

FIGURE 10.8. Portfolio insurance with hypothetical unlisted index options

Consider these theoretical values for 240.00-strike-price, European S&P 500 Index puts, assuming a volatility of 15%, dividend yield of 15%, and riskless interest rate of 7%. As time until expiration increases, the theoretical value of the put increases as well. But at the same time, value *per unit of time* decreases. A vivid demonstration of this principle is to note that a one-year put is valued at 10.58, but two consecutive six-month puts total 16.58. More astonishing, one year's worth of consecutive one-week puts would cost 100.08.

Time until expiration	Theoretical value	Value per month
1 week	1.92	8.34
1 month	3.85	3.85
2 months	5.26	2.63
3 months	6.27	2.09

6 months	8.29	1.38
9 months	9.62	1.07
1 year	10.58	0.88

The source of this effect is the way the option valuation procedure defines and analyzes risk. Recall from our earlier discussions that the procedure requires an estimate of the volatility of the underlying index, a prediction of how widely its returns will be dispersed in a random diffusion process. We said that as an intuitive approximation, when an index has an annual volatility of 15%, *two-thirds of the time* its price will be changed by *less* than 15% at the end of one year. *One-third of the time* its price will be changed by *more* than 15%.

For the S&P 500 starting with an index price of 240.00, we are estimating that at the end of one year the index's price will be changed by *less* than 36.00 *two-thirds of the time. One-third of the time*, however, the price will be changed by *more* than 36.00.

Recall that we learned that to adjust volatility from an annual rate to a periodic rate, we would divide the annual rate by the square root of the number of periods. If we wished to convert the S&P 500's annual volatility of 15% into a six-month volatility, we would divide by the square root of 2:

Six-month volatility		Annual volatility		Square root of number of periods in a year
10.6%	=	15%	÷	$\sqrt{2}$

Six months is half a year, but the value of a six-month put is more than half the value of a one-year put precisely because 10.6% is more than half of 15%. As the valuation model deals with it, *risk does not increase linearly with time.* Rather it increases at a much slower rate, *with the square root of time.*

This explains why, as time until expiration increases, put values become cheaper *per unit of time.* But another effect, not observed until maturities lengthen beyond any ever listed on exchanges, causes put values to decrease *absolutely* as well. At first this idea violates common sense. It is virtually a truism that long-term puts must be more expensive in absolute dollars than short-term puts. After all, given the choice of a long-term put and short-term put at the same price, would an alert investor not always take the long term? Let's look at more put values, extending beyond the one-year maturity we examined before.

Time until expiration	Theoretical value	Value per month
2 years	12.67	0.53
3 years	13.45	0.37
4 years	13.62	0.28
5 years	13.45	0.22
10 years	10.85	0.09
20 years	5.66	0.02
30 years	2.74	0.008
40 years	1.29	0.003
50 years	0.60	0.001
100 years	0.01	0.00001

Note that as time until expiration extends to four years, the put value increases to 13.62. But then, at five years, we find that a five-year put has a lower value than a four-year put, and the same value as a three-year put—13.45. After this, the theoretical values continue to decrease until finally a 100-year put is valued at one penny.

The reason for this is in the fundamental definition of a put option— it is a contract that allows its owner to sell an underlying asset and receive the put's strike-price. All things being equal, the earlier the investor can receive the strike-price, the better because he can reinvest it at interest. But in the case of a European option he cannot receive the strike-price until expiration. The longer the time remaining until expiration, the longer this receipt is deferred, so the *present value* of the strike-price to the investor is reduced.

To illustrate how profound this effect can be we will have to make recourse to a transcendental number known as *e*. Like pi, its decimal expression extends to an infinite number of digits; its first nine are 2.71828183. It can be defined as what an investment of 1 would grow to in one year, continuously compounded at an annual rate of 100%. Without compounding, $1.00 would grow to $2.00 at a 100% rate; with continuous compounding, $1.00 would grow to *e*.

To calculate the present value of the strike-price we raise *e* to the power of -1 times the annual interest rate times the number of years until maturity and then multiply the strike-price by this result; for example, the present value of 240.00 in one year is 223.77.

Present value		Negative one		Annual interest rate		Years till maturity		Strike price
223.77	= e	(–1	×	0.07	×	1)	×	240.00

As time till expiration increases, this calculation lowers the present value of the strike-price further and further. For instance, the present value of 240.00 in 50 years is only 7.24.

Present value		Negative one		Annual interest rate		Years till maturity		Strike price
7.24	= e	(–1	×	0.07	×	50)	×	240.00

Although the present-value effect operates to create lower put values as time until expiration increases, the benefit of ever-wider dispersion of possible future index prices countervails to increase them. But, as we've seen, dispersion only increases with the square root of time—the present-value calculation is relentless, heading asymptotically toward zero. At the point at which it overwhelms increasing dispersion the theoretical value of the put begins to decline with additional time until expiration.

It is important to understand this process because it explains a fundamental inadequacy of exchange-traded put options in portfolio insurance. For an investor who prefers insurance for a 10-year period, valued theoretically, at 10.85, it would be drastically uneconomical to buy 40 consecutive three-month puts, valued at 250.80.

Given the problem of unavailability of contracts with sufficiently long maturities and the other drawbacks we have discussed—position limits, possible mispricing, American contract terms, standardized indexes, no dividend protection, and unavailability of customized strike-prices—it would appear that puts are not useful tools for buyers of portfolio insurance. Fortunately there is a viable alternative, a strategy of using index futures contracts to create customized "synthetic puts" that overcome most of these problems.

The idea of creating a synthetic put has already been discussed in great detail in connection with the option valuation procedure. We proved that a "synthetic option" with all the characteristics of a real option could be created out of a combination of shares of the underlying index and borrowing or lending. In 1981, Hayne Leland and Mark Rubinstein (of the Cox–Ross–Rubinstein model) published a paper entitled "Replicating Options with Positions in Stocks and Cash," in which they suggested that the idea was more than an abstraction—investors might actually employ synthetic options just as they would real options.

Recall that in the valuation procedure we generated a different combination of shares of the index and borrowing or lending at every isolated segment of the index price tree. Leland and Rubinstein noted that to actually create a synthetic option that would replicate the results of a real option through maturity, the investor would have to frequently rebalance the index shares and borrowing or lending in accordance with the prescriptions of the valuation procedure as time passes and the price of the underlying index fluctuates. Because this process involves ongoing reallocation of assets between shares and borrowing or lending, Leland and Rubinstein dubbed it Dynamic Asset Allocation®. This expression is a trademark of Leland O'Brien Rubinstein Associates, Inc., the firm they created to market investment management strategies based on this concept, including synthetic puts for portfolio insurance. Such strategies are known, in general, by the generic expression *dynamic hedging.*

Earlier, in an example of how the two-iteration valuation procedure valued a put, we saw that when the underlying index price rose into the upper isolated segment of the index price tree, the synthetic option consisted of 0.54 index shares sold short and $134.27 in lending. Conversely, when the index price declined into the lower segment, the synthetic option consisted of 1.00 index share sold short and $237.97 in lending. If an investor creating a synthetic put for portfolio insurance had set up a hedging account in which to sell short shares of the index and lend, he would *decrease* the short position and lending as the index *rose,* and *increase* the short position and lending as the index *declined.*

Figure 10.9 illustrates an idealized version of this process. The upper chart depicts positions taken in the hedging account—the value of the combination of shares of the index sold short and lending as a percentage of the value of the index to be insured with the synthetic put. On the left, in the region of the chart representing index declines, the percentage of shorting and lending ultimately reaches 100% of the value of the index—the index would have fallen so much as to be entirely hedged. On the right, in the region of the chart representing index rises, the percentage ultimately falls to zero, indicating that there would be no shorting and lending at all—the index would have risen so much as to need no further hedging.

The lower chart depicts the pattern of risks and returns associated with managing the hedging account in this way. On the down-side, increasing the level of shorting and lending as the index declines creates a large profit—the exercise value of the synthetic put, or the payoff of the portfolio insurance policy. But on the upside, decreasing the level of shorting and lending as the index rises will cut losses to a finite maximum—the cost of the synthetic put or portfolio insurance policy.

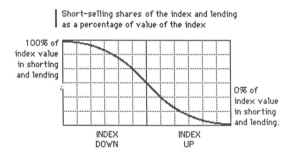

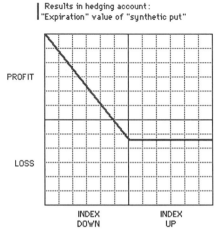

FIGURE 10.9. Managing a hedging account to create a "synthetic put" for portfolio insurance

Figure 10.10 is a detailed, though still idealized, example of creating a synthetic put with dynamic hedging. The goal is to replicate a one-year, European, 240.00-strike-price put; we've assumed an initial index price of 240.00, volatility of 15%, annual simple interest rate of 7%, and, for the sake of simplicity, no dividends. According to the valuation procedure at two iterations, the value of such a put is 6.27 (it is a distracting coincidence, a random artifact of using only two iterations, that this put is valued identically to the put we used at the beginning of this section, when there were only three months till expiration and the index had a 4% yield).

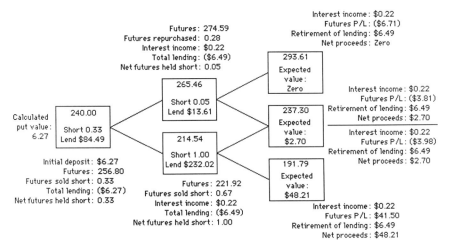

Index price: 240.00
Strike-price: 240.00
Exercise terms: European
Time until maturity: 1 year
Annual volatility: 15%
Interest rate: 7%
Dividend yield: Zero

Periodic volatility: 10.6%
Periodic interest rate: 3.44%

FIGURE 10.10. Creating a "synthetic put" with dynamic hedging

At expiration there are three possible index prices: 293.61, at which the put will be worth zero; 237.30, at which the put will be worth 2.70; and 191.79, at which the put will be worth 48.21. At each point in the index price tree, the combination of index shares sold short and lending required to create the synthetic option is listed in the box beneath the index price.

Next to each box is a summary of transactions in the hedging account. The first step, when the index price is 240.00, is to deposit the value of the option—$6.27—in the hedging account. Next, we sell short 0.33 share of the index, realizing proceeds from the sale of $78.22. Finally, we lend out the proceeds and the initial deposit, for total lending of $84.49.

Whether the index price now moves up or down, a revision in the hedging account will be required. For instance, if the index price declines to 214.54, the procedure calls for increasing the short position to 1.00 share. This would require selling 0.67 share, and would create proceeds of $144.62. Lending these proceeds, added to the existing lending and the

283

interest of $2.91 earned on it over the period, brings the total lending to $232.02.

Now, whether the index price moves up or down at expiration, this position will provide exactly the expected value of a real put. If the index price moves up to 237.30, we repurchase the short 1.00 share for $237.30, and retire the borrowing of $232.02. Including interest of $7.98 earned over the period, the liquidating value of the position is $2.70, exactly the value of a real put. If the index price moves down to 191.79 at expiration, we would repurchase the short 1.00 share for $191.79, and retire the borrowing of $232.02. Including $7.98 interest, the liquidating value of the position is $48.21, again exactly the value of a real put.

The process works just as perfectly for the other possible paths through the index price tree. If, in the first iteration, the index price has risen to 265.46, we would have had to repurchase 0.28 share, leaving a net short position of 0.05 share. The $73.79 cost of the repurchase would diminish the lending position to $13.61, including interest income of $2.91 over the period.

Again, whether the index price moves up or down, the position will provide exactly the expected value of a real put. If the index price moves up to 293.61 at expiration, we would repurchase the short 0.05 share for $14.08. Upon retiring the lending of $13.61, and including $0.47 interest, the liquidating value of the position is zero, exactly the value of a real put. If the index price moves down to 237.30 at expiration, we would repurchase the short 0.05 share for $11.38. On retiring the lending, and including interest, the liquidating value of the position is $2.70, once again exactly the value of a real put.

For clarity we have illustrated this process with only two iterations, but in practice, an investor could employ as many iterations as desired. The accuracy of the process increases with each iteration and the subsequent frequency of revisions. Because this strategy can require such frequent trading, many investors who employ it prefer to sell index futures contracts rather than stocks in order to minimize commission and market impact. Figure 10.11 illustrates this approach. At every point in the index price tree index futures are sold with identical underlying value to the shares of the index specified in the valuation procedure. Because selling an index futures contract against a stock position creates a synthetic money market instrument, it automatically accomplishes both short-selling and lending—premium erosion in the futures contracts takes the place of interest income.

Dynamic hedging successfully overcomes most of the deficiencies of exchange-listed puts that we discussed earlier. First, there are no position limits on synthetic puts, and it is often possible for bona fide hedgers

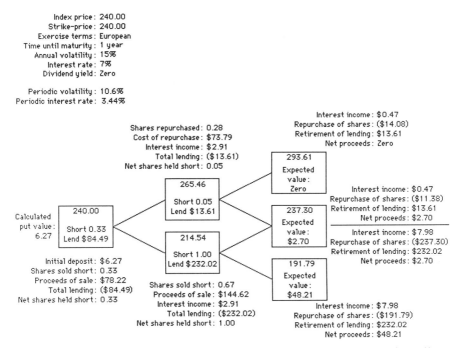

Index price : 240.00
Strike-price : 240.00
Exercise terms : European
Time until maturity : 1 year
Annual volatility : 15%
Interest rate : 7%
Dividend yield : Zero

Periodic volatility : 10.6%
Periodic interest rate : 3.44%

Shares repurchased : 0.28
Cost of repurchase : $73.79
Interest income : $2.91
Total lending : ($13.61)
Net shares held short : 0.05

Interest income : $0.47
Repurchase of shares : ($14.08)
Retirement of lending : $13.61
Net proceeds : Zero

265.46

Short 0.05
Lend $13.61

293.61

Expected value : Zero

Calculated put value : 6.27

240.00

Short 0.33
Lend $84.49

237.30

Expected value : $2.70

Interest income : $0.47
Repurchase of shares : ($11.38)
Retirement of lending : $13.61
Net proceeds : $2.70

Interest income : $7.98
Repurchase of shares : ($237.30)
Retirement of lending : $232.02
Net proceeds : $2.70

214.54

Short 1.00
Lend $232.02

Initial deposit : $6.27
Shares sold short : 0.33
Proceeds of sale : $78.22
Total lending : ($84.49)
Net shares held short : 0.33

191.79

Expected value : $48.21

Shares sold short : 0.67
Proceeds of sale : $144.62
Interest income : $2.91
Total lending : ($232.02)
Net shares held short : 1.00

Interest income : $7.98
Repurchase of shares : ($191.79)
Retirement of lending : $232.02
Net proceeds : $48.21

FIGURE 10.11. Creating a "synthetic put" with dynamic hedging, by selling futures contracts instead of shares of the index

who wish to implement the strategy with futures contracts to obtain an exemption from position limits from the exchanges. Second, synthetic puts can be designed with European exercise terms, lowering expected costs relative to exchange-listed American options. Third, if the strategy is implemented by trading shares of an investor's portfolio, the investor is not dependent on tracking a standardized index. Of course, use of futures contracts reintroduces this risk. Fourth, synthetic puts can be designed to be dividend protected. Fifth, synthetic puts can be designed with any desired lifetime and with any desired strike-price.

But dynamic hedging goes beyond merely improving the imperfect details of listed puts. It can be used to create "synthetic optionlike instruments" totally outside the scope and purpose of any instrument ever likely to be listed on an options exchange. For instance, while all listed options offer the investor the choice between the better performing of an underlying asset and cash, dynamic hedging could create an option that would offer the choice between, say, a stock index and long-term bonds, or between gold and the consumer price index, or between corn and soybeans.

For all its benefits, in practice dynamic hedging is not entirely perfect. First, success in delivering the expected put values at expiration is contingent on the accuracy of the volatility and interest rate estimates on which the valuation procedure is based. Since volatilities and interest rates can fluctuate during the life of the process, its results can be somewhat unpredictable.

Second, even when futures contracts are used, transaction costs will increase the cost of synthetic puts. As Hayne Leland pointed out in his paper "Option Pricing and Replication with Transaction Costs," because transaction costs implicitly act to make assets higher priced from the buyer's perspective and lower priced from the seller's, they could be said to systematically increase experienced index volatility. Making an appropriate adjustment in the volatility estimate allows transaction costs to be correctly accounted for in the process.

Third, the strategy presumes, as does the valuation procedure, that the index price will fluctuate in a smooth, random diffusion process. In reality, index prices can move in discontinuous jumps that may not allow an investor to make the proper adjustments to the position in the hedging account. For example, if a catastrophic news event caused stock and futures exchanges to be closed and then, when they reopened, index prices were drastically lower, adjustments to the hedging account could only be made after it was too late. For investors who expect portfolio insurance to protect them in this sort of scenario, exchange-listed puts may be preferable to synthetic puts despite their many drawbacks.

Whether implemented with puts or dynamic hedging, portfolio insurance has proven to be a very popular institutional investment strategy. Although its most obvious application is capital preservation, several academic and institutional studies have indicated that it may enhance long-term performance as well. The first such study was published in 1978 in a paper called "The Returns and Risks of Alternative Call Option Portfolio Investment Strategies" by Robert C. Merton, Myron S. Scholes, and Mathew L. Gladstein.

This study compared returns and risk of the 30 stocks in the Dow Jones Industrial Average with a portfolio of options on the same stocks, constructed in a manner that is functionally equivalent to a stock portfolio insured with put options. Examining the 12 1/2-year period from July 1, 1963, to December 31, 1975, these researchers found that the insured portfolio exhibited both lower risk and higher returns than the uninsured portfolio. Insuring lowered average volatility of the portfolio from 13.7% to 10.6%, and raised the average compound return from 3.3% to 4.7%.

To create their simulation, Merton, Scholes, and Gladstein assumed a series of six-month periods, each assuring a loss no greater than about 7% (including the cost of insurance). The simulation calculated the parameters of the insurance with the Black–Scholes options valuation model, using historical measures of volatility, dividends, and interest rates as inputs. Their simulation did not include the effects of transaction costs or taxation.

Other studies conducted by investment managers and brokerage firms, one going back over 100 years, have confirmed these findings. But intuitively, it seems hard to believe that any strategy can both reduce risk and enhance returns. Certainly none of the authors of these studies would guarantee that these results will necessarily obtain in the future. As Merton, Scholes, and Gladstein expressed it, "The relative risk characteristics of the strategies described by the simulations are representative of the strategies. The specific levels of the returns generated, however, are strongly dependent on the actual experience of the underlying stocks during the simulation period."

There may be significant doubt that an insured portfolio can deliver superior long-term returns compared with an uninsured portfolio, but for many institutional investors, who allocate only a portion of their total portfolio to stocks, this is not the relevant comparison. If, by using portfolio insurance, an investor can allocate more of his total portfolio to stocks than he would otherwise have dared, he can raise the expected return of the overall portfolio.

An example designed by Leland O'Brien Rubinstein Associates, Inc. illustrates this point. It shows two approaches open to an investor who seeks to maximize expected return consistent with limiting losses in any single year to 5%. Stocks are presumed to have an expected return of 18%, and Treasury bills 10%. The first approach is static asset allocation, in which the investor deploys assets in an unvarying mix of 55% stocks and 45% Treasury bills. Historically, this mix has proven adequate to meet the investor's risk control requirement with 95% confidence. The expected return of this approach is 14.4%, the average of the expected returns of stocks and Treasury bills, weighted by the proportions in which they are held.

The second approach is Dynamic Asset Allocation, in which the investor starts out with 72% of assets in stocks and 28% in Treasury bills. This mix will be varied continuously in accordance with the synthetic put strategy, but on average the mix will be about 78%/22%. The expected return of Dynamic Asset Allocation is 16.2%, 1.8% higher than that of static allocation, because it permits a greater exposure to stocks. It is important to note that in addition to providing a higher expected return, Dynamic Asset Allocation will meet the investor's risk control requirement with confidence approaching 100%.

	Initial Mix	On-Average Mix	Expected Return
Static asset allocation	55%/45%	55%/45%	14.4%
Dynamic Asset Allocation	72%/28%	78%/22%	16.2%
Gain from Dynamic Asset Allocation			1.8%

Assumptions:	Volatility	Correlation	Expected Return
T-Bill	2%	0.2	10%
Stocks	20%		18%

For investors like the one in this example, who define risk as the maximum loss they will tolerate over a given time horizon, the dynamic portfolio will tend to dominate the static. But if risk is defined as the standard deviation of returns, the reverse is true: a static portfolio will tend to have a higher expected return than a dynamic portfolio with the same standard deviation. In other words, portfolio insurance makes the most sense for an investor who explicitly prefers its uniquely skewed distribution of risks and returns.

OVERWRITING WITH INDEX CALL OPTIONS

Although *overwriting*—selling (or "writing") index call options against a portfolio of stocks—is certainly a form of hedging, it is, in many ways, the exact opposite of buying portfolio insurance. The buyer of portfolio insurance *pays a premium*, which is lost if the market is unchanged at the end of the holding period; the call seller *receives a premium*, his to keep if the market is unchanged, up or down. If the market rises, the portfolio insurance buyer *participates in the up-side*, minus the premium paid; the call seller puts a *cap on up-side gains*. If the market declines, the portfolio insurance buyer *loses no more than the premium* paid; the call seller *suffers any losses greater than the premium received*.

Figure 10.12 illustrates an idealized comparison of these two strategies. Theoretically, by paying a premium for limited risk, the portfolio insurance buyer lowers the expected return relative to holding a completely unhedged portfolio: simulated historical evidence to the contrary notwithstanding, the TANSTAAFL rule suggests that this must be so. The overwriter argues that by accepting the bulk of the down-side risk of a portfolio and selling off much of the up-side potential he is shifting his risk to scenarios that are unlikely to occur while raising his expected

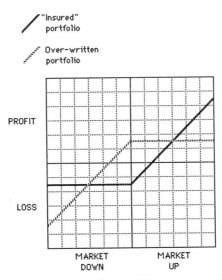

FIGURE 10.12. Idealized patterns of "portfolio insurance" and "overwriting"

return in the more likely scenario in which the index remains more or less unchanged. Of course, the logic of the options valuation procedure takes into account the relative likelihood of various scenarios, so if these strategies are implemented with fairly priced options, both will be rewarded equitably on a risk-adjusted basis over the long term. So the choice between the two strategies should focus on which pattern of returns a particular investor prefers.

Let's compare three strategies for the investor with a $1,200,000.00 portfolio who bought portfolio insurance in the previous section. The first strategy is simply to hold the portfolio unhedged; the other two are overwriting strategies, one conservative and one aggressive. We'll assume that the S&P 500 Index is at 240.00, its volatility is 15%, its yield is 4%, and the riskless interest rate is 7%. According to the options valuation procedure, the three-month, European, 240.00-strike-price calls have a value of 7.96.

For the more conservative of the two overwriting strategies, recall that in our discussion of market risk we saw that selling calls creates an exposure to potentially limitless up-side losses. To avoid this exposure the conservative investor would sell no more calls than could be offset by gains in his portfolio in the event of a major rally. To calculate the number of calls that create this kind of *covered* position, in this case 50, we divide the portfolio's value by the index price, multiplied by the options' contract multiplier:

Number of calls in covered position	Portfolio value		Index price		Contract multiplier
50	= $1,200,000.00	÷	(240.00	×	$100.00)

By selling 50 calls at 7.96 the investor creates an immediate positive cash flow of $39,800.00, which can be invested in Treasury bills:

Proceeds from sale of calls		Quantity sold		Call price		Contract multiplier
$39,800.00	=	50	×	7.96	×	$100.00

The more aggressive overwriting strategy seeks to take in greater initial proceeds by selling more calls than are covered by the stock portfolio. The exact number that the investor might sell is arbitrary, but for the sake of example let's say it is 100, resulting in proceeds of $79,600.00:

Proceeds from sale of calls		Quantity sold		Call price		Contract multiplier
$79,600.00	=	100	×	7.96	×	$100.00

Figure 10.13 illustrates the patterns of risks and returns associated with these three strategies. If the index is unchanged at the end of the holding period, the investor earns $12,000.00 in dividends in the unhedged portfolio. But in the conservative and aggressive overwriting portfolios his profits are higher by the initial proceeds from the call sales and the interest earned by reinvesting them—$52,496.50 and $92,993.00, respectively.

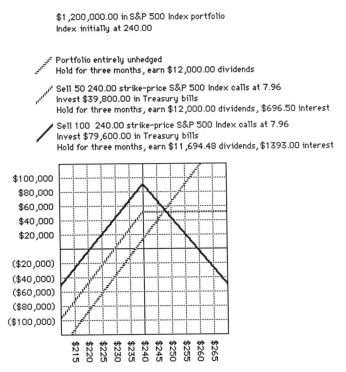

$1,200,000.00 in S&P 500 Index portfolio
Index initially at 240.00

Portfolio entirely unhedged
Hold for three months, earn $12,000.00 dividends

Sell 50 240.00 strike-price S&P 500 Index calls at 7.96
Invest $39,800.00 in Treasury bills
Hold for three months, earn $12,000.00 dividends, $696.50 interest

Sell 100 240.00 strike-price S&P 500 Index calls at 7.96
Invest $79,600.00 in Treasury bills
Hold for three months, earn $11,694.48 dividends, $1393.00 interest

FIGURE 10.13. Overwriting with index options

INDEX UNCHANGED

	Unhedged Portfolio	Sold 50 Calls	Sold 100 Calls
Cost of stocks	($1,200,000.00)	($1,200,000.00)	($1,200,000.00)
Sale of stocks	$1,200,000.00	$1,200,000.00	$1,200,000.00
Profit (loss) in stocks	0	0	0
Proceeds from calls		$ 39,800.00	$ 79,600.00
Expiration value of calls		0	0
Profit (loss) from calls		$ 39,800.00	$ 79,600.00
Interest income on T-bills (7% on $39,800.00 for 3 months)		$ 696.50	
Interest income on T-bills (7% on $79,600.00 for 3 months)			$ 1,393.00
Dividend income	$ 12,000.00	$ 12,000.00	$ 12,000.00
TOTAL PROFIT	$ 12,000.00	$ 52,496.50	$ 92,993.00

If the index declines by 10%, the unhedged portfolio suffers the full brunt of the decline, less dividends of $12,000.00, for a total loss of $108,000.00. The overwritten portfolios, cushioned by the proceeds from selling calls, show losses of only $67,503.50 (for the more conservative) and $27,007.00 (for the more aggressive). Although in neither case does overwriting act as "portfolio insurance," it nonetheless provides a partial hedge.

INDEX – 10%

	Unhedged Portfolio	Sold 50 Calls	Sold 100 Calls
Cost of stocks	($1,200,000.00)	($1,200,000.00)	($1,200,000.00)
Sale of stocks	$1,080,000.00	$1,080,000.00	$1,080,000.00
Profit (loss) in stocks	($ 120,000.00)	($ 120,000.00)	($ 120,000.00)
Proceeds from calls		$ 39,800.00	$ 79,600.00
Expiration value of calls		0	0
Profit (loss) from calls		$ 39,800.00	$ 79,600.00
Interest income on T-bills (7% on $39,800.00 for 3 months)		$ 696.50	
Interest income on T-bills (7% on $79,600.00 for 3 months)			$ 1,393.00
Dividend income	$ 12,000.00	$ 12,000.00	$ 12,000.00
TOTAL LOSS	($ 108,000.00)	($ 67,503.50)	($ 27,007.00)

When the index rises by 10%, the unhedged portfolio participates fully and earns dividends, showing profits of $132,000.00. But the conservative overwriting portfolio shows the same $52,496.50 profit as when the index was unchanged. In fact, because the position is a covered one, no matter how high the index rises it can never show profits any higher than this. The more aggressive overwriting portfolio, on the other hand, shows a loss of $27,007.00. Because more calls were sold than could be covered by offsetting gains in the portfolio, the more the index rises, the greater the loss.

INDEX + 10%

	Unhedged Portfolio	Sold 50 Calls	Sold 100 Calls
Cost of stocks	($1,200,000.00)	($1,200,000.00)	($1,200,000.00)
Sale of stocks	$1,320,000.00	$1,320,000.00	$1,320,000.00
Profit (loss) in stocks	120,000.00	120,000.00	120,000.00
Proceeds from calls		$ 39,800.00	$ 79,600.00
Expiration value of calls		($ 120,000.00)	($ 240,000.00)
Profit (loss) from calls		($ 80,200.00)	($ 160,400.00)
Interest income on T-bills (7% on $39,800.00 for 3 months)		$ 696.50	
Interest income on T-bills (7% on $79,600.00 for 3 months)			$ 1,393.00
Dividend income	$ 12,000.00	$ 12,000.00	$ 12,000.00
TOTAL PROFIT (LOSS)	$ 132,000.00	$ 52,496.50	($ 27,007.00)

A method to preserve the greater down-side protection and higher expected return afforded by the more aggressive overwriting strategy, while attempting to mitigate the losses it can lead to on the up-side, might operate something like the well-known *martingale* betting systems devised for casino gambling. In a martingale system the player doubles his bet every time he loses. This way, when the player finally wins, the payoff will compensate all prior losses.

To see how this concept might apply to overwriting, consider how an investor might have employed it in the preceding example. Let's say he makes a rule that anytime the index rises from one strike-price to the next higher one, he will repurchase his short calls and sell enough calls of the next closest out-of-the-money strike-price to offset the cost of repurchase. Let's explore the sequence of trading events triggered by this rule during a 10% rise in the index over three months.

The first trade occurs when the index rises from 240.00 to 245.00. If we assume that it takes place one month into the three-month holding period, the 240.00-strike-price calls he originally sold for 7.96 would now be valued at 9.41, and the 250.00-strike-price calls, the next closest out of the money, would be valued at 4.28. To repay the $94,100.00 cost of repurchasing the 240.00 calls the investor would have to sell 219.9 of the 250.00 calls.

Now let's say the market rises further, from 245.00 to 250.00 by midway through the three-month holding period. The 250.00-strike-price calls sold at 4.28 would be valued at 5.70, and the 255.00-strike-price calls would be valued at 3.52. To repay the $125,343.00 cost of repurchasing the 250.00 calls the investor would have to sell 356.1 of the 255.00 calls.

Next, let's say the market rises from 250.00 to 255.00 by two months into the three-month holding period. At this point the 255.00 calls sold at 3.52 would be valued at 4.69 and the 260.00 calls would be valued at 2.58. To repay the $167,010.90 cost of repurchasing the 255.00 calls the investor would have to sell 647.3 of the 260.00 calls.

Now, let's say the market rises from 255.00 to 260.00, with only two weeks to go in the three-month holding period. At this point the 260.00 calls sold at 2.58 would be valued at 2.86, and the 265.00 calls would be valued at 1.02. To repay the $185,127.80 cost of repurchasing the 260.00 calls, the investor would have to sell 1814.9 of the 265.00 calls.

Finally, at expiration, the index closes at 264.00, a 10% rise from 240.00, where it began three months earlier, and the 1814.9 265.00-strike-price calls will expire worthless. From a call position that grew over 18 times its original size, the investor captures exactly the same $79,600.00 he was expecting at the beginning. But, coupled with the appreciation in his stock portfolio and dividends and interest received, his total profit is $213,193.00—higher than anything that could have been expected with a less active strategy.

	Index Up 10%
Initial cost of stocks	$1,200,000.00
Sale of stocks	$1,320,000.00
Profit from stocks	$ 120,000.00
Proceeds from sale of 240.00 calls (7.96 × 100 × $100.00)	$ 79,600.00
Repurchase of 240.00 calls (9.41 × 100 × $100.00)	($ 94,100.00)
Proceeds from sale of 250.00 calls (4.28 × 219.9 × $100.00)	94,100.00
Repurchase of 250.00 calls (5.70 × 219.9 × $100.00)	($ 125,343.00)
Proceeds from sale of 255.00 calls (3.52 × 356.1 × $100.00)	$ 125,343.00
Repurchase of 255.00 calls (4.69 × 356.1 × $100.00)	($ 167,010.90)
Proceeds from sale of 260.00 calls (2.58 × 647.3 × $100.00)	$ 167,010.90
Repurchase of 260.00 calls (2.86 × 647.3 × $100.00)	($ 185,127.80)
Proceeds from sale of 265.00 calls (1.02 × 1814.9 × $100.00)	$ 185,127.80
Expiration value of 265.00 calls (expire worthless)	0
Profit from calls	$ 79,600.00
Interest income on T-bills	
(7% on $79,800.00 for 3 months)	$ 1,393.00
Dividends	$ 12,000.00
TOTAL PROFIT	$ 213,193.00

If an investor has confidence that the martingale strategy can control losses on the up-side, aggressive overwriting becomes not just a down-side hedge, but a strategy for overall performance enhancement. Unfortunately the martingale system has serious drawbacks. First, there is the risk that the investor will run out of margin funds. Second, there is the risk that he will hit the exchange's position limits—in the S&P 500 Index options we have been using in the example the limit is 15,000 contracts; therefore if the investor's initial position had been nine times larger (900 calls instead of 100) he would not have been able to make the final trade (16,334.1 contracts instead of 1814.9). Finally, there is the risk that the investor will simply run out of courage—it takes real conviction to adhere unflinchingly to a program that requires selling greater and greater numbers of uncovered calls as the market rises.

In practice, the investment managers who specialize in overwriting have a variety of approaches specifying the optimal number of calls to sell at the beginning of the holding period, and the precise trading rule to govern future adjustments. But to the extent that these approaches mitigate the drawbacks we have mentioned, they also mitigate the expected returns; for example, all the drawbacks can be dealt with by starting off selling fewer calls, but this obviously lowers expected returns when the index is unchanged or lower. Alternative adjustment rules, including rolling out from one expiration month to the next, can control the number of calls sold, but ultimately they just move the skeleton from one closet to another. In a sufficiently powerful market rally—however unlikely—any adjustment system will exhaust margin funds, hit position limits, and shake the confidence of even the most courageous trader.

Once the decision to sell index calls is made, regardless of the exact strategy that will be used to manage the position, an investor must choose specific calls to sell, at specific points in time, from among the hundreds available. Several simple criteria can narrow down the choice immediately:

The choice of underlying index flows either from concerns with correlation, performance, or both. Of course, overwriters must be concerned with selecting an index that will adequately track their underlying portfolios. On the other hand, they may prefer some unique attribute of a particular index, regardless of how poorly it correlates; for example, one might wish to sell calls on the Value Line because its geometric average construction gives it a downward bias relative to all other indexes.

The choice of strike-price and expiration term may be dictated by an investor's outlook for the performance of the index over the holding period or his willingness to bear the consequences of exercise. On the other hand, it may be the result of the requirements of a particular martingale rule.

These criteria can narrow down the universe of index options to a manageable number of choices, among which an investor will be effectively indifferent. The only criterion left by which to make the final selection is *advantageous mispricing*—the opportunity to sell calls higher than their theoretical values. Unfortunately, it is not always obvious which calls are the most mispriced.

Consider two calls. The first is a three-month, American call on the S&P 100 Index, with a strike-price of 240.00; the underlying index is at 235.00, its volatility is 17%, its yield is 4%, and the riskless interest rate is 7%. The theoretical value of this call is 6.22, and its delta (the call's sensitivity to a given move in the price of the underlying index) is 0.45. It can be sold in the marketplace at 7.25, a 1.03 advantage over theoretical value. The second is a two-month, American call on the NYSE Composite Index, with a strike-price of 145.00; the underlying index is at 140.00, its volatility is 15%, and its yield is 4%. The theoretical value of this call is 1.71, and its delta is 0.32. It can be sold in the marketplace at 2.50, a 0.79 advantage over theoretical value.

To choose between these calls we'll have to make their advantageous mispricings cross-comparable between them. We'll begin by accounting for price and volatility differences between the two underlying indexes. To do this we calculate each index's *annual dollar volatility* by multiplying the price of the underlying index by its estimated annual percentage volatility:

S&P 100 annual dollar volatility		Index price		Annual percentage volatility
39.19	=	230.00	×	17%

NYSE annual dollar volatility		Index price		Annual percentage volatility
21.00	=	140.00	×	15%

These annual dollar volatility figures mean that, about two-thirds of the time, the price of the S&P 100 will move *no more* than 39.19 points in a given year; but, about two-thirds of the time the price of the NYSE Composite will move *no more* than 21.00 points. With this knowledge we have already established an extremely important difference between the two indexes, which will help us choose the most mispriced call.

Next, we'll take into account that the two calls have differing times remaining until expiration. To do this we deannualize the annual dollar volatility by dividing it by the square root of the number of periods in a year equal to the time remaining. To adjust the S&P 100's annual dollar volatility of 39.19 for three months remaining, we divide 39.19 by the square root of 4. To adjust the NYSE's annual dollar volatility of 21.00 for two months remaining we divide 21.00 by the square root of 6:

S&P 100 dollar volatility		Annual dollar volatility		Square root of periods in a year
19.59	=	39.19	÷	$\sqrt{4}$

NYSE dollar volatility		Annual dollar volatility		Square root of periods in a year
8.57	=	21.00	÷	$\sqrt{6}$

Next we must adjust the dollar volatilities to account for the fact that the two calls represent different levels of risk to the seller because they have different sensitivities to given price changes in their underlying indexes. To do this, we multiply the dollar volatilities by the calls' deltas. For the S&P 100 we multiply 19.59 by 0.45. For the NYSE composite we multiply 8.57 by 0.32.

S&P 100 call's risk		Dollar volatility		Delta
8.81	=	19.59	×	0.45

NYSE call's risk		Dollar volatility		Delta
2.74	=	8.57	×	0.32

Finally, we divide the amount of mispricing by the call's risk. The result is a reward/risk ratio by which we can rank the two options. For the S&P 100 call we divide the mispricing of 1.03 by the risk of 8.81 to get a reward/risk ratio of 0.117. For the NYSE call we divide the mispricing of 0.79 by the risk of 2.74, to get a reward/risk ratio of 0.288:

S&P 100 call's reward/risk ratio		Mispricing		Call's risk
0.117	=	1.03	÷	8.81

NYSE call's reward/risk ratio		Mispricing		Call's risk
0.288	=	0.79	÷	2.74

Although the S&P 100 call appeared at first to be the more advantageous sale, with a mispricing of 1.03, as opposed to the NYSE Composite call's mispricing of only 0.79, exactly the opposite turns out to be the case when all the relevant risks are taken into account. This ratio is more than an arbitrary statistical convention. It has a literal, intuitive meaning and is universally cross-comparable between all options on all indexes. It represents the dollar amount of advantageous mispricing in a 1.00 delta position per dollar of dollar volatility.

11. INTERMARKET TRADING WITH INDEX OPTIONS AND FUTURES

Traditionally, investment decisions are focused on the timing and direction of "the market" as though it were a monolith. But although the underlying indexes on which options and futures trade have many similarities, they have intriguing differences as well. A unique and fascinating application for index options and futures is to exploit the subtle differences between the indexes by buying one and selling another. For the investor who seeks to establish this kind of position the conceptual challenge is to scale the two sides of the trade in such a way as to filter out the *absolute* performance of the broad market. In the ideal intermarket position the only element that counts is the *relative* performance between market sectors.

The arbitrage approach to intermarket trading takes an even more refined view. Rather than build intermarket positions in anticipation of a particular sector displacement, the arbitrageur buys underpriced options or futures on one index and sells overpriced ones on another. He is not betting on any particular relative performance; rather he is anticipating that the mispriced options or futures will return to equilibrium by expiration, at which time he will unwind the position at a profit.

This is a very different kind of arbitrage than any we have considered so far. In the synthetic money market instrument we have as close to a classic, *riskless arbitrage* as we are likely to find in modern markets. When an investor short-sells overpriced index futures contracts and simultaneously buys the stocks that constitute the underlying index, the mispricing virtually *must* resolve in the investor's favor by expiration because the futures cash-settle against the index price. But when an investor seeks to exploit mispricings between futures or options on *two different indexes*, he is engaging in *risk arbitrage*, for technically there is nothing to prevent the two indexes from diverging wildly, never to reconverge, and causing substantial losses on *both* sides of the position. The conceptual challenge for the arbitrageur is to quantify the risk of sector displacement and then determine whether anticipated arbitrage profits will be sufficient to compensate for it.

INTERMARKET POSITIONING AND ARBITRAGE WITH INDEX FUTURES

Consider an investor who is neither bullish nor bearish on the broad market—he doesn't know or care if, when, or in which direction the market will move. But there is one opinion he feels very strong about: he believes that macroeconomic factors (e.g., inflation, war, new tax legislation) will lead to relatively poorer performance by large, old-line industrial companies, as opposed to smaller high-tech or service companies. By simultaneously buying futures on the Value Line Average and short-selling futures on the Major Market Index, the investor has a practical, highly levered strategy for acting on just this kind of opinion.

The MMI is comprised of 20 large-capitalization, blue-chip stocks that represent "smokestack America." The Value Line, on the other hand, is comprised of more than 1500 stocks of all sizes, equally weighted so that the tiniest over-the-counter issue is as great a factor in determining the index price as is IBM. By buying one index and selling the other the investor is not betting on the timing or direction of broad market moves because, in general, both indexes tend to rise and fall together. Regardless of the *absolute* performance of either index, to the extent that the sector of the market represented by the Value Line *relatively* outperforms that sector represented by the MMI the investor will profit from his opinion.

To explore the implementation and possible outcomes of this strategy let's use actual historical data from the three months from June 24 to September 20, 1985. At the beginning the Value Line was priced at 197.38 and the MMI was priced at 259.38. To establish a position to profit from anticipated divergence between the indexes the investor would have to scale positions properly in the two indexes' futures contracts to take account of their different prices and contract multipliers. The Value Line contract, with a $500.00 multiplier, had on June 24 an underlying value of $98,690.00, but the MMI contract, with a $250.00 multiplier, had an underlying value of only $64,845.00:

Underlying value		Value Line price		Contract multiplier		Number of contracts
$98,690.00	=	197.38	×	$500.00	×	1

Underlying value		MMI price		Contract multiplier		Number of contracts
$64,845.00	=	259.38	×	$250.00	×	1

If the investor naively buys one Value Line contracts and sells one MMI contract, his investment on the long side would so overshadow his investment on the short side that he would, in fact, be making nothing but an up-side bet. To scale the number of MMI contracts to the underlying value of one Value Line contract we simply divide the two underlying values. The result is 1.52 contracts.

Number of MMI contracts = 1 Value Line contract		Value Line underlying value		MMI underlying value
1.52	=	$98,690.00	÷	$64,845.00

Underlying value		MMI price		Contract multiplier		Number of contracts
$98,690.00	=	259.38	×	$250.00	×	1.52

If the riskless interest rate were 9% and both indexes had dividend yields of 4%, the theoretical values of the Value Line and MMI contracts would have been 199.85 and 262.62, respectively. By buying one Value Line contract and selling 1.52 MMI contracts not only are the *underlying values* of the two positions equivalent, their *contract values* are equal, as well:

Contract value		Value Line contract price		Contract multiplier		Number of contracts
$99,923.62	=	199.85	×	$500.00	×	1

Contract value		MMI contract price		Contract multiplier		Number of contracts
$99,923.62	=	262.62	×	$250.00	×	1.52

This means that not only has the investor created an approximate hedge against moves made by both indexes but he has hedged the effects of premium erosion as well. If, at expiration in three months both underlying indexes close exactly unchanged or both are up or down by the same percentages, the investor will precisely break even.

	Both Indexes Unchanged	Both Indexes + 10%	Both Indexes − 10%
Initial contract value: Value Line	($99,923.62)	($ 99,923.62)	($99,923.62)
Expiration value: Value Line	$98,690.00	$108,559.00	$88,821.00
Profit (loss) from Value Line	($ 1,233.62)	$ 8,635.38	($11,102.62)
Initial contract value: MMI	$99,923.62	$ 99,923.62	$99,923.62
Expiration value: MMI	($98,690.00)	($108,559.00)	($88,821.00)
Profit (loss) from MMI	$ 1,233.62	($ 8,635.38)	$11,102.62
TOTAL PROFIT	0	0	0

If the two indexes do *not* move by the same percentages, the position will show either a profit or a loss, as illustrated in Figure 11.1. In this chart the horizontal axis no longer represents the price of the underlying index; now it represents the *percentage divergence between the two underlying indexes*. A positive number indicates divergence in the investor's favor: the Value Line outperforms the MMI. Conversely, a negative number indicates divergence to the investor's disadvantage: the MMI outperforms the Value Line.

But now let's look at Figure 11.2 to see what actually occurred between June 24 and September 20, 1985. As the investor had anticipated, the Value Line did, in fact, outperform the MMI. The broad market rallied in the first month of the holding period, taking the Value Line up 5.78% to 208.13—but the MMI rose only 2.60%, to 266.13. From there the broad market drifted lower but the Value Line continued to outperform the MMI until the final week of the holding period. One week before expiration the situation reversed, with the Value Line down 4.18% to 189.13 and the MMI down only 3.47% to 189.13. Virtually on expiration day itself the situation reversed again and the Value Line finished as the slightly better performer, down 3.36% to 190.75 versus the MMI down 3.42% to 250.50.

Figure 11.3 illustrates the daily cumulative profit or loss the investor could have realized every day in the position. At the point in July when the Value Line had most outperformed the MMI the investor had a profit

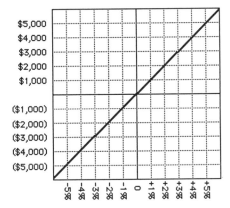

Buy 1 Value Line futures contract at 198.86
Sell 1.52 Major Market Index futures contracts at 198.86
Value line initially at 197.38
MMI initially at 259.38
Hold for three months

FIGURE 11.1. Dollar-balanced intermarket futures position

of $3139.10, which he could have elected to realize at that point simply by closing both sides of the position. At the point in September just before expiration, when the MMI temporarily outperformed the Value Line there was a loss of $746.43. Finally, at expiration, with the Value Line slightly outperforming the MMI, the investor's profit was $63.70.

Now let's go back to the beginning and look at this trade from the perspective of an arbitrageur, rather than a risk positioner. Although the positioner was motivated by a conviction about relative performance of the indexes, the arbitrageur would be motivated only by relative price discrepancies in the futures. Let's say that instead of their theoretical values of 199.85 and 262.62, respectively, the Value Line futures were *over*priced at 201.00 and the MMI contracts were *under*priced at 262.00. At these prices an investor might wish to simultaneously buy the underpriced MMI contract and short-sell the overpriced Value Line contract, regardless of how he thought the indexes might perform relatively.

He could proceed as earlier, setting up a position of equivalent *underlying value* on both sides, by buying 1.52 MMI contracts for every Value Line contract sold short:

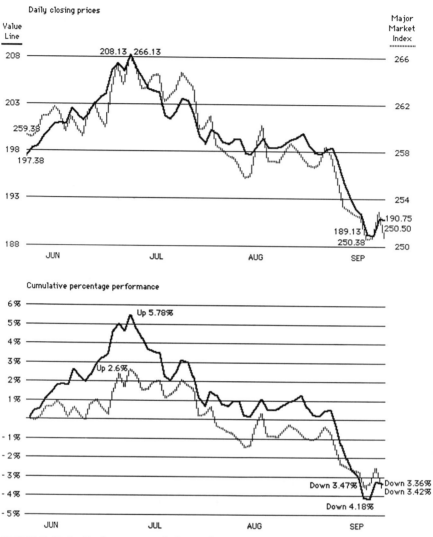

FIGURE 11.2. Performance of the Value Line Average and the Major Market Index, June 24 to September 20, 1985

Underlying value		MMI price		Contract multiplier		Number of contracts
$98,690.00	=	259.38	×	$250.00	×	1.52 (rounded)

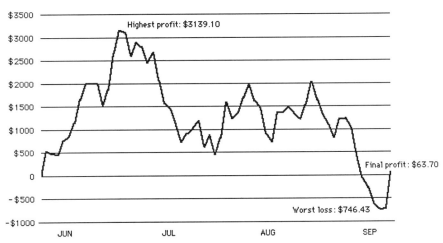

Buy 1 Value Line Index Futures Contract at 199.85
Sell 1.52 Major Market Index Futures Contracts at 262.62

FIGURE 11.3. Dollar-balanced intermarket futures position, cumulative daily profit and loss

Underlying value		Value Line price		Contract multiplier		Number of contracts
$98,690.00	=	197.38	×	$500.00	×	1

This time, however, the *contract values* of the two sides of the position will *not* be equal because one was bought below its theoretical value and the other was sold above:

Contract value		MMI Contract price		Contract multiplier		Number of contracts
$99,686.87	=	262.00	×	$250.00	×	1.52 (rounded)

Contract value		Value Line contract price		Contract multiplier		Number of contracts
$100,500.00	=	201.00	×	$500.00	×	1

There are two ways to determine the anticipated profit in the arbitrage.

One is to multiply the mispricing per contract by the respective contract multiplier and the number of contracts in the position and then sum the results for the aggregate position. Using this method, the result is an anticipated profit of $813.13.

Anticipated MMI profit		MMI mispricing		Contract multiplier		Number of contracts
$238.13	=	0.62	×	$250.00	×	1.52 (rounded)

Anticipated Value Line profit		Value Line mispricing		Contract multiplier		Number of contracts
$575.00	=	1.15	×	$500.00	×	1

Aggregate anticipated profit		Anticipated MMI profit		Anticipated Value Line profit
$813.13	=	$238.13	+	$575.00

The other way to determine anticipated profit is to calculate the difference between the *contract* values of the two contracts and subtract the result from the difference between the *underlying* values of the two contracts. With this method the result is the same—an anticipated profit of $813.13:

Difference in underlying values		Value Line (short) underlying value		MMI (long) underlying value
0	=	$98,690.00	−	$98,690.00

Difference in contract values		Value Line (short) contract value		MMI (long) contract value
$813.13	=	$100,500.00	−	$99,686.87

Anticipated profit		Difference in contract values		Difference in underlying values
$813.13	=	$813.13	−	0

$813.13 is what the investor can expect to earn if, at any time during the holding period, he can unwind the position at theoretical value—provided, however, that the two indexes do not diverge.

	Both Indexes Unchanged	Both Indexes +10%	Both Indexes -10%
Initial contract value: Value Line	$100,500.00	$100,500.00	$100,500.00
Expiration value: Value Line	($ 98,690.00)	($108,559.00)	($ 88,821.00)
Profit (loss) from Value Line	$ 1,810.00	($ 8,059.00)	$ 11,679.00
Initial contract value: MMI	($ 99,686.87)	($ 99,686.87)	($ 99,686.87)
Expiration value: MMI	$ 98,690.00	$108,559.00	$ 88,821.00
Profit (loss) from MMI	($ 996.87)	($ 8,872.13)	($ 10,865.87)
TOTAL PROFIT	$ 813.13	$ 813.13	$ 813.13

If the underlying indexes diverge, the investor's profit will deviate from the expected $813.13, as illustrated in Figure 11.4. If the MMI outperforms the Value Line, the profit will be greater; conversely, if the Value Line outperforms the MMI, the profit will be lower. Potentially it could even be a loss.

Let's return to the historical evidence and see how this arbitrage would have actually worked out. Figure 11.5 illustrates what we already knew from the preceding example: the Value Line so outperformed the MMI during most of the three months that the arbitrage position had a cumulative unrealized loss more often than not, despite the advantage of

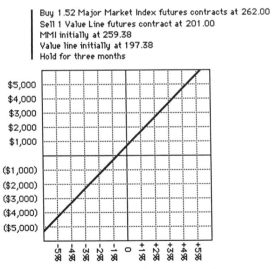

FIGURE 11.4. Dollar-balanced intermarket futures arbitrage

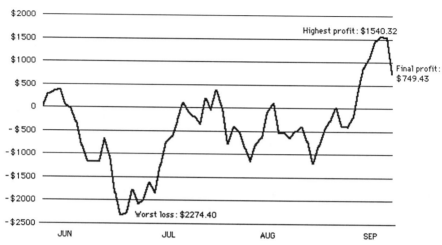

FIGURE 11.5. Dollar-balanced intermarket futures arbitrage, cumulative daily profit and loss

an $818.13 relative pricing discrepancy. At the worst point in early July the position showed an unrealized loss of $2274.40. At the best point, however, just before expiration, the position showed an unrealized profit of $1540.52. At expiration, despite the Value Line's slight final under-performance, the arbitrage ended up with a profit of $749.43.

The reduction of the anticipated profit of $813.13, attributable to the slight final divergence between the indexes at expiration, can be calcu-lated by multiplying the initial underlying value of one side of the po-sition by the percentage divergence:

Loss attributable to divergence		Initial underlying value of one side		Percentage divergence
$63.70	=	$98,690.00	×	0.06454%

The divergence lowered the profit in the arbitrage from the anticipated $813.13 to $749.43.

Final profit		Anticipated profit		Loss attributable to divergence
$749.43	=	$813.13	−	$63.70

There is a statistical technique that the investor could have used to predict the risk of divergence and then determine whether the anticipated reward of $813.13 was sufficient compensation. The technique begins with estimates of the volatility of the two indexes. Earlier, in the section on options valuation, we discussed the many ways of estimating volatilities, but for this example we'll settle for measurements of the indexes' historical volatilities during the three months prior to the holding period—6.5% annualized for the Value Line and 9.1% annualized for the MMI.

Along with the volatilities, we'll use the *correlation coefficient* of the daily percentage price changes of the two indexes, a historical measurement of the accuracy with which they track one another. For the three months prior to the holding period the correlation coefficient for the Value Line against the MMI was 0.784678, a good match, but not perfect (1.00 indicates perfect positive correlation).

By combining the correlation coefficient with the higher of the two indexes' volatilities, we can estimate the annualized volatility of the arbitrage position—3.5%.

Annual volatility of arbitrage		Higher index volatility		One minus correlation coefficient squared
3.5%	=	9.1%	×	$(1 - 0.784678^2)$

To convert this result into quarterly terms relevant to the three-month holding period we divide the annual figure by the square root of the number of holding periods in a year and get 1.75%:

Quarterly volatility of arbitrage		Annual volatility		Square root of number of periods in year
1.75%	=	3.5%	÷	$\sqrt{4}$

Assuming that divergences between the index will be normally distributed, this figure can be interpreted to mean that in only about *one trial out of three*, the underlying values of the two sides of the position will diverge by *more* than 1.75%, or $1727.07, by the end of the holding period. The investor can use this information to determine whether the anticipated profit of $813.13 is commensurate with the risk.

Following are tables giving the historical volatilities and correlation coefficients for the indexes on which options or futures are actively traded, as of August 7, 1986, and the quarterly volatility of the intermarket arbitrage between each pair of indexes. The highest volatility is between the very indexes we have been using in our example, the Value Line and the MMI: the quarterly volatility is now 3.22%, almost twice as high as that calculated for the June 1985 example. It is hard to imagine finding profit opportunities in intermarket arbitrages sufficient to justify this risk.

The lowest volatility is between the S&P 500 and the NYSE Composite, only 0.08%—eight-hundredths of one percent. Clearly, an investor would be willing to implement intermarket arbitrages between these two indexes with relatively low anticipated profits.

ANNUAL PERCENTAGE VOLATILITY*

MMI	NYSE	S&P 100	S&P 500	VLA
14.35%	11.64%	13.73%	12.83%	9.70%

*Based on daily data over three months.

CORRELATION COEFFICIENTS*

	MMI	NYSE	S&P 100	S&P 500	VLA
MMI	1.0000	0.9207	0.9553	0.9342	0.7418
NYSE		1.0000	0.9661	0.9940	0.8885
S&P 100			1.0000	0.9796	0.7944
S&P 500				1.0000	0.8522
VLA					1.0000

*Based on daily data over one year.

QUARTERLY VOLATILITY OF INTERMARKET ARBITRAGE POSITIONS

	MMI	NYSE	S&P 100	S&P 500	VLA
MMI	0	1.09%	0.63%	0.91%	3.22%
NYSE		0	0.46%	0.08%	1.22%
S&P 100			0	0.27%	2.53%
S&P 500				0	1.76%
VLA					0

Using this kind of information, the investor could attempt to structure his arbitrage to absorb the divergences experienced during the holding period. Obviously we can look back over historical data and determine what would have been the optimal structure. But let's put ourselves in the position of the investor having to make decisions on June 24, 1985, without benefit of knowing what would transpire in the upcoming three months.

One logical approach would have been to balance the futures positions with respect to the volatilities of the two indexes. The historical evidence available on June 24, 1985, would have shown the Value Line's annual volatility at 6.5% and the MMI's at 9.1%. To determine the position weighting factor appropriate to these volatilities we divide the smaller one by the larger one to get 0.7143:

Weighting factor		Value Line volatility		MMI volatility
0.7143	=	6.5%	÷	9.1%

We use this weighting factor to reduce the MMI position the investor would have ordinarily taken, considering that the MMI is apparently much more volatile than the Value Line. To do this we multiply the MMI position—1.52—by the weighting factor. The resulting volatility-weighted position is 1.087 contracts. Ironically, after using this elaborate weighting technique we have returned pretty much to the one-to-one position we dismissed earlier as naive:

Volatility-weighted position		Position size		Weighting factor
1.087	=	1.52	÷	0.7143

Now the two sides of the position will have very different underlying values:

Underlying value		MMI price		Contract multiplier		Number of contracts
$70,492.86	=	259.38	×	$250.00	×	1.087 (rounded)

Underlying value		Value Line price		Contract multiplier		Number of contracts
$98,690.00	=	197.38	×	$500.00	×	1

And the contract values of the two sides of the position will be very different as well:

Contract value		MMI contract price		Contract multiplier		Number of contracts
$71,204.91	=	262.00	×	$250.00	×	1.087 (rounded)

Contract value		Value Line contract price		Contract multiplier		Number of contracts
$100,500.00	=	201.00	×	$500.00	×	1

Determining the anticipated profit in the arbitrage structured this way is a conceptually more complicated problem than it was before, when both sides of the position had equal underlying values. Let's begin as we did earlier by multiplying the mispricing per contract by the contract multiplier and the number of contracts in the position:

Anticipated MMI profit		MMI mispricing		Contract multiplier		Number of contracts
$168.50	=	0.62	×	$250.00	× 1.087 (rounded)

Anticipated Value Line profit		Value Line mispricing		Contract multiplier		Number of contracts
$575.00	=	1.15	×	$500.00	×	1

Aggregate anticipated profit		Anticipated MMI profit		Anticipated Value Line profit
$743.50	=	$168.50	+	$575.00

By using this method we arrive at $743.50, slightly lower than the $813.13

we had expected earlier. This is because we have bought fewer under-priced MMI contracts. But next, when we try an alternate method for calculating anticipated profit, we arrive at an entirely different figure—$1097.95:

Difference in underlying values		Value Line (short) underlying value		MMI (long) underlying value
$28,197.14	=	$98,690.00	−	$70,492.86

Difference in contract values		Value Line (short) contract value		MMI (long) contract value
$29,295.09	=	$100,500.00	−	$71,204.91

Anticipated profit		Difference in contract values		Difference in underlying values
$1097.95	=	$29,295.09	−	$28,197.14

Of the two different anticipated profits, each is correct—but we must be careful to understand what each means. The $743.50 is the investor's *immediate advantage*; it's what he would earn *immediately*, if he could unwind the position at theoretical value. The $1097.95, on the other hand, is his *ultimate advantage*; it's what he will earn *at expiration*, provided that the two underlying indexes move with exactly the relative volatilities we used in the weighting calculation (in this case, the ratio 6.5:9.1; when the Value Line moves by 10%, the MMI must move by 14%). The reason the two figures are different and the expiration figure is higher is that the short side of the position is bigger than the long side—the investor has now sold more premium than he has bought. As time passes and the premium erodes, the anticipated profit will rise from $743.50 today to $1097.95 at expiration.

	Both Indexes Unchanged	MMI +14% Value Line +10%	MMI −14% Value Line −10%
Initial contract value: Value Line	$100,500.00	$100,500.00	$100,500.00
Expiration value: Value Line	($ 98,690.00)	($108,559.00)	($ 88,821.00)
Profit (loss) from Value Line	$ 1,810.00	($ 8,059.00)	$ 11,679.00
Initial contract value: MMI	($ 71,204.91)	($ 71,204.91)	($ 71,204.91)
Expiration value: MMI	$ 70,492.86	$ 80,361.86	$ 60,623.86
Profit (loss) from Value Line	($ 712.05)	$ 9,156.95	($ 10,581.05)
TOTAL PROFIT	$ 1,097.95	$ 1,097.95	$ 1,097.95

Let's look back at the historical evidence and see how the volatility-weighted arbitrage actually performed. Figure 11.6 overlays the cumu-

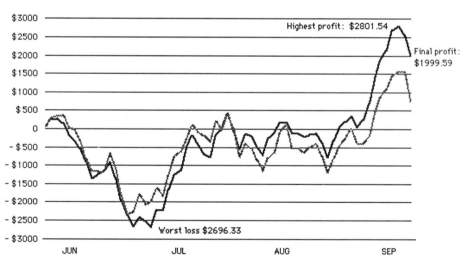

FIGURE 11.6. Volatility-weighted intermarket futures arbitrage compared with dollar-balanced arbitrage, cumulative daily profit and loss

lative daily profit and loss for the volatility-weighted arbitrage on the dollar-balanced arbitrage we examined previously. When the two indexes moved higher in the first third of the holding period, the volatility-weighted arbitrage sustained a worse unrealized loss than the dollar-balanced arbitrage; conversely, when the two indexes moved lower in the last two-thirds of the holding period, the volatility-weighted arbitrage had greater unrealized profits. Fortunately both indexes had declined by expiration and the volatility-weighted arbitrage finished with a profit of $1999.59.

Apparently the volatilites of the two indexes were not so different as the investor anticipated because the volatility-weighted position behaved as though it were excessively short—losses on the up-side and profits on the down-side. If the MMI had actually been more volatile than the Value Line, the smaller underlying value of the long MMI side of the position would have been a better hedge for the larger short Value Line position. In point of fact, measurement of the volatilities during the holding period confirms this intuition perfectly: the volatilites of the two indexes were not the widely divergent 9.1% for the MMI and 6.5% for the Value Line, as anticipated, but rather an almost identical 8.7 and 8.5%, respectively.

INTERMARKET POSITIONING AND ARBITRAGE WITH INDEX OPTIONS

In our examination of intermarket trading with index futures we saw that when an investor has long futures on one index and short futures on another, his profit or loss is a simple linear function of the correlation or divergence of the two indexes. When an investor establishes similar positions with index *options*, he can create more complex patterns of risks and returns than any we have examined so far.

Let's return to the historical example we used previously—the Value Line and the Major Market Index over the three months from June 24 to September 20, 1985. At the beginning of the period, with the Value Line priced at 197.38, a volatility of 6.5%, a yield of 4%, and a riskless interest rate of 9%, the three-month, American 195.00-strike-price puts would be valued at 1.14. With the MMI priced at 259.38, a volatility of 9.1%, and a yield of 4% the three-month, American 255.00-strike-price puts would be valued at 2.26. If, anticipating that the Value Line will outperform the MMI, the investor wanted to use these puts instead of futures, he could buy the MMI puts and sell the Value Line puts.

First, he'd have to deal with the problem of scaling the riskiness of the long and short sides of the position. At first glance, because the Value Line put is 2.38 out-of-the-money and the MMI put is 4.38 out-of-the-money, the two puts appear quite dissimilar; but a closer analysis reveals that they are comparable. To see this we'll compare the out-of-the-money amounts with the annual dollar volatility of each index. Recall, from our earlier discussion of screening calls for overwriting, that the annual dollar volatility of an index is its price multiplied by its annual percentage volatility:

MMI annual dollar volatility		Index price		Volatility
23.60	=	259.38	×	9.1%

Value Line annual dollar volatility		Index price		Volatility
12.83	=	189.38	×	6.5%

Next we'll determine the percentage of the annual dollar volatility represented by the amount out-of-the-money. This compares the amounts out-of-the-money with the probability that the prices of the respective indexes will move by that amount:

MMI percentage of annual dollar volatility		Out-of-the-money amount		Annual dollar volatility
18.56%	=	4.38	×	23.60

Value Line percentage of annual dollar volatility		Out-of-the-money amount		Annual dollar volatility
18.55%	=	2.38	×	12.83

The results, 18.56% for the MMI and 18.55% for the Value Line, are close enough to make the two puts functionally identical. In other words, given the respective prices and volatilities of the two indexes, *the two puts are equivalent amounts out-of-the-money.*

But this is not to say that the optimally hedged position would be structured simply by buying and selling the same number of contracts because the amount a put is out-of-the-money is not its only relevant measure of risk. To see why this would be so, consider two exactly *at-the-money* puts, one on an index priced at 100.00 and the other on an index priced at 50.00. Although the two puts are obviously equivalent in terms of amounts out-of-the-money, they clearly represent unequal levels of risk because, all else being equal, the index priced at 100.00 has the greater likelihood of making a given dollar price move simply because it's higher priced. To account for this principle the investor must weight the number of contracts on each side of the position by the ratio of the annual dollar volatilities of the two indexes, 23.60 and 12.83, respectively. The result is 1.84:

Ratio of annual dollar volatilities		MMI annual dollar volatility		Value Line annual dollar volatility
1.84	=	23.60	÷	12.83

The optimally hedged position would be to sell 1.84 Value Line puts at 1.14 for each MMI put bought at 2.26. Establishing this position would result in a small net cost of $16.00, which we'll assume could be financed at 7%:

Proceeds from Value Line puts		Put price		Number of contracts		Contract multiplier
$210.00	=	1.14	×	1.84	×	$100.00

Cost of MMI puts		Put price		Number of contracts		Contract multiplier
$226.00	=	2.26	×	1	×	$100.00

Net cost		Cost of MMI puts		Proceeds from Value Line puts
$16.00	=	$226.00	−	$210.00

With futures we were able to use a single two-dimensional chart to show the pattern of risks and returns associated with intermarket positions: the vertical axis represented profit or loss and the horizontal axis represented divergence between the indexes. Now, using index options instead of futures, profits and losses will be a function of an additional factor: the amount by which the options are in the money. If the options expire *out*-of-the-money, only the most extreme divergences can possibly be relevant: options on both indexes will expire worthless. But, when the options expire *in*-the-money, divergences lead to profits and losses as surely as they did for the futures position we examined earlier.

As Figure 11.7 illustrates, *multiple* two-dimensional charts can, when taken together, approximate the true shape of risks and returns associated with intermarket options positions. In this idealization we have assumed that both indexes are trading at the same price and have the same volatility and that both options are priced at their respective, identical theoretical values.

As with intermarket positions in futures, the vertical axes represent profit or loss (this time, as a percentage of the underlying value of one side of the position); the horizontal axes represent divergence between the indexes. Each chart represents a different *percentage amount in the money* for the long option in the position, ranging from 5% in the money (the large chart in the upper left-hand corner) to 5% out of the money (the large chart in the lower right-hand corner).

Note that when the *long* option in the position is 5% *in*-the-money (the large chart in the upper left-hand corner) the risk/reward line is perfectly *diagonal*. The investor can *gain* as much as 5% of the underlying value of one side of the position; this occurs if the indexes diverge *positively* by 5% or more, putting the *short* option *out*-of-the-money,

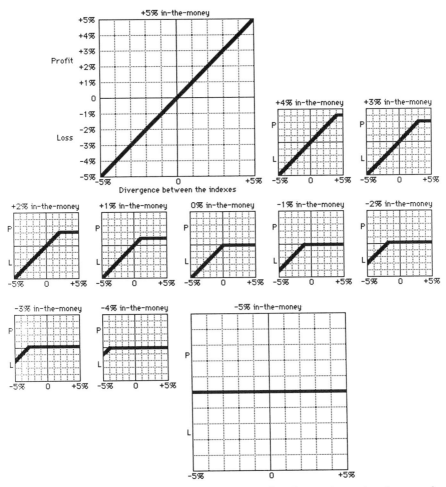

FIGURE 11.7. Idealized intermarket position with index options: simultaneously buy and sell either equivalent calls or equivalent puts on two underlying indexes

where it would expire worthless. On the other hand, the investor could *lose* 5% or more if the indexes diverge *negatively* by 5% or more, putting the *short* option more deeply *in*-the-money than the long option.

When the *long* option is 5% *out*-of-the-money (the large chart in the lower right-hand corner), the risk-reward line is perfectly *flat*. The investor breaks even at all points because both options will be out of the money, where they will expire worthless. If *negative* divergence exceeds

321

5% (not shown on the chart), the short option would expire in the money and the investor would experience a loss.

The small charts represent points in between the two large graphs, showing the investor's risk/reward lines for various amounts by which the long option expires in-the-money. The risk/reward lines of the eleven charts in Figure 11.7 are discrete cross sections of a continuous three-dimensional risk/reward *surface*, illustrated in Figure 11.8.

Note that the risk/reward surface is tangent to all points along the intersection of the *break-even plane* and the *nondivergence plane*. This illustrates that, regardless of whether the options in the position expire in-the-money, the position will break even as long as the underlying indexes do not diverge.

To apply this to the example we've developed consider what happens when the market is unchanged or higher. Provided that the two indexes move together with the relative volatilities we estimated, both puts expire worthless and the investor takes a small loss of $16.28, his initial cost, plus financing. If the market is lower, let's say the Value Line declines by 10% and the MMI by 14%, both puts will expire in-the-money. But the two puts are so closely aligned that they hedge each other almost perfectly: the investor's loss is $16.42.

	Both Indexes Unchanged	MMI +14% Value Line +10%	MMI −14% Value Line −10%
Initial cost MMI put	($226.00)	($226.00)	($ 226.00)
Expiration value MMI put	0	0	$3,193.32
Profit (loss) MMI put	($226.00)	($226.00)	$2,967.32
Initial proceeds Value Line puts	$210.00	$210.00	$ 210.00
Expiration value Value Line puts	0	0	($3,193.46)
Profit (loss) Value Line puts	$210.00	$210.00	($2,983.46)
Financing cost ($16.00 at 7%)	($ 0.28)	($ 0.28)	($ 0.28)
TOTAL LOSS	($ 16.28)	($ 16.28)	($ 16.42)

We know from earlier discussions of the historical evidence that the Value Line marginally outperformed the MMI during the three month holding period. Yet, when we calculate the final value of this options position, we find that the investor has taken a loss. The Value Line

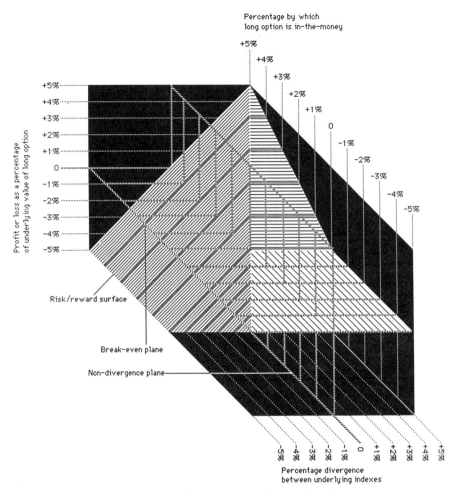

FIGURE 11.8. Continuous risk/reward surface

finished at expiration at 190.75, placing the short 195.00 puts 4.25 in-the-money, for an aggregate exercise value of $781.90. The MMI finished at 250.50, placing the long 255.00 puts 4.50 in-the-money, for an aggregate exercise value of $450.00. Altogether, including the $16.00 initial cost to set up the position and the $0.28 financing cost, the position showed a net loss of $348.18.

	MMI −3.42%; Value Line −3.36%
Initial cost MMI put	($226.00)
Expiration value MMI put	$450.00
Profit (loss) MMI put	$224.00
Initial proceeds Value Line puts	$210.00
Expiration value Value Line puts	($781.90)
Profit (loss) Value Line puts	($571.90)
Financing cost ($16.00 at 7%)	($ 0.28)
TOTAL LOSS	($348.18)

This position showed a loss—despite the investor's correct prediction of divergence between the indexes—for the same reason that, in the earlier example of an intermarket arbitrage with index futures, the investor experienced a windfall profit. Namely, the relative volatility estimates used in calculating the number of contracts on each side of the position turned out to be incorrect. Because the Value Line's estimated volatility of 6.5% was so much lower than the MMI's estimated 9.1%, the investor sold more Value Line puts than he would have had the two volatility estimates been equal. As we noted earlier, the actual volatilities exhibited by the Value Line and the MMI during the period were quite similar—8.5 and 8.7% respectively.

It is interesting to note how differently this position would have resolved if it had been executed with calls instead of puts and the indexes had finished higher rather than lower. The investor would have bought more Value Line calls than he sold MMI calls to make up for the Value Line's lower estimated volatility. When the market rose and the two indexes ended up exhibiting almost the same volatility, the greater-than-necessary number of long calls would have finished in the money at expiration and the investor would have had a windfall profit.

As with futures, index options can be used not only for intermarket positioning, as we have just seen, but for arbitrage as well. Let's consider how the trade we just examined would have fared if it had been executed, not to exploit an anticipated divergence, but to exploit advantageous prices; for example, let's assume that the Value Line puts could be sold at 1.50 rather than at 1.14, and let's assume that the MMI puts could be bought for 2.00 rather than for 2.26. Instead of a cost of $16.00, at these prices the investor would receive proceeds of $75.92, which he can reinvest in Treasury bills:

Proceeds from Value Line puts		Put price		Number of contracts		Contract multiplier
$2755.92	=	1.50	×	1.84	×	$100.00

Cost of MMI puts		Put price		Number of contracts		Contract multiplier
$200.00	=	2.00	×	1	×	$100.00

Net proceeds		Proceeds from Value Line puts		Cost of MMI puts
$75.92	=	$275.92	−	$200.00

Now, provided that the two indexes move together with the relative volatilities we estimated, when the market is unchanged or higher both puts expire worthless, and the investor will have a small profit of $77.25—his $75.92 initial cost plus $1.33 interest. If the Value Line declines by 10% and the MMI by 14%, the two puts hedge each other almost perfectly: the investor's profit is $77.11.

	Both Indexes Unchanged	MMI +14% Value Line +10%	MMI −14% Value Line −10%
Initial cost MMI put	($200.00)	($200.00)	($ 200.00)
Expiration value MMI put	0	0	$3,193.32
Profit (loss) MMI put	($200.00)	($200.00)	$2,993.32
Initial proceeds Value Line puts	$275.92	$275.92	$ 275.92
Expiration value Value Line puts	0	0	(3,193.46)
Profit (loss) Value Line puts	$275.92	$275.92	($2,917.54)
Interest income from T-bills (7% on $75.92 for 3 months)	$ 1.33	$ 1.33	$ 1.33
TOTAL PROFIT (LOSS)	$ 77.25	$ 77.25	$ 77.11

In intermarket arbitrage positions with futures the risk of divergence was symmetrical, omnipresent whether the indexes rose or declined. There was little that could be done effectively to manage the risk, so the key decision for the investor was to determine when his potential reward was sufficient to compensate for it. But with options the risk of divergence occurs only in the direction in which the options become in-the-money, so the risk/reward decision can be augmented by structural decisions designed to create more effective hedges.

By arbitraging index options that are far out-of-the-money, the investor sets up a position in which no single event can cause a loss; rather, a four-stage *chain of negative events* must occur. First, the indexes must move in the *direction* in which the options become in the money. Second, they must move with sufficient *magnitude* to place the options actually in the money. Third, they must *diverge*. And fourth, they must *diverge negatively*.

In this example, on returning to the historical evidence, we find that only the first three of these four events occurred. Yet the investor still suffered a loss because a fifth event intervened—the *misestimation of relative volatilities*. In the preceding example an investor would have lost $348.18; in this arbitrage mispricing reduced the loss to $254.65.

	MMI −3.42%; Value Line −3.36%
Initial cost MMI put	($200.00)
Expiration value MMI put	$450.00
Profit (loss) MMI put	$250.00
Initial proceeds Value Line puts	$275.92
Expiration value Value Line puts	($781.90)
Profit (loss) Value Line puts	($505.98)
Interest income on T-bills	
(7% on $75.92 for 3 months)	$ 1.33
TOTAL PROFIT	$254.65

QUESTIONS & ANSWERS

Today, barely five years after their introduction, it would be easier to imagine a modern society without automobiles or television than a marketplace without index options and futures. Yet many in the investment community question the value of their proliferation, for any profoundly new technology has the power to alter the environment into which it is introduced.

Ever since listed stock options were introduced in 1973 derivative securities of all kinds have been accused of everything from increasing the volatility of their underlying markets to siphoning off investment capital. It is difficult to measure whether the presence of index options and futures siphons capital away from the stock market. In their defense it could be argued that, by providing an otherwise unavailable risk-transfer mechanism, they actually encourage investment in the stock market. Since index options and futures began trading the New York Stock Exchange has traded the highest volume in its history and has even had to expand its trading hours.

The most urgent complaint about index options and futures is the "expiration effect," that rush of market-on-close orders on the New York Stock Exchange that is always alleged to be linked to options and futures expirations. So unpredictable and unsettling is this effect that the financial press has dubbed the last few moments of trading on expiration day the "witching hour."

If a product's acceptance in the marketplace is proof of its legitimacy, then whatever the problems associated with expiration index options and futures have received the investing public's enthusiastic seal of approval. If they are superfluous in an already complete market structure, then there is no explanation for their phenomenal success with every class of investor, great and small, institutional and individual.

The charge that index options and futures are mere speculative playthings for the unwary and the unsophisticated has been just as soundly refuted in the marketplace, as risk-averse institutional investors have rushed to embrace them as a unique, indispensable hedging opportunity.

The preceding chapters were written to shed some light on the quantitative and strategic issues concerning index options and futures. This chapter is intended to address the qualitative issues. To do so we should begin by placing index options and futures in their proper context, for they are only a small part of a larger conceptual revolution in the investment field.

The modern attitude is to conceive of a portfolio not as a collection of *individual assets* but rather as a single *composite asset*. This attitude amounts to the "commoditization" of securities. The perception of portfolios as composite assets has flourished in the era of institutional investment in which enormous collectives manage the investment of the majority of traded securities. The sheer magnitude of the funds controlled by these institutions necessitates their broad diversification across securities. The larger and better diversified these portfolios get, the more identical each one becomes with all the others; ultimately, they all begin to look pretty much like the very indexes used as benchmarks for measuring their performance.

Modern Portfolio Theory has arisen as a descriptive language to account for the slight divergencies in performance among these substantially identical portfolios. It is a science of optimal diversification in which individual stocks are relegated to the role of modular building blocks, elements to be plugged in or detached in the service of the overall architecture of the portfolio.

An increasing number of investment managers would now prefer to trade their portfolios as aggregate commodities through *program trades* that buy and sell entire portfolios all at once, as though they were single assets. The formal commoditization of portfolios into generic exchange-traded contracts is nothing more than an extension of this preference. Given this conceptual environment, it is not surprising to see index options and futures flourishing.

12. DO INDEX OPTIONS AND FUTURES AFFECT THE STOCK MARKET?

Like all fundamental innovations, index options and futures were born into a world of hostility, skepticism, and doubt. Criticized as corrupt gambling instruments, trivialized as toys for small-time speculators, and feared for their potential to sap capital from the stock market, the doubters argued that index options and futures should not be permitted. But they were permitted, and the rest, as they say, is history—the initial fears appear to have been largely groundless.

Although index options and futures are certainly used for gambling purposes—and what securities are not?—they have proved to be infinitely more useful for hedging and asset allocation. Although certainly enchanting their share of small-time speculators, they've attracted an army of institutional adherents, many of whom would scarcely have considered the idea of trading options or futures before. And far from sapping capital from the stock market, they've grown to prominence against a background of historically high levels of both price and volume on stock exchanges around the world. In short, index options and futures have developed into arguably the most successful new products in the history of the securities industry.

Yet for all their success—in fact, probably because of it—a vexing problem with index options and futures has emerged. Curiously, for all the initial doubts, it is a problem that was utterly unanticipated by anyone before it occurred. The problem, of course, is that expiring index options and futures apparently cause drastic price fluctuations on the New York Stock Exchange. Now that this "expiration effect" has burst into the investment community's awareness, it is blasted across headlines and magazine covers in language normally reserved for acts of terrorism. The September 29, 1986, cover of *Business Week* screamed, "ZAP! How Chicago Drives Wall Street"; and an October 22, 1985, cover story in the *Wall Street Journal* was headlined "Linked Deals in Stocks and Futures Contracts Roil Prices, Critics Say." For all the controversy the cause of the expiration effect appears to be really quite simple and straightforward. It is a side effect of implementing and unwinding the synthetic money-market instrument strategy discussed earlier.

The effect was first documented on Thursday, April 19, 1984, on the Chicago Board Options Exchange. This particular expiration day fell on Thursday because the next day was Good Friday, and the nation's exchanges were to be closed for its observance. Trading in stocks, options, and futures was light, as many traders left early for the three-day holiday weekend. Fifteen minutes before the close of New York Stock Exchange trading the S&P 100 Index stood at about 154.75. At this index price expiring index call options with the strike-price of 155.00 were essentially worthless and were offered in the trading crown on the CBOE floor at the minimum allowable price of $\frac{1}{16}$ (or $6.25 per contract). Despite the seeming certainty that these options would expire worthless in just a few minutes, a suspicious volume of orders to buy them arrived in the crowd.

As the floor-traders greedily shorted the April 155.00 calls at $\frac{1}{16}$, the expiration effect began to be felt for the first time. In the final 15 minutes of NYSE trading a wave of buy orders hit the market and the S&P 100 Index was driven up to about 155.35. Because the value of the cash-settled options would be determined by subtracting their strike-price from the closing index price (155.35 minus 155.00, or 0.35), the options sold a few minutes earlier for $6.25 were now worth $35.00, an almost 600% appreciation in 15 minutes.

But the effect was not over. After the closing bell stocks continued to uptick in the runoff, most $\frac{1}{4}$ or $\frac{3}{8}$ of a point, and one (Eastman Kodak) a full point. Even after the NYSE had apparently closed the index rose by another 0.40, closing at approximately 155.75. The April 155.00 calls finally settled at approximately $75.00, causing staggering losses for the unsuspecting floor-traders who had just shorted them at $6.25.

At first, traders attributed this strange activity to a bald-faced, if innovative, attempt to manipulate the prices of the April 155.00 calls. In fact, there was good reason to suspect this, because all the stocks that had been affected were major components of the index. The Chicago Board Options Exchange conducted an extensive investigation into the incident and determined that the motive behind the late buying was not to manipulate the index but to unwind a large position in the synthetic money market instrument strategy. Since this incident the same explanation has been advanced to explain similar effects experienced on almost every subsequent expiration.

To understand how trading the synthetic money-market instrument strategy might affect stock prices at expiration consider the position of the arbitrageur utilizing the strategy as expiration approaches. Let's assume that the arbitrageur has purchased the component stocks of the S&P 500 Index and has sold an equivalent dollar value in S&P 500 futures contracts.

On expiration the futures are settled in cash on the basis of the final value of the index, and then they simply vanish, leaving the arbitrageur holding only the stocks. Unless he wants to bear the risk of continuing to own the stocks unhedged, he must sell them on the close, just as the futures expire. The arbitrageur isn't concerned with the market impact of his selling program; any loss he takes by driving stock prices down will be perfectly offset in a better cash settlement for his short futures. This kind of crash selling program can drive prices significantly lower, often right in the closing runoff. This produces the expiration effect: the appearance of a massive selling wave hitting the market virtually after the close of trading.

The expiration effect can work in reverse as well, driving stock prices higher. Paradoxically, this reverse effect is also caused by trading in the synthetic money-market instrument strategy. Arbitrageurs who implement the strategy by buying the near-term futures and selling the far-term futures must replace the near-term futures with long stock when the futures expire. Such a trader will buy the component stocks of the index right at the close without regard for market impact; any penalty he pays by driving prices higher will be perfectly offset in a better cash settlement for the expiring long futures.

In the case of the April 1984 incident on the CBOE, arbitrageurs had implemented the *reverse* synthetic money-market instrument strategy by simultaneously buying index calls, short-selling puts, and short-selling the stocks in the S&P 100 Index. As the options expired they unwound the position by buying back the short stocks.

On March 15, 1986, a report studying the expiration effect was published by Hans R. Stoll of Vanderbilt University and Robert E. Whaley of the University of Alberta and the University of Chicago. Titled "The Expiration Day Effects of Index Options and Futures," this report was commissioned jointly by the options and futures exchanges and the Securities and Exchange Commission.

The report reached a number of interesting conclusions about the effect, on the basis of extensive analysis of empirical data. Some of these conclusions are controversial because they do not match intuitive surmises drawn by many observers. Basically, the study confirms that an expiration price effect does, in fact, exist. It found that the effect is small on expirations when only index options expire; it is stronger on quarterly expirations when S&P 500 Index futures expire. Last-hour NYSE volume on quarterly expiration Fridays is twice as great as it is on nonexpiration Fridays.

The magnitude of the expiration effect is about 0.33 to 0.50% of the value of the index, depending on which index is used and exactly how one defines the price effect. The impact of about 0.25% is attributable simply to buying at the offer or selling on the bid. Because the magnitude of the expiration effect is twice as great, it can be said that it truly moves the market. To put the seriousness of the effect in context the report points out that even larger price effects, closer to 0.75%, occur frequently in large block transactions in individual stocks. In light of these and other findings, Stoll and Whaley evaluated the various proposals aimed at alleviating the effect that have been put forward by exchanges, regulators, and industry gadflies.

1. *"Telescoping" Position Limits.* This proposal would require holders of index options and futures positions to liquidate them gradually as expiration approached rather than all on expiration day, defusing the expiration effect by spreading its impact out over a period of weeks. The report criticizes this proposal harshly for a number of separate reasons. First, the report claims that telescoping would diminish the effectiveness of index options and futures as risk management tools for legitimate hedgers. By forcing investors to liquidate positions in the market, rather than letting the positions settle for cash at the index value on expiration day, investors would have to bear the risk that the prices at which they liquidate may be unfair. Second, the report argues that telescoping would not work to alleviate the expiration effect because it would not prevent the arbitrage that creates it. It would merely limit the size of the position that could be held to expiration by any one arbitrageur. This might help for a while, but telescoping would not prevent a large number of small arbitrageurs from entering the market and creating the effect all over again.

2. *Physical Delivery.* This proposal would substitute the cash-settlement mechanism for the physical delivery of the actual stocks that make up the underlying indexes. The report points out that this solution is not possible in today's regulatory environment, since the Commodities Futures Trading Commission would have no jurisdiction to regulate a futures contract that resulted in the delivery of equity securities. If this stumbling block were overcome, physical delivery would involve impossibly cumbersome and costly administrative procedures.

3. *Averaged Settlement Price.* This proposal suggests that index options and futures be settled on expiration not against the closing value of the index, but against an average of index values experienced during the day. The report argues that this would be unfair to unsophisticated public investors who might not fully understand the settlement procedure.

4. *Increased Disclosure.* This proposal suggests regulations that would require arbitrageurs to disclose their positions in advance of expiration day. The report argues that besides the requirement of disclosure of confidential information, policing this requirement would be an administra-

tive impossibility. It does concede, however, that voluntary disclosure might allow the free-market mechanism to better absorb the expiration effect.

5. *Shifting Expiration Days.* This proposal would stagger expirations of various index options and futures throughout the month, rather than concentrating them on a single Friday. The report contends that most of the expiration effect is caused by the S&P 500 Index futures alone, so the timing of expiration of the other contracts is almost irrelevant. Additionally, the report points out that spreading the effect throughout the month would not necessarily be desirable, even if it could be achieved—it may be better to leave the effect segregated to just one day of the month, where it can easily be avoided by investors wishing to steer clear.

As of this writing, it appears that a solution not discussed in the report is the most likely to be adopted. The Chicago Mercantile Exchange has unilaterally applied to the CFTC to allow settlement of expiring contracts against the *opening* price of the underlying indexes (rather than against the *closing* price, as is currently the practice). Advocates claim that this proposal would not disrupt the efficiency of any current uses of the contracts. By diverting the flood of arbitrage-related stock orders to the opening, NYSE specialists would have time to make fair markets without the pressure of an imminent market close. And the NYSE would then have all day to readjust, creating the impression of more orderly markets (at least when measured from close to close).

None of the proposed reforms addresses the fact that expiration is not the only time that the synthetic money-market instrument strategy can move the market. Because arbitrageurs can set up and unwind the strategy at any time during market hours, the effect can occur at almost any moment. When futures prices are sufficiently high in relation to their theoretical values, arbitrageurs will sell the overpriced futures and buy stocks, driving stock prices higher. Conversely, when futures prices are sufficiently low, arbitrageurs will buy the underpriced futures and liquidate their stocks, driving stock prices lower.

Another way in which index options and futures can affect the market is through the interaction of the synthetic money-market instrument strategy with other strategies. As an example, consider an investor who uses index futures to create a "synthetic put" for portfolio insurance. Recall that to do this, the investor would generally have to buy index futures in response to market rises and sell index futures in response to market declines. Let's say the market rises sufficiently to cause the insurer to buy futures contracts, and that this trading activity in an already frothy marketplace drives the futures price above its theoretical value.

An arbitrageur could step in to sell the temporarily overpriced futures, simultaneously buying stocks on the NYSE to complete the synthetic money market instrument strategy. Next, let's say the arbitrageur's trading activity on the NYSE drives the stock market even higher, causing the portfolio insurer to buy even more futures contracts. The insurer's buying will drive futures prices higher still, triggering another round of arbitrage, which will trigger a further rise in the stock market—and so on and so on, in an infinite regress. On the down-side, the same effect could occur in reverse, driving the market lower and lower until it finally hits zero. While these scenarios are admittedly somewhat fantastical, the huge amounts of money devoted both to the synthetic money-market instrument strategy and to portfolio insurance are sufficient to cause thoughtful investors to ponder the possibilities.

Beyond the complaints associated with these effects themselves is the possibility of a deliberate market manipulation. If a single arbitrageur, or a group acting in concert, could be certain that their market impact on expiration (or at any other time) would be significant enough, they could exploit this nonpublic information by buying options or making other highly leveraged investments in anticipation of their own future actions. Trading options and futures with foreknowledge of price changes in the underlying markets is called front-running, and every futures and options exchange has regulations prohibiting it.

Although it was not proved conclusively in the investigation conducted by the Chicago Board Options Exchange following the April 1984 incident, many CBOE traders who witnessed the event believe that advance knowledge of the expiration effect was used to unfair advantage. It will never be known for sure whether the influx of buy orders for the April 155 calls was motivated by advance knowledge, but to the floor-traders, several of whom were forced out of business by the size of their losses in those few horrendous minutes, it may as well have been.

As with all manipulations—in fact, as with crimes of any type—the benefit of policing must be judged against its cost. Perhaps the best approach would be to wait to see if the free marketplace imposes its own solutions. No one can predict with absolute certainty whether a given month's expiration effect will move the market higher or lower, even someone with foreknowledge about his own future actions in the market. Under such circumstances, the danger of manipulation is relatively trivial. Those who would take advantage of the expiration effect are demoted from the status of "insider" to the normal status of any market speculator—risking capital on predictions of an uncertain future.

13. CAN INDEX OPTIONS AND FUTURES PREDICT THE MARKET?

Among many investors S&P 500 Index futures are called Spooze, after the Quotron symbol for the September contract SPU.Z. So great is the general belief that S&P 500 futures are a leading indicator of intermediate-term market behavior that some traders swear by the maxim, "Spooze Don't Lie." It is difficult to determine from simple observation whether this bit of folk wisdom is really true. Sometimes it seems that whenever S&P 500 futures make a major move, the New York Stock Exchange follows. But as with so many market indicators, it is all too easy to remember the times when this indeed happens and ignore the time when it doesn't.

To test the predictive ability implicit in prices of S&P 500 futures, parameters must first be set to define what is meant by a prediction. Using the futures valuation formula, it is easy to determine a benchmark price that can be assumed to contain no prediction; any variation from this price can be attributed to a prediction. For a three-month contract, when the index is at 240.00, the dividend yield is 4%, and the riskless interest rate is 7%, the predictionless price would be the theoretical value of 241.80.

Predictionless price (theoretical value)		Index price		Interest		Dividends
241.80	=	240.00	+	$4.20	−	$2.40

For the sake of argument let's assume that a "buy signal" would be given whenever the futures price in the marketplace, when plugged into the valuation formula, implies an index price 1% higher than the actual index price. Conversely, a "sell signal" would be given whenever the futures price implies an index price 1% lower. For instance, a buy signal would be given when the futures price is higher than 244.24, and a sell signal would be given when the futures price is lower than 239.35:

Buy signal futures price		Index price +1%		Interest +1%		Dividends
244.24	=	242.40	+	$4.24	−	$2.40

Sell signal futures price		Index price −1%		Interest −1%		Dividends
239.35	=	237.60	+	$4.16	−	$2.40

Figure 13.1 shows the history of signals generated in this way over the first three years of S&P 500 Index futures trading, from April 1982 to April 1985. Although there can usually be some ambiguity regarding what we mean by *correct* predictions, we can nonetheless derive an intuitive sense of the overall predictive ability of the signals simply by scanning these charts.

In 1982 and the first quarter of 1983 the signals were almost universally wrong—sell signals at short-term bottoms and buy signals at short-term tops. Consistently wrong predictions are as useful as consistently right ones, but after this period the pattern changed. In the last three quarters of 1983 there were no signals at all. And then in 1984 and 1985 there were (with one exception) nothing but buy signals. And the only ones that presaged an immediate rally of any consequence were those given in January 1985.

Overall, perhaps the most flattering analysis of the buy and sell signals is that they were worthless. And yet, especially in light of our discussion of how index options and futures can affect the stock market, it stands to reason that they should have some positive predictive ability, even if only in the sense of self-fulfilling prophecies.

Earlier, in our discussions of the synthetic money market instrument strategy, we described trigger points—key futures prices in relation to the current index price that would trigger an investor to set up or unwind the strategy, or its reverse. When futures prices are extremely high in relation to their theoretical values, arbitrageurs will sell the overpriced futures and buy stocks, driving stock prices higher. Conversely, when futures prices are extremely low, arbitrageurs will buy the underpriced futures and liquidate their stocks, driving stock prices lower. This process should create the appearance that the stock market follows the futures market in the ultra-short term: when futures are high, the stock market moves up as the arbitrageurs buy stocks; when futures are low, the market moves down as they sell stocks.

To anticipate where trigger points might lie at any given time we would simply calculate the theoretical value of a futures contract using

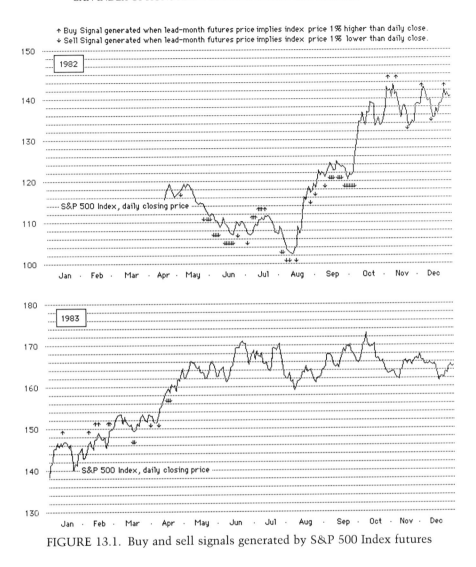

FIGURE 13.1. Buy and sell signals generated by S&P 500 Index futures

the interest rate we deemed sufficient to merit trading the synthetic money-market instrument strategy. If the prevailing riskless rate were 7%, and we estimate that an arbitrageur would want to earn 2% profit in excess of this after all transaction costs (estimated earlier at 1.29%), we would arrive at a trigger interest rate of 10.29%:

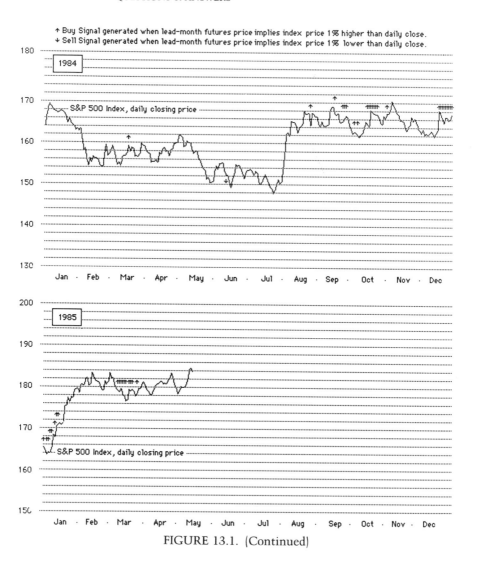

FIGURE 13.1. (Continued)

Trigger interest rate		Riskless rate		Profit margin		Transaction costs
10.29%	=	7%	+	2%	+	1.29%

To calculate the trigger futures price, we plug the trigger interest rate into the valuation formula. With the index priced at 240.00 and a dividend yield of 4%, we get a trigger futures price of 243.77.

Trigger futures price		Index price		Interest at trigger rate		Dividends
243.77	=	240.00	+	$6.17	−	$2.40

Recall that the synthetic money market instrument strategy can be implemented with index options as well. The trigger point with index options is not a single option price, but rather the net proceeds from simultaneous sale of a call and purchase of an otherwise identical put; for example, by using the trigger interest rate of 10.29% we calculate a trigger point of 3.53. If the arbitrageur could sell a call and buy an otherwise identical put for net proceeds of 3.53, he could earn 10.29% in the synthetic money market instrument.

Trigger: Call price − Put price		Fraction of year		Target interest rate: Index price Annual dividends One plus riskless rate
				$(10.29\% \times 240.00) - \$9.60$
3.53	=	0.25	×	$\overline{1.07}$

Mathematically it is no harder to calculate trigger points for the reverse strategy—trigger points that would motivate an arbitrageur to *sell* futures or simultaneously *buy* a call and *sell* a put; the difficult part is to estimate the relevant trigger interest rate. Given the differential rates at which various investors can earn interest on the proceeds from short-sales and the risks associated with executing them under the plus-tick rule, it is impossible to generalize the level of reward that might tempt the marginal arbitrageur.

14. SHOULD "MORAL INVESTORS" TRADE INDEX OPTIONS AND FUTURES?

Critics of the securities industry may hold that the expression *moral investor* is a contradiction in terms. Nonetheless, the industry has been swept in recent years by a movement toward evaluation of investment opportunities in terms of their moral, ethical, social, and environmental impacts. Many state and local government pension funds, and many university endowments, will not invest in the stocks of companies that participate in South Africa's racial policies. Some will not invest in companies that make weapons, cigarettes, or alcoholic beverages. Others will not invest in companies that pollute the environment with toxic waste.

Moral investors pay a price for their principles. Because many companies fail to meet the necessary standards of morality, investment managers have difficulty structuring optimally diversified *moral portfolios*. The worst problems are those encountered by moral investors who seek to create indexed portfolios: many of the most heavily weighted components of the recognized indexes cannot be included.

Earlier, in our discussion of index options and futures as alternatives to portfolios of stocks, we saw that index instruments could act as the perfect surrogates for "market portfolios." These strategies represent an opportunity for moral investors to participate in diversified portfolios in a way that explicitly avoids direct support of immoral companies. For moral investors trading index options and futures is the ultimate expression of the perception of portfolios as aggregate commodities. It become the strategy of choice specifically because it divorces the aggregate char acteristics of an index from the attributes of its individual components

Arguing in favor of this approach, it should be noted by moral investors that even though the underlying indexes may include immoral companies, index options and futures contracts are issued and guaranteed by the exchanges' clearing houses, not by the companies that comprise the index. They are not part of those companies' equity structures. By holding index options and futures, an investor in no sense owns an equity share, percentage ownership, or voting interest in any of the component companies. Inclusion in an underlying index and the trading of index options and futures contracts on an index does not benefit the component companies in any direct way whatsoever. The companies receive no royalties or licensing fees of any kind for being included in an index. And they derive no commissions or other payments as a result of options or futures trading activity.

On the other hand, moral investors may argue that component companies do, in fact, derive certain indirect benefits from inclusion in an underlying index, in the form of prestige and goodwill. When a company is included in an index for the first time, its stock becomes the target both of index fund managers who must include it in their indexed portfolios and of investment managers governed by guidelines of prudence that forbid them from holding stocks *not* included in a recognized index. Further, a stringently moral investor may not wish to trade options and futures that may encourage arbitrage activity ultimately including the stocks of immoral companies.

BIBLIOGRAPHY

Black, Fischer. "Fact and Fantasy in the Use of Options." *Financial Analysts Journal 31* (July–August 1975):36–41, 61–72.

Black, Fischer. "The Pricing of Commodity Contracts." *Journal of Financial Economics 3* (January–March 1976):167–179.

Black, Fischer. "One Way to Estimate Volatility." *Fischer Black on Options 1* (May 17, 1986).

Black, Fischer. "Screening Options." *Fischer Black on Options 1* (September 20, 1976).

Black, Fischer, and Myron Scholes. "The Pricing of Options and Corporate Liabilities." *Journal of Political Economy 81* (May–June 1973):637–659.

Board of Governors of the Federal Reserve System, Commodity Futures Trading Commission, and Securities and Exchange Commission. "A Study of the Effects on the Economy of Trading in Futures and Options." Washington, D.C.: Government Printing Office, 1984, pp. VII-8–VII-49.

Chiras, Donald P., and Stephen Manaster. "The Information Content of Option Prices and a Test of Market Efficiency." *Journal of Financial Economics 6* (June–September 1979):213–234.

Cornell, Bradford, and Kenneth R. French. "The Pricing of Stock Index Futures." *Working Paper Series*, Center for the Study of Futures Markets, Columbia Business School, Working Paper CSFM-43 (October 1982).

Cox, John C., Stephen A. Ross, and Mark Rubinstein. "Option Pricing: A Simplified Approach." *Journal of Financial Economics 7* (September 1979):229–263.

Cox, John C., and Mark Rubinstein. "A Survey of Alternative Option Pricing Models." In Menachem Brenner, Ed., *Option Pricing.* Lexington, MA: Heath, 1983, pp. 3–33.

Cox, John C., and Mark Rubinstein. *Options Markets.* Englewood Cliffs, NJ: Prentice-Hall, 1985, pp. 127–358.

Figlewski, Stephen. "Hedging with Stock Index Futures: Theory and Application in a New Market." *Working Paper Series*, Center for the Study of Futures Markets, Columbia Business School, Working Paper CSFM-62 (July 1983).

Figlewski, Stephen. "Explaining the Early Discounts on Stock Index Futures: The Case for Disequilibrium." *Financial Analysts Journal 40* (July–August 1984):43–47.

Jarrow, Robert A., and Andrew Rudd. *Option Pricing.* Homewood, Il.: Dow-Jones Irwin, 1983.

Laderman, Jeffrey M., and John N. Frank. "A New Breed of Investor is Whipsawing Wall Street." *BusinessWeek* (September 23, 1985):84–86.

Laderman, Jeffrey M., John N. Frank. "How Chicago Zaps Wall Street." *BusinessWeek* (September 29, 1986):92–102.

Laderman, Jeffrey M., John N. Frank, Vicky Cahan, and Alice Z. Cuneo. "Those Big Swings on Wall Street." *BusinessWeek* (April 7, 1986):32–26.

Lee, Susan. "What's with the Casino Society?" *Forbes* (September 22, 1986):150–158.

Leland, Hayne. "Who Should Buy Portfolio Insurance?" *Journal of Finance 35* (May 1980):581–594.

Leland, Hayne. "Option Pricing and Replication with Transaction Costs." *Journal of Finance 40* (December 1985):1283–1301.

Margrabe, William. "The Value of an Option to Exchange One Asset for Another." *Journal of Finance 33* (March 1978):177–186.

Merton, Robert C. "Theory of Rational Option Pricing." *Bell Journal of Economics and Management Science 4* (Spring 1973):141–183.

Merton, Robert C., Myron S. Scholes, and Mathew L. Gladstein. "The Returns and Risks of Alternative Call Option Portfolio Investment Strategies." *Journal of Business 51* (April 1978):183–242.

Modest, David M., and Mahadevan Sundaresan. "The Relationship Between Spot and Futures Prices in Stock Index Futures Markets: Some Preliminary Evidence." *Working Paper Series*, Center for the Study of Futures Markets, Columbia Business School, Working Paper CSFM-45 (November 1982).

Parkinson, Michael. "The American Put." *Journal of Business 50* (January 1977):21–36.

Rubinstein, Mark, "Alternative Paths to Portfolio Insurance." *Financial Analysts Journal 41* (July–August 1985) 42–52.

Rubinstein, Mark, and Hayne Leland. "Replicating Options with Positions in Stocks and Cash." *Financial Analysts Journal 37* (July–August 1981):63–72.

Sebastian, Pamela. "Street Fight; Linked Deals in Stocks and Futures Contracts Roil Prices, Critics Say." *Wall Street Journal* (October 22, 1985):1.

Seligman, Daniel. "Don't Fret About Program Trading." *Fortune* (October 13, 1986):86–92.

Singleton, Clay J., and Robin Grieves. "Synthetic Puts and Portfolio Insurance Strategies." *The Journal of Portfolio Management 10* (Spring 1984):63–69.

Stoll, Hans R., and Robert E. Whaley. "Expiration Day Effects of Index Options and Futures." Study commissioned by the American Stock Exchange, Chicago Board Options Exchange, New York Stock Exchange, Pacific Stock Exchange, Philadelphia Stock Exchange, and the National Association of Securities Dealers (March 1986).

INDEX